Contemporary Humanitarian Action and Emergency Management

Series Editor

Diego Fernández Otegui, Imara-IHG
Henrico, VA, USA

Humanitarian action and emergency management are two distinct, though deeply interrelated social systems where those concerned with the well-being of others converge. They have been of great interest to scholars and have increasingly become the subject of introspection by practitioners as well. Still, many aspects of their practice are rarely studied and only vaguely understood.

One of the most significant challenges in understanding their nature is the diversity of their essential parts: the humanitarian worker and the emergency practitioner. The voices of the people doing the work, we believe, are critical in working out how to articulate what constitutes them. The vast majority of existing literature, however, is imbued with the point of view of the scholars that produced it. Furthermore, they discuss what each author considers necessary for the world to know.

With this series, we want to give expert practitioners a chance to speak for themselves and present their divergent opinions without neglecting the expertise of scholars who dedicate their lives to systematically and rigorously creating knowledge. To do so, it benefits from a mixed editorial board of highly renowned practitioners and scholars. Experts from both worlds work together, from the conception of an idea to the publication of each book.

We want to help the public learn how those involved in assisting others practice their craft and experience their life within this unique space dedicated to meeting human needs. To do so, it covers a wide variety of topics and encourages the submission of proposals from all fields of study. It also welcomes proposals from leaders who might not be directly involved in either discipline but have a vested interest and substantial knowledge in either area, such as corporate executives, religious leaders, public officials, and community representatives.

The series accepts both solicited and unsolicited proposals to publish edited volumes and authored monographs.

Elena Cherepanov

Humanitarian Competencies for Global Mental Health Professionals

Guidelines for Responding to Humanitarian Emergency

Springer

Elena Cherepanov
Graduate School of Psychology & Counselling
Cambridge College
Boston, MA, United States

ISSN 2731-4839 ISSN 2731-4847 (electronic)
Contemporary Humanitarian Action and Emergency Management
ISBN 978-3-031-74267-5 ISBN 978-3-031-74268-2 (eBook)
https://doi.org/10.1007/978-3-031-74268-2

This Springer imprint is published by the registered company Springer Nature Switzerland AG
The registered company address is: Gewerbestrasse 11, 6330 Cham, Switzerland

Preface

One of the most unsettling calls a global mental health (GMH) specialist can receive from a peer is: "I am [on a disaster site]. What do I do now, and how can I start helping?"

This book equips MH professionals with essential competencies to respond to disasters, conflicts, famines, and other humanitarian emergencies both nationally and internationally.

Frankly, I was not planning on writing this book. Furthermore, throughout this process, I was struggling with bouts of disappointment in humanity while watching the unfolding apocalyptic scenes of violence and the flywheels of hatred spinning around the world.

The writing process, however, became therapeutic because it made me realize how much is being accomplished by GMH professionals who have been on the front line of humanitarian relief, reminding people of the importance of humanistic values during troubled times.

I saw the overwhelming and passionate response by the international MH professionals to the recent high-profile disasters and conflicts, such as the earthquake in Syria and Turkey, the Russia-Ukraine war, the Israel-Hamas conflict, and the uptick of violence in Haiti.

MH professionals and paraprofessionals from all over the world and across political spectrums have risen to the occasion, helping those in need, regardless of borders or barriers, and bringing attention to the needs of the most vulnerable and neglected people. They have been providing MH services, bearing witness, supporting humanitarian aid workers, informing policies, and shaping global agenda. Their voices and testimonies against violence are now louder than ever.

They have been working in the most impoverished and dangerous places of the world, assisting refugees and other marginalized and disenfranchised groups. They worked in Ebola-affected regions, supporting survivors, victims' families, and health providers. They have been supporting, raising awareness, and advocating for victims of gender-based violence and providing MH assistance to survivors of wars and genocide. They are aiding children and adolescents in most troubled regions ravaged by crime and severe poverty, offering them skills for resilience and instilling hope for the region's future.

I have seen the power of professional mission and compassion. I also recognized the ultimate need for specialized professional and humanitarian competencies in MH providers responding to humanitarian emergencies. These competencies are necessary to ensure that helping interventions are conducted effectively and ethically. Without such competencies, MH interventions risk becoming fragmented and uncoordinated, adding more disorganization and confusion to the already chaotic situations. The lack of coordination makes MH's response far less effective and coherent, potentially interfering with the natural process of healing and overcoming.

The goal of this book is to support MH providers in their global mission. I hope this book will be a next step toward forming specialized professional expertise in GMH, part of which is recognizing ethically problematic practices and navigating unique ethical dilemmas plentiful on a disaster site.

And for those who will not have time to read this book, I compiled the abbreviated answers to the most frequently asked questions:

No—Under no circumstance shall the MH providers travel alone to a disaster or war zone. Such travel requires extensive coordination with humanitarian relief agencies and NGOs for security purposes and to avoid service redundancy and fragmentation.

No—If you are a seasoned MH provider with expertise in trauma and experience in working with multicultural populations, you still must not travel to a disaster site or war zone alone.

No—If you believe that "If I don't do it, no one will," it still does not justify a solo trip.

No—It is generally not a good idea to travel to a disaster site just to show solidarity with victims and demonstrate to them that they are not alone and that you care. The people are busy surviving and need more tangible assistance.

No—You will not be able to figure out what to do on the disaster site. An ethical response to humanitarian emergencies calls for specialized competencies and planning.

No—You must not bring your family or a pet to a disaster zone. It is not tourism or vacation.

No—We cannot understand what people in a humanitarian emergency feel and what they need. We must ask them.

No—Survivors are not required to trust MH providers or express gratitude. If they do—it is a bonus.

No—Testing new interventions on a disaster site is never a good idea.

No—Delivering charitable goods to a disaster site is also not a good idea unless those are educational materials. Send money to the relief agency instead.

No—Local MH providers do not need patronizing. They are the main people there and will stay after we leave. Instead, ask them if you can help.

No—GMH professionals must refrain from using their diagnostic and counseling skills on their co-workers unless it is a clearly spelled part of the professional role.

No—Humanitarian relief is not the same as human rights advocacy activity. While advocacy for victims of human rights violations and demands for cessation of violence are integral to GMH mission, as health professionals, we are primarily committed to the principle of Neutrality. This principle dictates that when acting in a professional capacity internationally, professionals must refrain from participating in political activities, such as calling for regime change, joining political rallies and protests, or engaging in infighting. Instead, GMH professionals use other powerful tools at their disposal to get their viewpoints across, such as bear witness.

No—Do not expect all your colleagues or family members to commend you on or even care about the work you feel so proud of: "We have enough of our own problems over here." The best way to receive true support and understanding is to stay in touch with peers.

No—Don't expect to remain the same after a humanitarian mission. Much will change in you and how you perceive the world. It would help if you gave yourself time to readjust before making life-changing decisions or jumping to another mission. Reach out for peer support, if needed.

No—The GMH work is not for idealists. This professionally and personally rewarding work is only for those who are fully aware of all the challenges and risks and still choose to contribute to the humanistic agenda of making the world safer and kinder.

And, yes—By responding to humanitarian emergencies, you will gain the unique, often life-changing experience that allows to learn about self and others, and reveal the true importance of professional mission along with a clear realization that you can make a real difference in people's lives.

My hope is that this book will inspire, educate, and empower mental health professionals to directly contribute to a more compassionate and resilient future by joining the global mental health work, which is the intersection between professional mental health and humanitarian relief.

Boston, MA, United States Elena Cherepanov

Acknowledgment

My appreciation goes to my humanitarian colleagues who all the way supported the idea of this book and generously shared their experiences and expertise.

I am grateful to students who took my classes in trauma-specific interventions, cultural trauma, and global mental health studies at Cambridge College (USA) and Briva Universitate/Free University (Latvia) for their participation and challenging questions.

Contents

About the Author

Elena Cherepanov, PhD is a clinical psychologist by training. She is an independent consultant with expertise in global mental health and trauma. She has over 20 years of humanitarian experience working with Caritas International, MSF, UNICEF, and other humanitarian organizations and has provided mental health support to populations affected by wars, disasters, and political violence. Dr. Cherepanov is a professor of the trauma studies program at Cambridge College, Boston, USA) and teaches at Briva Universitāte/Free University (Riga, Latvia). Her research focuses on trauma and recovery systems, refugee mental health, and cultural trauma. The most recent works examine the lingering mental health impact of the dictatorship and other political dysfunction. Elena is the author of over 80 papers and books translated into different languages.

List of Abbreviations

ACEs	Adverse childhood events
AMA	American Medical Association
APA	American Psychiatric Association
APA	American Psychological Association
CDC	Center for Disease Control and Prevention
CE	Complex emergency
CPC	Complex political context
GBD	Global Burden of the Disease
GBV	Gender-based violence
GMH	Global Mental Health
HIC	High-income country
IASC	the Inter-Agency Standing Committee
ICRC	International Committee of the Red Cross
IFRC	International Federation of Red Cross and Red Crescent Societies
INGO	International Non-Governmental Organization
IPV	Intimate person violence
ITQ	The International Trauma Questionnaire
LMIC	Low- and middle-income country
MGMH	The Movement for Global Mental Health
MH	Mental Health
mhGap	Mental Health Global Action Plan
MHPSS	Mental Health and Psychosocial Supports in Emergency
MSF	Médecins Sans Frontières (Doctors Without Borders)
NGO	Non-Governmental Organization
OCHA	The United Nations Office for the Coordination of Humanitarian Affairs
PFA	Psychological First Aid
PTSD	Post-Traumatic Stress Disorder
RMH	Refugee Mental Health
SDGs	Sustainable Development Goals
SDOH	Social Determinants of Health
SGBV	Sexual gender-based violence

SPR	Skills for Psychological Recovery
UN	United Nations
UNHCR	The United Nations High Commission for Refugees
UNICEF	The United Nations International Children's Emergency Fund
US	United States of America
WHO	World Health Organization

List of Figures

List of Tables

Chapter 1
Introduction

The number, frequency, and scale of humanitarian emergencies worldwide are only expected to increase due to climate change and the crumbling world order. The changing global landscape calls for multidisciplinary professionals and practitioners to collectively redefine their role in the face of global processes and assume professional responsibility for alleviating suffering, building resilience, advocating for policy changes, and preventing future violence.

This book is written for psychologists, psychiatrists, MH counselors, social workers, psychotherapists, social workers, physicians, nurses, anthropologists, sociologists, researchers, and anyone else who is interested in global studies and advancing the global health and mental health agenda.

The book introduces humanitarian competencies that can be used by MH professionals, paraprofessionals, students, and other specialists who are interested in mitigating the impact of humanitarian emergencies. It orients readers to the humanitarian relief systems, humanitarian culture, ethics, and regulations and outlines the best practices in the humanitarian context.

In recent decades, the global mental health (GMH) work has achieved a significant presence and attained high public visibility. As such, GMH has been recognized as a powerful force in advancing both mental health and humanitarian agendas and influencing global processes by drawing attention to the detrimental impact of wars and conflicts.

Increased global-mindedness, cultural competencies, awareness of geopolitical processes, and a better understanding of the MH role in mitigating the effects of humanitarian emergencies have created a strong demand for humanitarian competencies. The interest in global aspects of MH is recognized in a raising number of academic publications on different aspects of GMH and the growing number of higher education programs now offering the GMH studies concentration.

Humanitarian emergencies refer to a broad range of situations such as disasters, wars, armed conflicts, famines, epidemics, political dysfunction, and other crises

E. Cherepanov, *Humanitarian Competencies for Global Mental Health Professionals*, Contemporary Humanitarian Action and Emergency Management,
https://doi.org/10.1007/978-3-031-74268-2_1

that exceed people's ability to cope and threaten their well-being, health, and, sometimes, lives. Humanitarian settings are characterized by the massive and interconnected humanitarian, health, and MH needs, insufficient resources to meet them, and the power differential between providers and people who need assistance.

The book presents a practical application of the theoretical framework previously outlined in my book *Ethics for Global Mental Health: From Good Intentions to Humanitarian Responsibility* (Cherepanov, 2018). These guidelines are envisioned as the next step in forming professional GMH specialization as an interdisciplinary field of study and practice concerned with providing MH support and interventions to people affected by humanitarian emergencies. Most of this work takes place internationally but can also include supporting refugees and migrants in the host countries.

The book steers away from providing one-size-fits-all protocols and solutions. Instead, it draws the framework, establishes points of reference and strategic vectors in decision-making, and offers practical guidance for finding solutions to a unique situation. Such an approach signals the main virtues of GMH work. They are the priority of humanitarian values, professionalism, high standards of practice, ethics, and humanitarian responsibility. In practice, it also means being open-minded, resourceful, thinking outside the box, using critical thinking skills, and conducting interventions appropriately for the situation.

The guidelines focus on establishing the integrity of the complex decision-making process in volatile and uncertain situations rather than focusing on poorly foreseeable outcomes. Navigating humanitarian situations and making informed decisions with limited information and under duress requires a higher level of professional skills than just those needed for following protocols. It explains why this book's most frequently used words are *decision-making* and *possible outcomes* but not *results*, which is most difficult to predict in a highly unpredictable environment.

For a long time, MH professionals who primarily work in private practice, offices, and clinics in countries with high resources have shared a belief that the nature of GMH work, which is often conducted in low- and middle-resource settings, is not much different. With this book, I intend to challenge this misperception and bring awareness of the importance of specialized skills and humanitarian competencies. The GMH professionals will be able to use this knowledge to inform their professional judgment when conducting contextually appropriate interventions, navigating ethical and moral dilemmas, and making difficult decisions in complex emergencies.

There are numerous papers and books examining MH needs in humanitarian crises that have been written by and for MH professionals. Much has also been written by and for professional humanitarians on the specific nuances of humanitarian work. The novelty of this book lies in offering a broad context for integrating these two professional frameworks because the GMH discipline focuses on providing MH interventions within humanitarian space.

This book outlines the set of humanitarian competencies required for MH professionals who may not be humanitarian workers but who respond to humanitarian emergencies along with other humanitarians and take advantage of the humanitarian relief systems. Because in the emergency MH and humanitarian needs are interconnected, the MH role involves providing direct MH support to those affected by crises, managing risks, and coordinating their efforts with existing relief systems established on the ground.

Global work takes MH professionals out of their comfort zone. In doing this work, they face unique professional and personal challenges. With the limited availability of professional support or referral systems, the providers sometimes have to make decisions entirely independently and take full responsibility for their choices. With this understanding, multidisciplinary MH professionals who are interested in responding to humanitarian emergencies now actively seek specialized and humanitarian competencies.

In humanitarian crises, providing aid to very vulnerable people require the highest professional and ethical standards of conduct and practice because the price for substandard care and ethical indiscretions can run exceptionally high and include the loss of trust in humanitarian aid agencies, increased risks for aid workers and recipients, and possible suspension of aid.

MH continues playing a vital role in various areas of people's life long after the end of the crisis. In addition to being a survival, functioning, and well-being factor, addressing MH needs reduces the impact of adversity on the population and remains a critical factor in determining the region's future. Better MH contributes to improving access to health care, reducing the global burden of the disease, preventing future violence, and strengthening resilience in the face of adversity. It helps to prevent the escalation of violence and reduce suicides and substance misuse that are often rampant in the wake of the disaster.

In recognition of the central role the MH plays in populations' health, resilience, and human rights, the United Nations has designated improvement of MH as a global priority and included it in the Sustainable Development Goals (SDGs), a plan for peace, well-being, and prosperity (UN, 2022). Addressing MH needs remains a significant consideration in the reduction of the global burden of disease (GBD) and achieving public health goals such as mitigation of the effects of adverse childhood events (ACE) and trauma (Kalmakis & Chandler, 2015).

The global experience has benefitted the professional MH field in numerous ways. It inspired and informed studies of cross-cultural phenomena and resilience and explored different ways of understanding the response to adversity. However, most of all, it ignited curiosity about how people cope and overcome severe adversities.

This new perspective opened the door to transformative changes in mainstream MH, where the GMH experience has become a mirror that allowed the MH to self-reflect and reevaluate its core assumptions. The humanitarian context also paved the way for reconciling multidisciplinary agendas under the overarching humanitarian umbrella mission of saving lives and relieving suffering.

This experience facilitated shifting the notion of MH pathology toward normalizing the adaptive reactions to severe stress. It refocused trauma interventions from "fixing" people to strengthening their resilience, supporting coping, and facilitating healing.

GMH's perspective spotlighted the significance of contextual factors, which are the meaning assigned to the adversity, its cultural and geopolitical context, access to the individual and collective resources, and systems of support, as well as previous experience of overcoming. The quality of community and social interactions can determine the availability of social support, which is a decisive factor in resilience. The problematic social support toward socially excluded groups, on the other hand, exposes social vulnerabilities and becomes a significant barrier to recovery and overcoming.

The GMH's path toward professional self-determination has not always been smooth. As GMH branched from the mainstream MH field, it had to sort out its complicated legacy. As a professional field, MH has long faced accusations of living in a professional ivory tower with its presumption of centrality and self-righteousness. In GMH, this translates to the challenging the illusion that people had never known how to survive and cope before MH professionals taught them how to grieve, experience trauma and depression, or handle adversities. I refer to it as *the original sin of MH*, which GMH has been in the perfect position to pinpoint and overcome for the sake of the whole profession.

This paternalistic attitude is similarly reflected in MH professionals' naive belief in the universal and absolute values of Western-originated concepts and practices and their transferability to vastly different situations and cultures. Recognizing the disconnect between how Western MH field sees the world and how the world sees MH work has already facilitated efforts to sensitize providers to their clients' diverse understanding of their needs. The introduction of cultural competencies, trauma-informed care, and, more recently, considerations of the impact of political experience (Cherepanov, 2023) represent significant steps toward embracing the diversity of human experiences. However, these efforts still fall short of capturing the systemic impact of humanitarian crises on people's entire lives.

The most vigorous critique around GMH targets the over-pathologizing trend in approaching, assessing, and treating human distress as something that must not be happening. Reducing complex human reactions to a norm-pathology dichotomy or labeling suffering as a mental disorder has already led to a situation where any deviation from the presumed "norm" is deemed pathological. This approach is blamed for lowering the tolerance for psychological distress in Western societies (the "snowflake" effect) and worsening the stigma associated with seeking help for MH issues.

The GMH experience has taught MH professionals about the miracle of human resilience. It spearheaded the development of newer assessments and interventions consistent with this normalization trend. However, the most pressing need has been for the developing humanitarian competencies, which involve understanding the humanitarian context and the systems of humanitarian relief.

The GMH framework used in this book is based on the assumption that most people are strong and capable of coping with adversity and healing. Still, those who are vulnerable and struggling to cope need more support in accessing internal and external resources and receiving MH treatment in most severe cases. Consequently, GMH prioritizes interventions that gear toward identifying and building on the available individual, family, or community resources and addressing the barriers to accessing them.

With this understanding, the GMH work emphasizes resilience, coping, and recovery rather than telling affected people what they must feel or trying to make them "healthy," whatever it can mean in severe adversity.

The GMH work also has made clear that MH professionals can no longer afford to be confined to their siloed areas of professional expertise. Attending to the complex and interconnected needs in humanitarian settings presents significant challenges to the traditionally siloed professional training. These challenges require developing integrated interdisciplinary concepts and approaches, contextually appropriate assessment tools, and integrated interventions.

In contrast to individual acts of altruism, humanitarian work always is an organized, coordinated, and collaborative helping activity that brings together different organizations and actors across disciplines and sectors who must closely collaborate because no one will be able to meet such complex and interconnected needs alone. Both humanitarian relief and GMH work can only be effective as these organized and concerted efforts. The GMH response to humanitarian emergencies conducted as a part of humanitarian action relies on estabilishing collaborations and partnerships between the interdisciplinary actors and the benefitiaries, united by shared core values and mission.

As a specialty with its distinct scope of services, practices, regulations, and ethics, GMH work, by and large, is defined by its interdisciplinary and collaborative nature and the humanitarian context. When responding to humanitarian crises, GMH providers become a part of a humanitarian action where all actors rely on shared humanitarian competencies, core values, and goals.

Humanitarian competencies offer an understanding of how these professionally and culturally diverse international humanitarian actors operate and work together, which is essential to maximize the mutual benefits of interventions and reduce risks.

Humanitarian competencies highlight the importance of professionalism in GMH work. These competencies include the knowledge of MH reactions to extreme and traumatic stress in humanitarian emergencies, awareness of relevant assessment tools and MH interventions, understanding of the humanitarian relief systems and humanitarian ethics, and cultural and geopolitical awareness. Professional self-awareness and self-care are essential factors for burnout management in humanitarian work.

The book maps the humanitarian competencies for GMH professionals and provides references for additional reading and training so that the readers can further explore the topics of interest. It prioritizes ethics, generously supplies exercises, discussion points and ethical dilemmas, and offers protocols for practicing decision-making.

The book consists of an introduction and 12 chapters, which sequentially describe the components of professional and humanitarian competencies of MH providers and offer the roadmap for obtaining them.

Here is a brief outline of the chapters:

Humanitarian emergencies create massive MH needs and limit access to services. Attending to these needs is recognized as a global priority on the path toward a healthy and resilient future.

The multidisciplinary GMH work's evolving role in collaborative humanitarian action contributes to the changing landscape of humanitarianism and determines prioritized directions.

The attributes of a humanitarian situation and the extreme vulnerabilities of aid recipients define the context of GMH work, create special challenges for providers, and place particular demands on professional competencies and understanding the humanitarian systems.

Humanitarian context of GMH work determines the understanding of the prioritized needs and tailoring interventions to different humanitarian situations: disasters, armed conflicts, genocide, political oppression, and other form of political dysfunction. GMH professionals assisting special populations such as refugees, child soldiers, or victims of war rape must be aware of their special needs and barriers to meeting them.

An essential component of humanitarian expertise is the knowledge of the humanitarian code of conduct and the GMH ethics, which assists with avoiding ethically questionable practices and negotiating intractable ethical and moral dilemmas that humanitarian emergencies supply in abundance.

The book offers practical steps and recommendations for engaging in humanitarian work and conducting contextually appropriate MH interventions. The knowledge of humanitarian landscape, the inventory of personal and personal values, and professional skills come in handy when exploring employment opportunities in the humanitarian sector or launching a humanitarian project or NGO.

GMH providers may be asked to provide MH and peer support to fellow aid workers and assist them with and supporting them in their readjustment. Self-awareness and self-care skills allow GMH providers to attend to these and their own MH needs, timely recognize countertransference and professional fantasies, and manage burnout.

The book comprises materials, protocols, and examples from different sources. Most are original and drawn from the author's experience, observations, and personal reports. Other examples have been published in literature by other researchers. The piece on trauma in humanitarian emergencies in Chap. 4 has been previously developed as teaching material for the trauma-specific interventions course taught at Cambridge College, where I incorporated students' and faculty's questions and the feedback.

Presented materials have several limitations. First, each humanitarian experience is unique. It is difficult to mechanically extrapolate onto other situations, and not everyone will find the suggested guidelines fully applicable to all aspects of their work. Second, this book is mainly practice-oriented. It touches upon modern conceptual developments and controversies in MH and the humanitarian field but avoids diving deep into ferocious theoretical debates plaguing both the humanitarian and GMH work. It generally proposes the best practices for a particular context, but examining the MH interventions in detail goes beyond this book's scope. Third, it uses generic examples and mostly avoids references to the specific events or countries where a specific case scenario could have occurred or mentioning specific humanitarian organizations that provided relief activities.

Instead, it maps the challenges of MH work in humanitarian settings, focuses on practical recommendations, provides guidance and protocols that can be helpful in GMH work in a variety of situations, and offers resources for further learning. The proposed curriculum for professional training is an attempt to standardize basic requirements for GMH competencies.

The case studies, exercises, and suggested discussion points can be used for training or education. They are loosely based on real-life scenarios. In contrast to the professional humanitarian literature, this book mostly omits references to specific regions or recognizable events. It is done for several reasons. Besides understandable concerns over the accidental disclosure of sensitive and personal information, political situations can change rapidly, and time perspective will reveal new information that can provide a different take on the same problem. With gained time distance, some aspects become more apparent, and others—more controversial. Revealed details can expose participants to dangerous ways many years later. Spotlighting the work of a particular humanitarian agency may raise concerns about the appearance of a conflict of interest or advertisements.

Finally, each real-life and identifiable example of a humanitarian emergency comes with way too many contextual nuances that can overshadow the main point of discussion. The overconcentration on details complicates recognition of the general patterns. Using generic situations allows the readers to improvise and fill in the examples from the regions that are the most familiar to them.

For brevity, the term *global mental health (GMH)* in this book is used broadly. It is similar to how we use *mental health (MH)* or *public health*. It equally refers to health status, an area of expertise, and the scope of service. The word *global* in global mental health refers to the problem's scope, not its location (Koplan et al., 2009).

The separately attached glossary explains and clarifies commonly used terms and notions that sometimes are used interchangeably or have several concurrent connotations.

References

Cherepanov, E. (2018). *Ethics for global mental health: From good intentions to humanitarian accountability*. Routledge. https://doi.org/10.4324/9781351175746

Cherepanov, E. (2023). Refugees from countries with complex political contexts: Politically informed approach to health and mental health services. *Frontiers in Public Health, 11*, 1323259. https://doi.org/10.3389/fpubh.2023.1323259

Kalmakis, K. A., & Chandler, G. E. (2015). Health consequences of adverse childhood experiences: A systematic review. *Journal of the American Association of Nurse Practitioners, 27*(8), 457–465. https://doi.org/10.1002/2327-6924.12215

Koplan, J. P., Bond, T. C., Merson, M. H., Reddy, K. S., Rodriguez, M. H., Sewankambo, N. K., Wasserheit, J. N., & Consortium of Universities for Global Health Executive Board. (2009). Towards a common definition of global health. *Lancet, 373*(9679), 1993–1995. https://doi.org/10.1016/S0140-6736(09)60332-9. Epub 2009 Jun 1. PMID: 19493564; PMCID: PMC9905260.

UNSTATS. (2022). *The Sustainable Development Goals report 2022*. https://unstats.un.org/sdgs/indicators/Global%20Indicator%20Framework%20after%202022%20refinement_Eng.pdf

Chapter 2
Mental Health in Humanitarian Emergency

Humanitarian Emergencies and Their Impact on MH

This chapter reviews what has been learned about the mental health (MH), health and social impact in emergencies, and the challenges for conducting the epidemiological research.

The ever-increasing frequency and severity of armed conflicts, disasters, epidemics, and famines all around the world with no seeming end in sight has become a reminder of the fragility and interdependency of humanity. It has inspired MH professionals to redefine their roles in the changing global landscape and actively contribute to saving lives and alleviating suffering.

The introduction of a global perspective has brought attention to the impact of humanitarian emergencies on MH and spearheaded humanitarian research and practical innovations. However, currently, we face a peculiar situation when empirical innovation outpaced the development of concepts, assessments, and the development of contextually appropriate interventions.

What Are Humanitarian Emergencies?

A *humanitarian emergency* is an event or series of events that represents a critical threat to a community's health, safety, or well-being (https://www.humanitariancoalition.ca/what-is-a-humanitarian-emergency). Examples include disasters, conflicts, famines, epidemics, or political violence.

E. Cherepanov, *Humanitarian Competencies for Global Mental Health Professionals*, Contemporary Humanitarian Action and Emergency Management,
https://doi.org/10.1007/978-3-031-74268-2_2

The impact of such events exceeds the community's capacity for coping and produce massive humanitarian needs, exacerbate vulnerabilities, and can worsen the social and political tensions, injustices, and violence.

(Data)

In June of 2023, the International Rescue Committee identified the ten top ongoing crises, with more information available on their website at https://www.rescue.org/article/top-10-crises-world-cant-ignore-2023.

10. Ukraine: The war has created the world's most significant displacement.
9. Haiti: Gang violence and climate change combine into chaos.
8. Burkina Faso: Armed group activity invites instability.
7. South Sudan: Climate change compounds the legacy of civil war.
6. Syria: Years of war trigger a health crisis.
5. Yemen: Failed truce could lead to renewed conflict.
4. Democratic Republic of Congo: Decades-long conflicts escalate.
3. Afghanistan: An entire population is pushed into poverty.
2. Ethiopia: Drought and conflict affect tens of millions.
1. Somalia: A catastrophic hunger crisis.

This watchlist has been expanding and now includes the 2023 earthquakes in Syria and Turkey, and the Gaza–Israel armed conflict. Many more disasters and wars are unfolding on a smaller scale, which does not make them less devastating or lethal.

These crises and wars have already led to the largest refugee crisis in modern history, which is worsening every day.

The United Nations High Commission for Refugees (UNHCR, 2023) estimates that there are 110 million people forcibly displaced worldwide as a result of persecution, conflict, violence, human rights violations, or events seriously disturbing public order. Among them

43.3 million are children.
52% originate from just three countries:

Syrian Arab Republic 6.5 million
Afghanistan 6.1 million
Ukraine 5.9 million.

Mental Health Impact

Humanitarian emergencies expose people to profoundly disempowering experiences of trauma and victimization while also compromising community and family support and access to care.

Evidence suggests humanitarian crises and deteriorating environmental conditions have catastrophic effects on health, MH, and well-being (Batniji et al., 2006; Tol et al., 2010). Humanitarian emergencies can trigger or exacerbate preexisting MH and related issues, such as mental illnesses, neurological conditions, and developmental problems, potentially leading to problematic behavioral health outcomes, including substance misuse, suicide, and an increase in community violence (Ventevogel et al., 2013).

> The MH impact of humanitarian emergency is recognized in people who give up hope and no longer strive to survive; those who can no longer attend to activities of daily living, care for themselves and their loved ones or reach out for help when help is needed and available. They can become a part of the problem by choosing self-destructive behavior or engaging in cycles of retaliatory violence.

What do we know about MH needs in conflict and humanitarian settings? Humanitarian research of the prevalence of MH symptoms remains the primary tool for understanding the state of MH. The massive body of the research has already been conducted to evaluate the extent of needs, identify the service gaps in services, and improve access to MH services. Why then are we still so far from being satisfied with the knowledge about the state of MH outside the Western countries? One issue seems to relate to the lens through which we approach this task.

Although no one has any doubts that humanitarian crises significantly affect MH, measuring this impact has proven tricky. Initially, researchers were primarily focusing on identifying rates of post-traumatic stress disorder (PTSD) and depression (de Jong et al., 2003; Neria et al., 2008; Steel et al., 2009) as they seemed to be most indicative of changes in well-being. And now efforts are made to develop tools allowing us to capture the complexity of the impact of adversity and the protective factors (i.e., culture) on various areas of people's functioning, health, and the well-being.

One common approach to collecting epidemiological data has been to rely on inventory trauma symptoms in different populations and specific emergencies and then compare the prevalence of symptoms to the existing norm.

This approach has indeed produced a host of data, which allowed researchers to decide on the prevailing issues. It has also brought questions about the relevance of these questionnaires to different cultures and situations and whether they can give us an accurate picture. Some scholars have challenged the underlying assumptions, such as over-pathologizing suffering in humanitarian settings (Summerfield, 2004). Other questioned the cultural appropriateness of Western assessments and the language they use (Bemme & D'Souza, 2014).

The rush to gather epidemiological data in humanitarian emergencies has highlighted yet another issue: significant variations in the research designs, assessment tools, samples, sample sizes, and the settings where the research took place create difficulties in comparing these results. One such method that allows us to reconcile these disparate results is meta-analysis.

Meta-analysis is a statistical method that identifies overall trends and patterns by combining and analyzing the results from multiple research studies conducted on the same topic (Oxford English Dictionary, s.v. "Meta-analysis").

The meta-analysis of the epidemiological surveys, which used random samples and diagnostic interviews, indeed confirmed a higher prevalence of MH and psychosocial problems in conflict-affected populations.

Meta-analysis of various studies revealed the following rates of MH issues in conflict settings: 15,4% for PTSD and 17,3% for depression (Hall, 2020; Tol et al., 2011). To compare, an estimated 3.9% people worldwide have had PTSD at some point of their life according to www.who.int/news-room/fact-sheets/detail/posttraumatic-stress-disorder". And the lifetime average prevalence of the most anxiety and major depression disorders in world population ranges from 6-12% and 4-10% respectively (Kessler et al., 2009).

These findings corroborate the empirical evidence indicating a high prevalence of mental disorders and psychosocial concerns that pose significant public health challenges in conflict zones.

Common Reactions to Extreme Stress

Following exposure to a disaster or armed conflict, many report symptoms of post-traumatic stress reactions and behavioral changes (de Jong & Kleber, 2003). Among the most commonly mentioned have been flashbacks, intrusive memories, hypervigilance, isolation, uncontrolled anger, depression, anxiety, sleep problems, substance abuse, suicidal behavior, sense of worthlessness, self-neglect, and chronic medical issues (de Jong et al., 2003).

Trauma exposure can alter beliefs about the self and the world, which can be at the core of difficulties with finding meaning in suffering. Janoff-Bulman (1992) proposed that violence and abuse make the world seem unpredictable, inherently hostile, and untrustworthy. Such social cognitions can persist long after adversity and shape future generations' social perceptions, assumptions, and choices.

Gender-based, ethnic, sectarian, or political violence adds another layer of victimization when a person is targeted based on their gender, ethnicity, or beliefs. The traumatized, divided, and polarized communities may not be able or willing to support survivors, which may further revictimize them. Subsequently, rebuilding support systems and facilitating changes in community attitudes become a powerful impetus to overcoming (Cherepanov, 2015).

Trauma can carry an intergenerational impact. Danieli (2007), who studied children of Holocaust survivors, demonstrated that traumatized parents exhibited characteristic parenting styles that affected the upbringing of children and made them more susceptible to depression, anxiety, and subsequent traumatization.

When stress becomes chronic, the hope for a better future can fade, and hopelessness, desperation, and demoralization set in. Chronic stress may increase the risk of further disintegration of community connections, and worsens the health outcomes. This destructive trauma cycle can be interrupted by a functional and inclusive community that has the resources to help survivors regain dignity and trust in the world.

Risk and Protective Factors

Braveman and Gottlieb (2014) identified several factors shaping MH responses to adversity. Some of these factors increase risks and vulnerabilities while others strengthen resilience. Three groups of risks have been found to be contributing to the reaction of extreme distress.

The first one is the exposure to severe and repeated trauma, violence, and loss, which increases the severity of trauma and the risk of developing serious MH conditions.

The second includes local and global threats and contextual factors such as exposure to violence, poverty, and discrimination. Examples include belonging to a marginalized and discriminated group, and not having access to resources, or social support.

And the third group comprises environmental factors, as well as health and social determinants of health (SDOH).

Protective factors, on the other hand, are those that strengthen resilience and facilitate coping and recovery. In addition to the quality of social support, they can include knowledge about reactions to extreme stress and its coping, a history of positive overcoming in the past and assigning meaning to suffering.

MH promotion and prevention assists with identifying individual, social, cultural, and historical sources of strength and then taking action to rebuild systems of social connectedness and support to help individuals and groups take responsibility for the collective future. These community-based interventions can be tailored for individuals, particular groups, or entire populations (Cherepanov, 2015).

Improving Mental Health as a Public Health Concern and Is the Matter of Human Rights

The emergencies' impact on MH extends far beyond individual distress and trauma to become a factor of public health and human rights.

MH as a Public Health and Human Rights Concern

Disasters and conflicts increase individual and collective vulnerabilities and spotlight human rights concerns. Bajbouj et al. (2022) write that it is a fundamental humanitarian right of disadvantaged and traumatized people to access the same assistance, protection, and care provided to others. In addition, MH providers must ensure that their work does not leave behind the most marginalized, underserved, and disadvantaged people such as children, older people, persons with disabilities or minorities whose needs are often ignored.

In an emergency, these groups often face discrimination, abuse, and violence and are denied access to resources. Supporting and protecting them is an undisputed humanitarian priority of MH work.

Physical health, suicide prevention, and substance misuse are the domains of overlap between MH and public health.

> *Public Health* aims to detect, prevent, and respond to diseases (Oxford English Dictionary, s.v. "Public Health").

The public health paradigm underscores that mental and physical health are equally important and interconnected components of overall health and well-being. MH plays an integral role in achieving public health goals, such as improving physical health and reducing the burden of disease, substance abuse, and suicides.

The recent response to the SARS pandemic demonstrated that medical treatment is only one part of multidisciplinary interventions. Other interventions involve engaging community response, health promotion and education, and delivering masks and the vaccines. MH influences how people perceive and interpret health information, and reach out and accept help, so they are not entangled in conspiracy theories, and do not stigmatize health care workers, survivors, victims, and their families, something that was routinely reported during the 2013–2016 Ebola virus epidemic in West Africa. Mobilizing community-based response became the main tool of curbing the epidemic. "We all are in this together" became a motto during the interdisciplinary pandemic response.

Social Determinants of Health

Social determinants of health (SDOH) include environmental impact and the conditions in which people are born, grow, work, live, and age. Economic, political, social, and other nonmedical factors such as food (in)security, housing, and access to healthcare influence physical and mental health outcomes. (Marmot et al., 2008)

Humanitarian emergencies tend to exacerbate preexisting unequal distribution of income, wealth, influence, power, and other social inequities (Braveman & Gottlieb, 2014), which carry direct implications for the health and MH of the affected populations.

It is estimated that the impact of SDOH accounts for 30–55% of health outcomes (Bhavnani et al., 2023), and the healthcare sector can substantially contribute to advocating and addressing SDOH.

Physical Health

Exposure to severe stresses, trauma, and adversity can significantly shape physical health throughout one's life, including influencing the development of various medical conditions. The scientific evidence has shown that adverse events experienced in childhood (adverse childhood events, or ACEs), such as severe stress, trauma, abuse, or neglect, may have a lifelong effect on physical and mental health. If not addressed, ACEs have been associated with persistent physical and MH problems later in life, such as diabetes, cardiovascular and autoimmune diseases, chronic obstructive pulmonary disease, metabolic disorders, substance abuse, and depression (Kalmakis & Chandler, 2015; Momen et al., 2020).

The opposite is also true: The presence of chronic medical conditions can increase anxiety and depression (NIMH, 2015). Medical conditions and symptoms of depression may continue long after adverse circumstances have improved and survivors are in a safe place, as we see in refugees (Mollica et al., 1993).

Suicide Prevention

A staggering increase in suicide rates around the world has made suicide prevention a high priority in the global public health agenda.

According to WHO statistics, more than 700,000 people die by suicide every year, where 77% of global suicides happen in low- and middle-income countries. (World Health Organization, 2019)

There is an established link between trauma, depression, alcohol abuse, and suicide. Other risk factors include loss, loneliness, relationship strain, financial problems, chronic pain, and illness, as well as exposure to violence, abuse, and conflict (Turecki & Brent, 2016). Such experiences are prevalent during humanitarian emergencies.

Substance Misuse

Substance misuse exponentially increases vulnerabilities in humanitarian crisis because it compromises self-preservation and survival focus, and increases reckless behavior, self-harm (overdose and suicide), and the risk of becoming a victim of violence and crime. When substance users are unable to get their substance of choice, they may develop a life-threatening withdrawal (IASC, 2007). Traumatized people can consume mood-altering substances to self-medicate, which harms their health.

In patients diagnosed with PTSD, the prevalence of comorbid alcohol abuse ranges from 36% to 52% (Banerjee & Spry, 2017). These estimates are even higher in certain groups. It has been estimated that one third of patients with major depressive disorder also suffer from substance use disorders (SUDs) (Vujanovic et al., 2017). Another study demonstrated that 63% of combat veterans with war trauma had comorbid alcohol use disorder and PTSD. (Acosta et al., 2017)

Mental Health as a Global Priority and Future Directions

Designating an area of human functioning as a global priority carries many consequences. This area of concern receives international attention, manpower, and the funding from the international governments and professional community, which facilitate establishing programs. The United Nations (UN), which has a mandate to coordinate the humanitarian response, has recognized the central role of MH in mitigating humanitarian emergencies and achieving health and wellness (CSIS, n.d.).

As a global priority, MH has been deemed a decisive factor in supporting human rights, public health, and suicide prevention, as well as for shaping international policies and achieving sustainable development for all. Protecting and restoring MH

Table 2.1 Seventeen Sustainable Development Goals (SDGs) (https://sdgs.un.org/goals)

(SDG 1) No poverty
(SDG 2) Zero hunger
(SDG 3) Good health and well-being
(SDG 4) Quality education
(SDG 5) Gender equality
(SDG 6) Clean water and sanitation
(SDG 7) Affordable and clean energy
(SDG 8) Decent work and economic growth
(SDG 9) Industry, innovation, and infrastructure
(SDG 10) Reduced inequalities
(SDG 11) Sustainable cities and communities
(SDG 12) Responsible consumption and production
(SDG 13) Climate action
(SDG 14) Life below water
(SDG 15) Life on land
(SDG 16) Peace, justice, and strong institutions
(SDG 17) Partnerships for the goals

is positioned at the core of strengthening resilience and recovery from adversity (World Health Organization, 2022). Problematic MH, on the other hand, undermines the ability to resiliently cope with adversity, engage in productive work, fulfill one's potential, and make meaningful contributions to the well-being of the family and the community.

The UN's Sustainable Development Goals (SDGs) are the 17 connected goals adopted by the United Nations in 2015, which outline the shared strategic priorities for peace and prosperity for people and the planet, now and into the future (Staglin, 2022). The UN underscored the importance of strengthening MH services by including them in most of their SDGs and set the goal of reducing the MH treatment gap to achieve sustainable development and reduce the burden of disease (Patel et al., 2018). Specifically, MH is placed in the SDG 3 group, which is the "Good health and well-being" goal. It is also positioned as a cross-cutting issue interlinked with physical health, sustainable economy, gender equality, and social inclusion. MH challenges can be both a contributor to and a result of poverty, poor health, violence, and various other global issues (Table 2.1).

Defining Mental Health in Humanitarian Crisis

The introduction of a global perspective has invited MH professionals in Western countries to self-reflect and reevaluate many core concepts that were previously taken for granted. Understandably, this task has revealed the difference in opinions. The only matter that all agree on is that suffering people need support.

One of the most scrutinized notions has become the concept of MH itself. The way this issue is framed determines the needs, goals, strategic directionality of interventions and how to measure their outcomes. Remarkably, the most contentious point has been what it means to be mentally (un)healthy in difficult circumstances. As a result, the professional community has been disproportionally focusing on treating mental disorders and illnesses (which is also very important) rather than supporting a great diversity of normal reactions to adversity.

Global work has also reignited concerns regarding the trend in MH to over-pathologize MH reactions (Caldas de Almeida, 2019). Global mental health (GMH) experience exposed the limitations of the "norm–pathology" dichotomy and questioned the efficacy of using medications when treating contextually appropriate (and, possibly adaptive) expressions of distress as a symptom of pathology (Briere & Scott, 2014; Bracken et al., 2016). Without having a clear answer to how we understand MH and what are the meaning of phrases "we want to improve mental health" and "we need to scale up MH interventions" lack merit.

In the history of MH field, there have been various attempts to delineate this difficult-to-define notion, including suggestions to view MH as an absence of disorders, or a state of total health and wellness—even complete happiness.

Some of these suggestions have been more instrumental than others. The main critique revolves around the unrealistic and misleading expectation for someone to be healthy, well, and happy in the middle of a catastrophe. Many may not be happy, healthy, or well, yet they can have a sense of purpose and live their lives to the fullest under the circumstances.

> This book uses the World Health Organization's (WHO) definition of *mental health* as "a state of mental well-being that enables people to cope with the stresses of life, realize their abilities, learn well, work well, and contribute to their community." (World Health Organization, 2013)

Such conceptualization emphasizes the situational congruency of reactions and feelings, self-determination, ability to function, and doing one's best in challenging circumstances. It highlights the active role of people in overcoming adversity, which is essential for the capacity to make informed choices, build connections, and regain control over one's life.

With respect to children, the WHO (2021) highlights developmental aspects of MH, such as developing a positive sense of identity, regulating emotions, building social relationships, and learning, ultimately enabling their full active participation in society.

This conceptualization positions MH as a critical factor determining physical survival, well-being, and resilience in conflict-ridden settings.

Global Burden of Disease (GBD)

The Lancet Commission on Global Mental Health and Sustainable Development emphasized MH as a fundamental human right imperative for global development (Patel et al., 2018). The Commission called for more investment in MH services and better integration of these services into the global response.

The Global Burden of Disease (GBD) is a measure that was developed to estimate a population's health status as well as the impact thereof on economic development and the population's well-being. GBD is measured by a metric called DALY: Disability-Adjusted Life Years. Conceptually, one DALY is the equivalent of losing 1 year in good health because of either premature death, disease, or disability. (Kabajulizi & Francis Awuku, 2022)

The GBD assesses both mortality (the number of deaths) and morbidity (the number of individuals affected by disabilities) to evaluate the socioeconomic impact caused by disease and injuries, accounting for country, time, age, and gender. This approach allows thinking in terms of improving healthcare systems and bridging disparities for better health outcomes.

A 30-year-long analysis of GBD via DALY published by *Lancet* concluded that mental disorders remain the tenth leading cause of disease burden worldwide (GBD 2019 Mental Disorders Collaborators, 2022). The recommended inclusion of the MH agenda in the SDGs has offered new opportunities for global initiatives to research the prevalence of MH disorders, such as PTSD, depression, substance use, and self-harmful behaviors.

This documented burden associated with mental disorders is compounded by the widening mental health treatment gap worldwide; more than 70% of persons who need MH services lack access to care (Kohn et al., 2004). Two decades later, this gap is expected to be even wider.

Barriers to Accessing MH Support and Services

Severe stress and trauma associated with humanitarian crises create massive MH needs. In low- to middle-income countries (LMICs), MH resources are often nonexistent or insufficient and problematic to access.

The treatment gap measures the accessibility of health and MH services. It is expressed as the percentage of individuals who require care but, for various reasons, do not receive treatment. (Kohn et al., 2004)

In a humanitarian emergency, people face numerous barriers to accessing the MH support and services. In addition to the limited availability of service providers, access is complicated by the religious, social, and cultural beliefs affecting what people know and how they feel about receiving MH care. Prevalent misconceptions about MH services with associated stigmas and prejudices are widespread and often deter people from seeking help even when this help is available.

Weinberg et al. (2017) have attributed the existence of the MH treatment gap to the stigma associated with mental illness, lack of providers, fragmented service delivery models, and lack of research that is needed for policy change.

A World Health Organization survey concluded that in LMICs, between 76% and 85% of people with severe mental disorders had not received any treatment for their MH conditions within a year before the interview, where alcohol abuse and dependence accounted for 78.1% of the respondents. (Demyttenaere et al., 2004)

However, the appeal to close the treatment gap as a primary goal in Global Mental Health (GMH) work has sparked controversy due to its likely disregard for culturally available specific forms of coping, resilience, and reliance on community strength (Jansen et al., 2015; Cosgrove et al., 2020). Furthermore, GMH professionals, medical anthropologists, and transcultural psychiatrists have deemed this approach concerning, as it imposes the Western healthcare model as the only one possible, without discussing its limitations and alternative options.

Future Directions

During a humanitarian crisis like war, natural disaster, or civil unrest, offering MH support to the affected people can be lifesaving. MH care is equally essential to physical and mental health because it influences an individual's capacity to survive and endure adversity (Moore, 2021). Failure to address MH issues in humanitarian emergencies will likely have long-lasting impacts on health and social issues of the region, lowering quality of life and reducing economic stability. Furthermore, high rates of MH issues can negatively impact a community's ability to cope and remain resilient.

In 2018, the Lancet Commission on Global Mental Health and Sustainable Development outlined the priorities for MH professionals working globally. The authors called for urgent action to translate current knowledge into concrete activities that should aim to promote MH, prevent mental disorders, and strengthen services allowing for the detection, treatment, support, and recovery of people with mental illnesses (Patel et al., 2018).

The current Comprehensive Mental Health Action Plan 2013–2020 (WHO, 2010) issued by the World Health Organization (WHO) recognizes the essential role that MH plays in achieving health and wellness for all people and outlines strategic objectives for MH. The mhGAP plan sets the future directions for MH as such:

Develop interventions and GMH-appropriate assessment tools.

Wessels (2009) has expressed a belief that universal approaches may not be effective and called for increased efforts to ensure contextually and culturally appropriate interventions. Development of such tools can be achieved by employing critical self-reflection, greater specificity in ethical guidance, a stronger evidence base for intervention, and improved methods of preparing GMH professionals.

Develop community-based approaches.

Community-based approaches have the answers to many lingering questions, as they delegate the responsibility for recovery and well-being back to the community. The interventions include engaging formal or informal community leaders and training and supporting community workers. (Abramowitz, 2017; Cherepanov, 2015)

Incorporate integrated approaches.

At a disaster site, medical, social, and MH needs are all intertwined, and integrating MH into the social services and primary care system reflects the structure of these needs.

Foster resilience.

Resilience is a core component that determines the effectiveness of recovery and the capacity to deal with future adversities. In MH, resilience means the ability to cope with hardships and challenges and to bounce back when confronted with traumatizing events. For example, MH and human resilience are critical components of mitigating and adapting to climate change. (World Health Organization, 2022)

Prioritize violence prevention.

Exposure to the collective trauma of violence can undermine the stability of recovery and raise concerns about the peaceful future of the region. Prevention of future incidents of violence becomes a priority in humanitarian settings, where MH providers not only respond to an immediate threat but contribute to breaking cycles of violence.

Counter effects of stigma and discrimination.

Psychoeducation, rejecting the pathologizing of MH, and emphasizing local culturally appropriate healing practices are primary strategies for reducing the MH stigma in affected populations.

Seek policy solutions.

Promoting and protecting MH is a growing area of interest that can be supported through legislation and funding. With the growing number of humanitarian crises, humanitarian action is committed to informing policy solutions to humanitarian challenges and improving humanitarian access. (CSIS, n.d.)

Trauma and Trauma-Specific Interventions in Humanitarian Settings

Disasters and conflicts expose people to adverse events, hardship, and other traumatizing experiences. Psychological trauma is the MH condition that GMH providers most commonly expect to encounter in a humanitarian crisis. In their work, they ponder how they can best serve people whose entire lives are affected and whose resilience is stretched to its limits.

I begin with examining post-traumatic stress disorder (PTSD), the diagnostic criteria associated with traumatic exposure, and examine how it influenced assessment tools, and how the concept of trauma is currently evolving. Then, I place trauma in the humanitarian context, explore the collective experience of trauma, and discuss implications for interventions.

Post-Traumatic Stress Disorder (PTSD) and Its Assessment

The professional and public interest in trauma has led to the explosion of various models, assessments, and interventions. Still, more attention has been given to PTSD, the severe, chronic, and sometimes debilitating disorder that is associated with neurological and endocrinological changes. PTSD is diagnosed when exposure to a traumatizing event is followed by the emergence of avoidance, intrusions, hypervigilance, and other specific symptoms. Consequently, the trauma treatment goals for PTSD are envisioned as elimination, reduction, or better management of these symptoms.

This symptoms-oriented approach has produced numerous diagnostic, assessment, and treatment tools. The data has been used in epidemiological research to study the prevalence of PTSD and trauma-associated MH disorders in the regions affected by disasters and conflicts. Trauma assessments and related treatment interventions have been a hallmark of GMH involvement from the get-go. Still, GMH experience questioned some tenets of the traditional trauma work, and the relevance of PTSD-specific and evidence-based practices in humanitarian emergencies.

The PTSD-based assessments have been used for measuring the MH impact of trauma on adults and children. They were developed and standardized for clinical settings and not all are GMH-friendly: some are way too long, too complicated, and contain difficult-to-translate instructions, questions, and statements. More contextually appropriate assessment tools rooted in different trauma concepts are currently being developed. The International Trauma Questionnaire (ITQ) (Hyland et al., 2017) is one such novel assessment.

Here are some commonly used assessment tools with brief annotations.

PTSD Checklist for DSM-5 (PCL-5)

The PCL-5 is a 20-item self-report measure that assesses the 20 DSM-5 symptoms of PTSD. The PCL-5 has a variety of purposes, including monitoring symptoms change during and after treatment, screening individuals for PTSD, and making a provisional PTSD diagnosis. (Weathers et al., 2013)

PTSD Symptom Scale—Interview for DSM-5 (PDS-5)

The PDS-5 is a 24-item self-report measure that assesses PTSD symptom severity in the last month according to DSM-5 criteria. The PDS-5 begins with two trauma screen questions to assess trauma history and identify an index trauma. An item for each of the 20 DSM-5 PTSD symptoms is included, and an additional four items ask about distress and interference caused by PTSD symptoms as well as onset and duration of symptoms. (Foa et al., 2016)

Impact of the Event Scale-Revised (IES-R) for DSM-IV

The IES-R is a 22-item self-report measure (for *DSM-IV*) that assesses subjective distress caused by traumatic events. Items correspond directly to 14 of the 17 *DSM-IV* symptoms of PTSD. Respondents are asked to identify a specific stressful life event and then indicate how much they were distressed or bothered during the past seven days by each "difficulty" listed. (Weiss & Marmar, 1996)

Trauma Symptom Inventory-2 (TSI-2)

The TSI-2 is a 136-item adult self-report measure of post-traumatic stress and other psychological sequelae of traumatic and stressful events. It is designed to assess the sequelae of a wide range of adversities, including DSM-5 trauma, but also stressful experiences such as emotional neglect and experiences of loss. The TSI-2 assesses PTSD symptoms but also broader psychological outcomes. Symptom responses are not tied to a particular event or timespan. (Briere, 2011)

The International Trauma Questionnaire (ITQ)

The ITQ is an 18-question self-report measure focusing on the core features of Post Traumatic Stress Disorder (PTSD) and Complex PTSD (CPTSD). The ITQ is designed for diagnosis and can discriminate PTSD from CPTSD by employing validated diagnostic rules. The scale has two major subscales with three symptom clusters in each: Post Traumatic Stress Disorder (PTSD) and Disturbances in self-organization (DSO). The ITQ is useful in the assessment of adults who have experienced trauma and asks them to answer questions in relation to a specific traumatic event. (Hyland et al., 2017). There is also a children's version of ITQ-CA (Haselgruber et al., 2020)

The Danieli Inventory of Multigenerational Legacies of Trauma

It is a self-reported behavioral measure for "assessing multidimensional multigenerational impacts of massive trauma. The questionnaire assesses the adaptation in children of trauma survivors to post-trauma parenting style (60 items per parent)". (Danieli et al., 2015a, b)

GMH work experience confirmed that there may be a wide variety of reactions to traumatic exposure that are not captured by PTSD-focused assessments. Making sense of these reactions helps to establish contextually appropriate assessments and trauma-informed and culture-sensitive interventions.

Trauma in a Humanitarian Emergency

Trauma work is emblematic of GMH practice and, not surprisingly, is often a focal point of GMH interventions. At the same time, the meaning of what we consider trauma has changed and expanded so far beyond its extreme presentation (i.e., PTSD) that almost any distressing life experience is now called trauma.

Traumatic exposure does not automatically mean the loss of functioning, but it still can affect MH in a significant way and alter emotional well-being, behavior, and social cognition. Trauma experience affects a person on multiple levels: physiologically, emotionally, cognitively, or socially. Severe reactions to traumatic events interfere with daily functioning and, in addition to pain and suffering, complicate coping, impede resilience, and interfere with survival tasks.

The broadening of the qualifying criteria for trauma in terms of what can cause traumatic stress and the range of expected reactions has made the notion of trauma less specific. Equating the experience of people directly subjected to violence, mistreatment, or injustice to those who watched it on TV or heard about it from witnesses does a disservice to both groups.

In GMH work, the word trauma is often used in its broadest sense, as a metaphor signifying the losses and fragmentation in a person's life incurred because of exposure to severe adversity (Cherepanov, 2020). Humanitarian emergencies tend to break social connections and disrupt the flow and fabric of personal and community life. This profoundly disempowering experience splits the person's life into before and after and is associated with multiple and ambiguous losses. They can be the loss of a loved one, home, property, or community connections. The loss of family and social support often compounds a loss of social identity or status. Traumatic exposure can instill mental fragmentation, where the "wounded" parts of self and painful memories are alienated and dissociated because they are too painful to handle.

On the other side, trauma experience can invoke strength, consolidate resources, and become an epitome of resilience, overcoming, and perseverance. It activates mutual support and reveals true strength and compassion.

In contrast to the universality of trauma, pain, and suffering experience, the expressions of distress, meaning-making, and coping are culturally and contextually conditioned.

Those who believe that people in other cultures do not grieve the same way, or love and care about their children as much as Westerners do, need to reevaluate their presumptions about humanity to avoid dehumanizing the people we serve.

In an African region with extremely high child mortality, GMH providers noticed that mothers are emotionally cold and distant with their children and do not show much affection. Based on their observation, providers presumed that these mothers don't feel much love for their babies. Several alternative explanations for this behavior were revealed during in-depth conversations with mothers. These women encountered so many losses in their lives that they were afraid to get emotionally attached to their children or show them their love. Another reason was that they feared the children would become attached to them. If something happens to parents, the children will be left to care for themselves. As terrible as it sounds, grieving may not be conducive to survival, and parents were trying to protect their children from this faith. Interestingly, I've encountered reports of similar emotional detachment from loved ones among survivors of the Great Purge during Stalin's repressions in the Soviet Union and from the survivors of Killing Fields in Cambodia. (Cherepanov, personal communication)

The evolving understanding of trauma reactions increased appreciation for natural healing and the contextual dimensions that inform treatment and coping strategies. They are cultural, social, and political influences.

Adaptive Role of Trauma Reactions

Understanding the trauma symptoms as adaptive has challenged the perception of traumatized people as being fundamentally deficient and damaged. It also questioned the absolute value of eliminating trauma symptoms without offering alternative ways to manage traumatic memories. For example, a person who overworks and is unable to relax or uses alcohol to cope with trauma may become inundated by traumatic memories if they just stop working or drinking. Concurrent development of alternative coping tools other than drinking helps to avoid maladaptive self-medication.

GMH work has consistently demonstrated the limitations of previously prevailing approaches, which reduce trauma to its pathological aspects. Such a pathologizing approach does not seem to explain much in a humanitarian emergency where most people share similar experiences and many report the same symptoms but, nevertheless, are able to continue functioning. The opposing optics involve strength-based approaches that focus on what makes a person persevere and what resources and strength that a person can access and use to overcome adversity and heal.

In this book, I follow the understanding of traumatic reaction formation as primarily adaptive (Briere & Scott, 2014; Correia-Santos et al., 2023). In this framework, the trauma symptom's function is to protect a person from toxic, intrusive, painful, and sometimes shameful traumatic memories, and to enhance the person's adjustment to a dangerous situation. For example, dissociation helps to avoid the reminders; anxiety or hypervigilance can be adaptive during active conflict and will help a person to stay alert and out of danger. On the other hand, staying relaxed in such a situation can make a person weak, defenseless, and more vulnerable in the hostile and unpredictable environment.

Practicing relaxation techniques in a dangerous situation can create a false sense of safety and weaken psychological defenses (this happens when we feel safe) and, as a result, increase vulnerability. Instead, such a person may benefit from, technoques that involve re-focusing and becoming mindful of external or internal objects to distract a person from traumatic memories while allowing them to remain alert and paying attention to their surroundings. For example, grounding, mindfulness techniques, or progressive muscle relaxation involve actively contracting muscles to create tension and progressively releasing them. (Toussaint et al., 2021)

The understanding of trauma reactions as adaptive has been gaining traction among GMH professionals, guiding them to support affected people in coping and recovery efforts and strengthening resilience instead of dwelling on weaknesses and deficiencies. This approach appears very promising because it normalizes the reactions and emphasizes the active role of people in shaping their coping and recovery.

Within this framework, the goal of trauma interventions is to assist people to regain control over their mind, feelings, and behavior. After the crisis is over and there is more life stability, targeted interventions can address persistant emotional and trauma-related needs.

This said, adaptation can sometimes also become problematic. First, like any other adaptation, trauma reactions can be adaptive to only particular circumstances, losing their adaptive potential or becoming maladaptive when the situation changes. A glaring example of such changed functionality is the PTSD symptoms in veterans, which are adaptive in the war zone but become problematic when veterans reach safety. Maladaptive behavior is also the form of adaptation that can turn problematic on the long run. An example is using alcohol or other psychoactive substances to self-medicate. Finally, too much adaptation can impede the survival instinct or create the “frog in boiling water” effect (Cherepanov, 2020). For example, some well-adapted people may fail to relocate while such an opportunity is still available.

Cultural and Contextual Dimensions of Trauma: Collective Trauma

In a humanitarian crisis, trauma is often severe, compounded, and chronic. At the same time, this experience may be normalized when many others have been exposed to the same adversity and hardship. This is different from sexual assault, which is always personalized and experienced as targeted victimization.

The situation on the ground, culture, the history of the region, and available supports all play a role in how adversity is perceived, understood, expressed, and coped with. For example, the descendants of the genocide survivors may interpret any adversity as a continuation of the historic genocidal victimization and freeze in response instead of seeking protection or fighting back.

Here are a few words about the role of culture in trauma interventions. The culture's powerful and complex presence in people's lives extends beyond beautiful traditions, rituals, or delicious cuisine. Culture is an infinite source of meanings, empowerment, and coping.

Culture plays an important role in forming mutual support and showing compassion, and the culture-bound idioms of distress determine how trauma and distress are expressed and communicated. Culture contributes to assigning meaning to the experience and provides prescriptions for survival, i.e., survival messages (SMs) (Cherepanov, 2020), which guide the survival efforts and remain a great resource of transgenerational wisdom, empowerment, strength, resilience, and healing.

Traditional cultures can also impose values, as it sets rigid norms and regulates behaviors, where any diversion from what culture deems "normal" has negative consequences and can be punished. Such "warden's" role of a traditional culture can partially explain the frequently encountered stigmatization of anything that appears different, whether it is a mental illness, severe trauma, or LGBTQ gender identity.

The limitations of reliance on culture on a disaster site has been noted by Dyregrov et al. (2002), who suggest that the people's resilience can become a more important factor in shaping people's reaction to traumatic stress than culture.

I hypothesize that culture is well equipped to mitigate the routine life events such as loss or grief. The traditional or faith-based healing practices and bereavement rituals are often examples of perfectly designed therapeutic interventions, and MH providers can only admire and learn from how the culture supports its members. However, traditional culture can misfire when encountering unusual or unfamiliar issues and reveal a hostile attitude toward people who survived, for instance, domestic violence or sexual abuse. In such cases, traditional culture can side with perpetrators and blame the victims, making survivors a social pariah and continuing victimizing them. GMH providers must scale up their support for survivors to substitute compromised community support.

I also must mention the caution when relying on traditional healing practices, which can include using mood-altering substances as well as elements of physical abuse.

Besides culture, trauma response is expected to be different in natural disaster or an "Act of God" when there is no one to blame, or in case of terrorism, genocide, or political violence and other instances of deliberate victimization. The culture and political context affect social cognitions and determine the help-seeking behavior and trust or lack thereof to the officials, including health care providers.

Trauma is also experienced differently, whether it is an individual or collective experience. Despite the belief that collective experience makes trauma experience worse, it is not always the case, thanks to the phenomenon of aggregation (Cherepanov, 2020).

> *Aggregation* occurs when many traumatized people interact, and this interaction creates a sort of mental space of trauma where people who share similar experiences can empathize, relate, and support each other. The experience of surviving political persecution or a dictatorship deeply affects trust, and the aggregation may not develop, leaving people feeling alone and isolated.

Trauma-Specific Interventions

The complexity of the phenomena of trauma can be compared only to life itself, which is never ideal, but it does not mean that it needs to be treated. Existing conceptualizations of trauma inform the choice of appropriate interventions. However, regardless of how trauma is understood, the GMH interventions usually aim at coping, improving functioning, and promoting healing. More about best practices in specific emergencies will be discussed in Chaps. 7 and 8.

I often receive questions about the relevance of psychoanalysis in an emergency. I agree with my peers who, in private conversations, questioned the utility of analytical approaches on a disaster site.

It is my belief that the analytical interventions can exacerbate the mental fragmentation in survivors affected by the ongoing or recent trauma, which is a common attribute of trauma experience. The second reason is that analytical approaches in therapy encourage self-reflection and invite a person to explore the distant past, which seems less relevant to the rapidly evolving situation. This distracts us from attending to the immediate needs and the concerns about the near future. Finally, analytical approaches thrive on identifying and challenging the "resistance," which is part of psychological defenses. This tactic contradicts trauma-informed care, which is based on the idea that we must meet the person where they are and not force upon them to go further than they feel safe to go.

In trauma work, resistance and resilience seems to come from the same source and are driven by the need in re-instating control over their mind and behavior. A trauma-informed service provider respects and strengthens mental defenses so the person feels safe enough to initiate changes in their life.

With this understanding, trauma-informed therapy gears toward repairing the ensued fragmentation and facilitating healing by restoring the sense of wholeness of self and the continuity of life. Examples of such approaches are art therapy or holistic approaches, which treat a client as a whole person who is not reduced to their traumatized part.

People are affected by adversity in different ways, and GMH work is moving away from making assumptions about the impact and focuses on coping and functioning. This way, the primary goal of trauma interventions is not curing trauma but providing emotional support and empowerment, supporting personal and collective resilience, and helping people access resources and regain a sense of control. Those who are severely impacted, most vulnerable, struggle to cope, have no support, or are rejected by the community are prioritized for MH support and may require higher intensity interventions.

When providing training and supervision to the GMH professionals, I often observed *a convergence of interventions*. It is the effect when GMH providers coming from different schools of thought and training end up using the same interventions and share a similar understanding of their goals. Their interventions equally involve active listening skills, offering emotional support, encouragement, and empowerment, and assisting with accessing the resources and problem-solving.

Common Misconceptions About Trauma

There are several pervasive myths and misconceptions about trauma in humanitarian emergencies that can affect our understanding of needs and priorities.

"Anyone who is exposed to adversity needs assistance."

Most people demonstrate tremendous strength and resilience and will be able to cope. MH support relieves pain and suffering and helps to overcome difficulties. It makes coping more effective and facilitates resilience and recovery.

"Distress is not normal and must be alleviated in the shortest time possible."

While lessening suffering is a main mission of MH work, distress unfortunately remains a predictable part of human existence and is an expected reaction to a horrific situation. A person's choice to stay with their feelings should be respected. In most instances, rushing for quick solutions and treatment deprives a person of the ability to use their own resources, heal naturally, and use this experience to build future resilience.

"Human suffering and trauma are culture-specific, and providers from different cultures will not be able to understand it."

Basic human emotions such as love, pain, anger, loss, fear, and desperation are universal. Regardless of the culture, anyone who just lost a loved one will have similar feelings and it allows people to relate to each other. Culture determines how these feelings are expressed and communicated, and it, in part, informs coping methods.

"MH treatment is always associated with stigma."

There is a widespread conviction that anything associated with MH carries stigma, which becomes an impassable barrier to receiving services. Indeed, deeply seeded fears associated with mental illness and psychiatry can be found across most cultures—the limited understanding of what psychologists and counselors do add to this prejudice. However, introducing MH counseling or treatment as something that can help with stress or sleep dramatically reduces the risk of stigmatization.

"People with underlying MH issues are more vulnerable to traumatization."

In many instances, this is an accurate statement. However, in a crisis, many can use their previous experience of overcoming to show great strength and resilience and to help others.

"Quickly jumping to meaning-making will help a person find a silver lining."

It is a common belief that finding meaning in suffering makes it easier to endure, but this has been challenged. Rushed meaning-making can worsen the outcome of traumatization and lead to higher PTSD rates. Updegraff et al. (2008) suggested that premature meaning-making efforts are linked to higher levels of posttraumatic stress symptoms. Furthermore, the meaning tends to change over time.

"Religious belief is always important in trauma recovery, and providers must do everything to help a person to reconnect with their faith."

Although having faith provides an important support in trauma recovery, some survivors may lose faith because of their experience. Many, however, maintain spirituality and the belief in higher power. This belief helps with perseverance and maintaining strength. There are also survivors who find their primary source of empowerment in other beliefs and meanings that are not religious, such as sense of duty, love, and devotion.

"A successful trauma work requires establishing trust with an MH provider."

Trust is never given and it must be earned, especially during humanitarian emergencies, when people have good reasons for distrust strangers. That said, much of trauma work in a crisis is skills-based and oriented toward symptom management. Teaching one about trauma symptoms and how they can improve their sleep or depressed mood does not require much interpersonal trust. In addition, being truthful has never been a qualifying requirement to receive MH services.

"Victims are good, honest and appreciative people."

This supposition in providers is linked to the "belief in a just world" (Janoff-Bulman, 1992), an illusion in which we tend to believe that if we help someone, this person will not harm us back. We must not make any assumptions about the nature of people based on their experience of suffering: The people we serve may or may not be good people; they may lie or tell the truth. The most important point is that it is totally irrelevant to our work, which is about helping people who suffer regardless of anything else. Being truthful or a good person is not a qualifying characteristic for receiving MH support and treatment. GMH providers shall not impose their moral judgment on people they service.

"Talking about the traumatic experience makes a traumatized person feel better."

Not always. Western MH has put many hopes in trauma processing, which is a part of cognitive-behavioral therapy. However, the universality of such an approach in different cultures and situations has been questioned. The indiscriminative use of trauma processing can lead to re-traumatization and does not always bring relief, especially when the person doesn't have a place of safety or sound support. In addition, a traumatized person may have committed deeds in the past that they may not be proud of. It must be totally up to the individual whether to share their traumatic experience, and they should not be coerced by false promises that they will feel relief if they do, especially when the effectiveness of such invasive approaches has not been exhaustively proven. (Murray et al., 2022)

"To deal with trauma, we need to talk about trauma."

There are many ways an MH provider can address trauma reactions without explicitly talking about trauma. One of the most powerful PTSD symptoms is avoidance, and talking about painful experiences can make a person feel worse unless they express such a preference. Better options may be using metaphors, expressive arts, playing games with children and adults, or just talking about a person's overcoming, support, successful coping, strength, and resilience.

"Trauma work relies on concept of hope as the main source of strength and resilience."

In trauma, the use of hope is possible but not necessary. First, hope implies having a positive future vision. Trauma survivors, especially those who continue to live in an unpredictable and unsafe environment, often have a hard time visualizing a time beyond the immediate conditions. This is the "effect of the foreshortened future," when one cannot imagine oneself in the future. (Ratcliffe et al., 2014)

Second, hope may be perceived as an unrealistic reassurance without facts to support it. And finally, hope can interfere with the acceptance of reality in cases of ambiguous losses such as when loved ones are missing in action.

Instead, sources of strength and hopefulness can come from historic survival experiences of overcoming, the "one day at a time" approach and (re)establishing daily routines. (Pearson & Cherepanov, 2012; Cherepanov, 2016)

Takeaways

- Humanitarian emergencies expose people to severe stress and trauma, and strain internal and external coping resources. Their impact is often systemic and affects the entire life of individuals and the community, complicating overcoming and recovery.

- Disasters, conflicts, famines, political violence, and other humanitarian emergencies undermine mental health, health, well-being, and resilience, creating barriers to accessing resources, support, and treatment.
- Strategic Development Goals (SDGs) make MH a public health and humanitarian concern and recognize improving MH a global priority.
- Strengthening resilience and supporting coping, community-based interventions, integrative approaches, future violence prevention, and seeking policy solutions are the prioritized directions in addressing MH needs.
- Trauma, pain, and suffering are universal experiences. However, their expression, assigned meaning, coping, and sources of strength have cultural and contextual determinants.
- The main goals of trauma-specific interventions are to provide emotional support and empowerment, strengthen individual and collective resilience, and help people access resources, improve functioning, and regain the mastery of their lives.

References

Abramowitz, S. (2017). Epidemics (especially Ebola). *Annual Review of Anthropology, 46*, 421–445. https://doi.org/10.1146/annurev-anthro-102116-041616

Acosta, M. C., Possemato, K., Maisto, S. A., Marsch, L. A., Barrie, K., Lantinga, L., Fong, C., Xie, H., Grabinski, M., & Rosenblum, A. (2017). Web-delivered CBT reduces heavy drinking in OEF-OIF veterans in primary care with symptomatic substance use and PTSD. *Behavior Therapy, 48*(2), 262–276. https://doi.org/10.1016/j.beth.2016.09.001

Bajbouj, M., Ta, T. M. T., Hassan, G., & Hahn, E. (2022). Editorial: The nine grand challenges in global mental health. *Frontiers in Psychiatry, 12*, 822299. https://doi.org/10.3389/fpsyt.2021.822299

Banerjee, S., & Spry, C. (2017). *Concurrent treatment for substance use disorder and trauma-related comorbidities: A review of clinical effectiveness and guidelines*. Canadian Agency for Drugs and Technologies in Health. https://www.ncbi.nlm.nih.gov/books/NBK525683/

Batniji, R., van Ommeren, M., & Saraceno, B. (2006). Mental and social health in disasters: Relating qualitative social science research and the Sphere standard. *Social Science & Medicine, 62*(8), 1853–1864. https://doi.org/10.1016/j.socscimed.2005.08.050

Bemme, D., & D'Souza, N. (2014). Global mental health and its discontents: An inquiry into the making of global and local scale. *Transcultural Psychiatry, 51*(6), 850–874.

Bhavnani, S. K., Zhang, W., Bao, D., Raji, M., Ajewole, V., Hunter, R., Kuo, Y. F., Schmidt, S., Pappadis, M. R., Smith, E., Bokov, A., Reistetter, T., Visweswaran, S., & Downer, B. (2023). Subtyping social determinants of health in all of us: Network analysis and visualization approach. [Preprint]. *medRxiv*. https://doi.org/10.1101/2023.01.27.23285125

Bracken, P., Giller, J., & Summerfield, D. (2016). Primum non nocere. The case for a critical approach to Global Mental Health. *Epidemiology and Psychiatric Sciences, 25*(6), 506–510.

Braveman, P., & Gottlieb, L. (2014). The social determinants of health: It's time to consider the causes of the causes. *Public Health Reports, 129 Suppl 2*(Suppl 2), 19–31. https://doi.org/10.1177/00333549141291S206

Briere, J. (2011). *Trauma Symptom Inventory-2 (TSI-2)*. Psychological Assessment Resources.

Briere, J. N., & Scott, C. (2014). *Principles of trauma therapy* (2nd ed.). SAGE Publications.

Caldas-de-Almeida, J. M. (2019). Four reflections on the new global mental health priorities. *Epidemiology and Psychiatric Sciences, 29*, e75. https://doi.org/10.1017/S2045796019000726

Center for Strategic and International Studies (CSIC). (n.d.). *Humanitarian agenda*. https://www.csis.org/programs/humanitarian-agenda

Cherepanov, E. (2015). It takes a village: Psychological recovery in complex emergencies. *International Journal of Psychology and Behavioral Sciences, 5*(1), 16–25.

Cherepanov, E. (2016). Role of the international trauma specialist in settings with complex trauma needs. In B. Ghafoori, Y. Caspi, & F. S. Smith (Eds.), *International perspectives on traumatic stress: Theory, access, and mental health services* (pp. 116–131). Nova.

Cherepanov, E. (2020). *Understanding the transgenerational legacy of totalitarian regimes: Paradoxes of cultural learning*. Routledge. https://doi.org/10.4324/9780429030338.

Correia-Santos, P., Ford, J. D., Maia, Â. C., & Pinto, R. J. (2023). Posttraumatic stress disorder symptoms and dissociation as serial mediators of the relationship between cumulative victimization and adjustment problems among poly-victimized at-risk youth. *Psychological Trauma, 15*(Suppl 1), S11–S19. https://doi.org/10.1037/tra0001383. Epub 2022 Oct 27. PMID: 36301298.

Cosgrove, L., Mills, C., Karter, J. M., Mehta, A., & Kalathil, J. (2020). A critical review of the Lancet Commission on global mental health and sustainable development: Time for a paradigm change. *Critical Public Health, 30*(5), 624–631. https://doi.org/10.1080/09581596.2019.1667488

Danieli, Y. (2007). Multicultural, multigenerational perspectives in the understanding and assessment of trauma. In J. P. Wilson & C. Tang (Eds.), *The cross-cultural assessment of psychological trauma and PTSD* (pp. 65–89). Springer-Verlag Publishers.

Danieli, Y., Norris, F. H., Lindert, J., Paisner, V., Engdahl, B., & Richter, J. (2015a). The Danieli Inventory of Multigenerational Legacies of Trauma, Part I: Survivors' post-trauma adaptational styles in their children's eyes. *Journal of Psychiatric Research, 68*, 167–175. https://doi.org/10.1016/j.jpsychires.2015.06.011. Epub 2015 Jun 23. PMID: 26228416.

Danieli, Y., Norris, F. H., Lindert, J., Paisner, V., Kronenberg, S., Engdahl, B., & Richter, J. (2015b). The Danieli Inventory of Multigenerational Legacies of Trauma, Part II: Reparative adaptational impacts. *The American Journal of Orthopsychiatry, 85*(3), 229–237. https://doi.org/10.1037/ort0000055. PMID: 25985110.

de Jong, K., & Kleber, R. J. (2003). Early psychosocial interventions for refugees and war-affected populations. In R. Orner & U. Schnyder (Eds.), *Reconstructing early interventions after trauma* (pp. 184–192). Oxford University Press.

de Jong, J. T., Komproe, I. H., & Van Ommeren, M. (2003). Common mental disorders in postconflict settings. *Lancet, 361* (9375), 2128–2130. https://doi.org/10.1016/s0140-6736(03)13692-6.

Demyttenaere, K., Bruffaerts, R., Posada-Villa, J., Gasquet, I., Kovess, V., Lepine, J. P., Angermeyer, M. C., Bernert, S., de Girolamo, G., Morosini, P., Polidori, G., Kikkawa, T., Kawakami, N., Ono, Y., Takeshima, T., Uda, H., Karam, E. G., Fayyad, J. A., Karam, A. N., et al. (2004). Prevalence, severity, and unmet need for treatment of mental disorders in the World Health Organization World Mental Health Surveys. *JAMA, 291*(21), 2581–2590. https://doi.org/10.1001/jama.291.21.2581

Dyregrov, A., Gupta, L., Gjestad, R., & Raundalen, M. (2002). Is the culture always right? *Traumatology, 8*(3), 135–145. https://doi.org/10.1177/153476560200800302

Foa, E. B., McLean, C. P., Zang, Y., Zong, J., Rauch, S., Porter, K., et al. (2016). Psychometric properties of the Post-traumatic Stress Disorder Symptoms Scale Interview for DSM-5 (PSSI-5). *Psychological Assessment, 28*, 1159–1165. https://doi.org/10.1037/pas0000259

GBD 2019 Mental Disorders Collaborators. (2022). Global, regional, and national burden of 12 mental disorders in 204 countries and territories, 1990-2019: A systematic analysis for the Global Burden of Disease Study 2019. *Lancet Psychiatry, 9*(2), 137–150. https://doi.org/10.1016/s2215-0366(21)00395-3

Hall, B. J. (2020). Everyday life experiences and mental health among conflict-affected forced migrants: A meta-analysis. *Journal of Affective Disorders, 264*, 50–68. https://doi.org/10.1016/j.jad.2019.11.165.

Haselgruber, A., Sölva, K., & Lueger-Schuster, B. (2020). Symptom structure of ICD-11 Complex Post-traumatic Stress Disorder (CPTSD) in trauma-exposed foster children: Examining the International Trauma Questionnaire – Child and Adolescent Version (ITQ-CA). *European Journal of Psychotraumatology, 11*(1), 1818974. https://doi.org/10.1080/20008198.2020.1818974

Hyland, P., Shevlin, M., Brewin, C. R., Cloitre, M., Downes, A. J., Jumbe, S., Karatzias, T., Bisson, J. I., & Roberts, N. P. (2017). Validation of post-traumatic stress disorder (PTSD) and complex PTSD using the International Trauma Questionnaire. *Acta Psychiatrica Scandinavica, 136*(3), 313–322. https://doi.org/10.1111/acps.12771

IASC. (2007). *Guidelines on mental health and psychosocial support in emergency settings*. Interagency Standing Committee.

Janoff-Bulman, R. (1992). *Shattered assumptions: Towards a new psychology of trauma*. Free Press.

Jansen, S., White, R., Hogwood, J., Jansen, A., Gishoma, D., Mukamana, D., & Richters, A. (2015). The "treatment gap" in global mental health reconsidered: Sociotherapy for collective trauma in Rwanda. *European Journal of Psychotraumatology, 6*, 28706. https://doi.org/10.3402/ejpt.v6.28706

Kabajulizi, J., & Francis Awuku, D. (2022). Do non-communicable diseases influence sustainable development in Sub-Saharan Africa? A panel autoregressive distributive lag model approach. *Health Policy and Planning, 37*(3), 337–348. https://doi.org/10.1093/heapol/czab131

Kalmakis, K. A., & Chandler, G. E. (2015). Health consequences of adverse childhood experiences (ACEs): A systematic review. *Journal of the American Association of Nurse Practitioners, 27*(8), 457–465. https://doi.org/10.1002/2327-6924.12215

Kessler, R. C., Aguilar-Gaxiola, S., Alonso, J., Chatterji, S., Lee, S., Ormel, J., Ustün, T. B., & Wang, P. S. (2009). The global burden of mental disorders: An update from the WHO world mental health (WMH) surveys. *Epidemiologia e Psichiatria Sociale, 18*(1), 23–33. https://doi.org/10.1017/s1121189x00001421.

Kohn, R., Saxena, S., Levav, I., & Saraceno, B. (2004). The treatment gap in mental health care. *Bulletin of the World Health Organization, 82*(11), 858–866.

Marmot, M., Friel, S., Bell, R., Houweling, T. A., Taylor, S., & Commission on Social Determinants of Health. (2008). Closing the gap in a generation: Health equity through action on the social determinants of health. *Lancet, 372*(9650), 1661–1669. https://doi.org/10.1016/s0140-6736(08)61690-6

Mollica, R. F., Donelena, K., Tor, S., Lavelle, J., Elias, C., Frankel, M., & Blendon, J. (1993). The effect of trauma and confinement on functional health and mental health status of Cambodians living in Thailand-Cambodia border camps. *JAMA, 270*(5), 581–586. https://doi.org/10.1001/jama.1993.03510050047025

Momen, N. C., Plana-Ripoll, O., Agerbo, E., Benros, M. E., Børglum, A. D., Christensen, M. K., Dalsgaard, S., Degenhardt, L., de Jonge, P., Debost, J. P. G., Fenger-Grøn, M., Gunn, J. M., Iburg, K. M., Kessing, L. V., Kessler, R. C., Laursen, T. M., Lim, C. C. W., Mors, O., Mortensen, P. B., et al. (2020). Association between mental disorders and subsequent medical conditions. *New England Journal of Medicine, 382*(18), 1721–1731. https://doi.org/10.1056/NEJMoa1915784

Moore, S. (2021). Mental health in humanitarian settings. *Medical Life Sciences*. https://www.news-medical.net/health/Mental-Health-in-Humanitarian-Settings.aspx

Murray, H., Grey, N., Warnock-Parkes, E., Kerr, A., Wild, J., Clark, D. M., & Ehlers, A. (2022). Ten misconceptions about trauma-focused CBT for PTSD. *Cognitive Behaviour Therapist, 15*, e33. https://doi.org/10.1017/S1754470X22000307

National Institutes of Health (NIMH). (2015). *Chronic illness & mental health*. National Institutes of Health, National Institute of Mental Health.

Neria, Y., Nandi, A., & Galea, S. (2008). Post-traumatic stress disorder following disasters: A systematic review. *Psychological Medicine, 38*(4), 467–480.

Patel, V., Saxena, S., Lund, C., Thornicroft, G., Baingana, F., Bolton, P., Chisholm, D., Collins, P. Y., Cooper, J. L., Eaton, J., Herrman, H., Herzallah, M. M., Huang, Y., Jordans, M. J. D.,

Kleinman, A., Medina-Mora, M. E., Morgan, E., Niaz, U., Omigbodun, O., et al. (2018). The Lancet Commission on global mental health and sustainable development. *Lancet, 392*(10157), 1553–1598. https://doi.org/10.1016/s0140-6736(18)31612-x

Pearson, A., & Cherepanov, E. (2012). Building a disaster behavioral health response to radiological nuclear disaster. *Journal of Emergency Management, 10*(6), 413–424.

Ratcliffe, M., Ruddell, M., & Smith, B. (2014). What is a "sense of foreshortened future?" A phenomenological study of trauma, trust, and time. *Frontiers in Psychology, 5*, 1026. https://doi.org/10.3389/fpsyg.2014.01026.

Staglin, G. (2022, February 23). The role of mental health in global sustainable development. *Forbes*. https://www.forbes.com/sites/onemind/2022/02/23/the-role-of-mental-health-in-global-sustainable-development/?sh=7e6a58422897

Steel, Z., Chey, T., Silove, D., Marnane, C., Bryant, R. A., & van Ommeren, M. (2009). Association of torture and other potentially traumatic events with mental health outcomes among populations exposed to mass conflict and displacement: A systematic review and meta-analysis. *JAMA, 302*(5), 537–549. https://doi.org/10.1001/jama.2009.1132

Summerfield, D. (2004). Cross-cultural perspectives on the medicalization of human suffering. In G. M. Rosen (Ed.), *Posttraumatic stress disorder: Issues and controversies*. Wiley. https://doi.org/10.1002/9780470713570.ch12

Tol, W. A., Kohrt, B. A., Jordans, M. J., Thapa, S. B., Pettigrew, J., Upadhaya, N., & de Jong, J. T. V. M. (2010). Political violence and mental health: A multi-disciplinary review of the literature on Nepal. *Social Science & Medicine, 70*(1), 35–44. https://doi.org/10.1016/j.socscimed.2009.09.037

Toussaint, L., Nguyen, Q. A., Roettger, C., Dixon, K., Offenbächer, M., Kohls, N., Hirsch, J., & Sirois, F. (2021). Effectiveness of progressive muscle relaxation, deep breathing, and guided imagery in promoting psychological and physiological states of relaxation. *Evidence-based Complementary and Alternative Medicine, 2021*, 5924040. https://doi.org/10.1155/2021/5924040. PMID: 34306146; PMCID: PMC8272667.

Tol, W. A., Barbui, C., Galappatti, A., Silove, D., Betancourt, T. S., Souza, R., Golaz, A., & van Ommeren, M. (2011). Mental health and psychosocial support in humanitarian settings: Linking practice and research. *Lancet, 378*(9802), 1581–1591. https://doi.org/10.1016/s0140-6736(11)61094-5.

Turecki, G., & Brent, D. (2016). Suicide and suicidal behaviour. *Lancet, 387*(10024), 1227–1239. https://doi.org/10.1016/s0140-6736(15)00234-2

UNHCR. (2023). Refugee Data Finder. from https://www.unhcr.org/refugee-statistics/

Updegraff, J. A., Silver, R. C., & Holman, E. A. (2008). Searching for and finding meaning in collective trauma: Results from a national longitudinal study of the 9/11 terrorist attacks. *Journal of Personality and Social Psychology, 95*(3), 709–722. https://doi.org/10.1037/0022-3514.95.3.709

Ventevogel, P., Jordans, M., Reis, R., & de Jong, J. (2013). Madness or sadness? Local concepts of mental illness in four conflict-affected African communities. *Conflict and Health, 7*(1), 1–16.

Vujanovic, A. A., Meyer, T. D., Heads, A. M., Stotts, A. L., Villarreal, Y. R., & Schmitz, J. M. (2017). Cognitive-behavioral therapies for depression and substance use disorders: An overview of traditional, third-wave, and transdiagnostic approaches. *American Journal of Drug and Alcohol Abuse, 43*(4), 402–415. https://doi.org/10.1080/00952990.2016.1199697

Weathers, F. W., Litz, B. T., Keane, T. M., Palmieri, P. A., Marx, B. P., & Schnurr, P. P. (2013). *The PTSD Checklist for DSM-5 (PCL-5)*. Scale available from the National Center for PTSD at www.ptsd.va.gov

Weinberg, R., Butt, L., Mellano, K., & Harmmoosion, R. (2017). The stability of mental toughness across situations: Taking a social-cognitive approach. *International Journal of Sport Psychology, 48*(3), 280–302.

Weiss, D. S., & Marmar, C. R. (1996). The impact of event scale – Revised. In J. Wilson & T. M. Keane (Eds.), *Assessing psychological trauma and PTSD* (pp. 399–411). Guilford.

Wessells, M. G. (2009). Do no harm: Toward contextually appropriate psychosocial support in international emergencies. *American Psychologist, 64*(8), 842. https://doi.org/10.1037/0003-066X.64.8.842

World Health Organization (WHO). (2010). *mhGAP intervention guide for mental, neurological and substance use disorders for non-specialist health settings*. World Health Organization.

World Health Organization (WHO). (2013). *Mental health action plan 2013–2020*. https://www.who.int/publications/i/item/9789241506021

World Health Organization (WHO). (2019). *Suicide prevention*. https://www.who.int/health-topics/suicide#tab=tab_1

World Health Organization (WHO). (2021, September 21). *Comprehensive mental health action plan 2013–2030*. https://www.who.int/publications/i/item/9789240031029

World Health Organization (WHO). (2022, June 3). *Why mental health is a priority for action on climate change*. https://www.who.int/news/item/03-06-2022-why-mental-health-is-a-priority-for-action-on-climate-change

Chapter 3
Humanitarian Action: The Global Mental Health Perspectives

What Is Humanitarianism?

The chapter outlines the landscape of the modern humanitarianism for mental health (MH) providers working with humanitarian emergencies.

Today's face of humanitarianism is incredibly diverse and complex, reflecting the complexity of global processes. It includes hundreds, if not thousands, of non-governmental organizations, humanitarian agencies, and individuals who provide a variety of relief, aid delivery, and development activities.

The informal ideology of humanitarianism is humanism, which is the active belief that every person deserves respect and dignity and should be treated accordingly. Humanistic values acknowledge the absolute value of every human life and inspire us to lessen suffering and promote human dignity during war, famine, or disaster. Humanitarian action puts this belief into practice by aiding vulnerable populations to improve their conditions in increasingly complex environments (Walzer, 2011).

The social phenomenon of humanitarianism is remarkable by itself because it showcases hope for humanity and remains an example of global collaboration. The desire to help those in need unites people from different countries and across the political spectrum. It brings together multidisciplinary actors who find the way to reconcile their political, social, and cultural differences.

Humanitarian relief activities aim at meeting imminent needs of people affected by a humanitarian crisis. Humanitarian aid organizations have been focusing on delivering essentials such as food, water, medical supplies, and shelter, and now they partner with health providers to respond to health and MH needs. In recent

E. Cherepanov, *Humanitarian Competencies for Global Mental Health Professionals*, Contemporary Humanitarian Action and Emergency Management,
https://doi.org/10.1007/978-3-031-74268-2_3

decades, MH, psychosocial, and integrated primary care modules for survivors of armed conflict, genocide, famine, or epidemic have become integral to humanitarian relief activities.

Over the past 30 years, the humanitarian sector has expanded, transformed, diversified, and professionalized. It has now become an industry that employs an estimated 570,000 people globally, mostly from countries experiencing conflicts and disasters, who serve millions worldwide (Alnap, 2017; Frennessonet al., 2022).

Humanitarian action is the system of humanitarian relief activities. It is tasked with orchestrating a humanitarian response to save lives, decrease human suffering, reduce vulnerabilities, and enhance capacity to cope and recover. In addition to direct aid provision and the coordination, its responsibilities include establishing technical, operational, and financial standards to ensure the highest effectiveness and accountability to the programs, beneficiaries and the organizations providing funding. (Ministerio de Asuntos Exteriores, 2023)

When the information of the humanitarian emergency reaches humanitarian agencies, and the needs assessment concludes that local and national resources are insufficiesnt to cope, international humanitarian action springs to action. The coodinating organizations activate the response, initiate establsishing partnerships, combine resources, and organize access to logistics and human resources required for rapid delievery of humanitarian aid.

There are two main modes of humanitarian operations. *Humanitarian relief* is the assistance used to mitigate the immediate consequences of emergencies. It is different from *development aid*, which is assistance in addressing preexisting, or long-term issues and works on systemic changes in the society or community.

When responding to humanitarian crises, MH providers become part of multinational and multidisciplinary action united by a common mission. To be effective in their work, every actor must understand the operations and be cognizant of their own role and contribution to the collaborative humanitarian activities.

Evolutionary, Spiritual, and Cultural Roots of Helping Behavior: The Healed Femur Story

Oxford Dictionary defines *humanitarianism* as the beliefs and practices of people who try to help and improve the living conditions of those who are suffering. It is also a way of thinking and a sort of culture defined by humanistic ideology, priorities, and the setting with humanitarian needs. It is based on the belief that everyone deserves respect and dignity. A practitioner joining humanitarian action commits to sharing its spirit, values, and mission. But why do people choose to help others?

Evolutionary, Spiritual, and Cultural Roots of Altruism and Helping Behavior

Understanding the evolutionary, spiritual, and cultural antecedents of altruism and helping behavior provides insight into how altruistic values shape the humanitarian profession.

The roots of altruistic and helping behavior are found throughout the animal kingdom, particularly in species with complex social structures such as insects like bees that are not capable of forming an intent. Okasha (2020) suggested that such behavior likely carries significant evolutionary benefits and improves the odds of collective survivorship.

In humans, helping and sharing resources with those in need has always been regarded as a virtue, reflected in most ancient and modern cultures and spiritual beliefs. This altruistic imperative exists, in almost identical forms, in all the major religions—Buddhism, Christianity, Islam, and Judaism—with the notion that doing good deeds is a source of human happiness and the ultimate way to express love for God (Batson, 2011, 2012).

Helping Behavior as a Staple of Civilization: The Healed Femur Story

Concern for the well-being of others has long been recognized as a staple of humanity. In *The Descent of Man* (1871), Darwin already linked the origin of altruistic behavior among humans to the origins of civilization. The Healed Femur Story is an example of this point of view.

According to a widely circulated (albeit questioned) account, an anthropology student once asked an American cultural anthropologist Margaret Mead about the earliest indicator of a civilized society. While there are various versions of this story, the core details remain consistent: Mead's unexpected response was that the first sign of civilization was a fractured and subsequently mended femur bone dating back 15,000 years, discovered at an archaeological site. The femur, the body's longest bone, connecting the hip to the knee, typically takes about 6 weeks to heal without the benefits of modern medicine.

Mead elaborated by suggesting that injured animals are typically preyed upon and consumed in the wilderness before their broken bones can heal. Consequently, a healed femur indicates that an injured individual must have received assistance from others. The healing of a fractured femur shows that another person had been caring for the injured individual, providing food and water, and protecting them until they could recuperate. Mead concluded, "Helping someone else through difficulty is where civilization starts" (Lasco, 2022).

Benefits of Volunteering

The psychologist Batson (2011, 2012) went on to suggest that helping others is a form of prosocial behavior with significant psychological and social benefits of feeling good about oneself.

Numerous studies have noted the beneficial impacts of volunteer work on happiness and well-being, such as the establishment of a robust connection between volunteering, health, overall quality of life, and longevity (Schwartz et al., 2003; Post, 2005).

Other benefits include an improved social standing and self-image, a sense of self-efficacy, and the enrichment of professional experience. Global involvement provides an excellent opportunity to travel, meet people from different cultures, and see the world for what it is, not just as a tourist.

Brief History of Humanitarian Action

While helping behavior has been present in some form throughout human history, the formal beginnings of humanitarianism as an organized activity can be attributed to 1876–1879 when the international community responded to the Northern Chinese Famine (China Famine Relief Fund, 1879).

While not all the developments in humanitarian action directly relate to MH, the following timeline summarizes historical milestones that led to forming the system of values governing global mental health (GMH) (Cherepanov, 2018):

1949. The Fourth Geneva Convention adopted the International Humanitarian Law. This body of regulations, motivated by humanitarian concerns, was designed to protect individuals affected by armed conflicts. The law restricts the tactics and tools employed in warfare. For example, it prohibits targeting civilians or assaulting medical facilities while also mandating unhindered access for humanitarian agencies. Violations of these rules constitute a war crime (ICRC, 1949).

1965. The International Federation of the Red Cross and Red Crescent (IFRC) societies adopted the fundamental principles of the movement: humanity, impartiality, neutrality, independence, voluntary service, unity, and universality. The principles have defined the humanitarian movement's identity and purpose (IFRC, 1965).

1960s–1970s. The Biafran Civil War in Nigeria, during which civilians were murdered and starved by government forces, spotlighted controversies around humanitarian neutrality in armed conflict or during genocide. Disagreement with this principle led to the emergence of Médecins Sans Frontières (MSF) or Doctors without Borders, which is the independent medical humanitarian organization. In 1971, MSF proposed that solidarity (with victims. ECh) replaces neutrality because the world needs to know about the events humanitarians are witnessing. MSF called this mission a *temoignage* (i.e., bear witness) (MSF, 2011).

1990. The inadequate response to the genocide in Rwanda renewed discussions about the values and limits of humanitarian action. The Rwandan genocide polarized humanitarian actors and challenged the principle of impartiality by questioning the provision of humanitarian aid to perpetrators (Storey, 1997).

1990s. Massive media coverage of the Ethiopian famine highlighted shortcomings in an uncoordinated, inefficient, and disorganized humanitarian response, prompting the emergence of interdisciplinary coordination initiatives.

1994. The world's largest disaster relief NGOs adopted the NGO Code of Conduct, which set up consistent expectations for conduct from humanitarian workers across sectors (IFRC & ICRC, 1994).

1997. The Sphere Project was charged with developing standards of quality and accountability for humanitarian response (IFRC, 2004).

2000s. "The War on Terror" was a name for the international military campaign launched by the US and UK governments and their allies after the September 11, 2001, attacks in the United States. It has made the environment more dangerous for humanitarian aid workers and brought attention to their safety and mental health needs (Schmitt & Shanker, 2005).

2002. In response to allegations of sexual abuse of refugees by peacekeepers and aid workers in West Africa, Congo, Kosovo, and Haiti (Jordan, 2004; Nichols, 2016; Dodds, 2017), united humanitarian action proclaimed a commitment to eradicate acts of sexual exploitation and abuse by aid workers and to proactively respond to all such incidents (IFRC, 2004).

Changing Landscape of Humanitarianism: Shifting Strategic Priorities and Emerging Trends

The humanitarian sector, which started with a small number of relief organizations, such as the International Committee of the Red Cross (ICRC) and Médecins Sans Frontiers (MSF), has exponentially grown and diversified (Schweer, 2011). This entire landscape has transformed into a more complicated domain, which, along with humanitarian organizations, now includes financial entities and the media.

The for-profit organizations and charities sometimes donate to the humanitarian projects as a pretext to improve the public image, but the humanitarians worry that these donations do not necessarily directly benefit humanitarian relief (Otegui, 2021). It can become concerning when such organizations either spend a large part of these donations on managing funds or the publicized administrations or celebrities' trips to the disaster zones, or request that donations are going to a specific program that may not be a humanitarian priority.

The humanitarian sector consists of established humanitarian actors and national, international, local, and grassroots organizations, where each has a different mission and institutional norms and culture. With all this diversity, humanitarian aid organizations are united by their mandate to aid people living in the most challenging political, social, and economic environments. There is an increased recognition of MH needs in the affected populations and in aid workers, and many large and small international and local humanitarian organizations have already instituted MH response as part of their routine activities.

Key Factors Influencing Modern Humanitarianism

Modern-day humanitarians work takes place in a significantly more complex and demanding environment with unique challenges. Various factors contribute to the evolving humanitarian relief models, and GMH plays an increasingly important role in forming and supporting the humanitarian agenda.

The changing strategic priorities in the humanitarian sector are reflected in different trends, practices, and models. The key factors influencing humanitarianism are the changing global context and the new developments in humanitarian industry (Table 3.1).

Shifting Priorities

Perhaps the most significant changes in the humanitarian sector have been seen in the expanding considerations for the morality of humanitarian decisions and giving more power to the beneficiaries in determining the priorities (Slim, 2015a).

Table 3.1 Key factors influencing modern humanitarianism

Rising nationalism, and localization of aid, suggests retreat from the idea of globalization in humanitarianism (Grenfell, 2017).
Increased frequency, scale, and complexity of crises due to accelerating impacts of climate change and the spread of infectious diseases (Church, 2007).
The rise of political, social, and economic instability, and the breakdown of global norms (Barrett, 2022).
Politization and increased competition for resources made humanitarian aid a politically divisive factor which contradicts the unifying nature of humanitarianism (Six Emerging Trends…, 2020).
New and emerging technologies are changing the way humanitarian relief is conducted (Six Emerging Trends…, 2020).
Changes in the nature of warfare make the provision of humanitarian aid riskier (Six Emerging Trends…, 2020).
Blurred military–humanitarian boundaries (Schweer, 2011) increase risks to humanitarian actors.
There has been an increase in violence against humanitarian workers (Schweer, 2011).

The diversification of humanitarian organizations has brought to the forefront the need for shared values, consistency, and operations coordination. The contemporary overarching trends in the humanitarian sector are the globalization and professionalization of humanitarian assistance, confronting neocolonialistic attitudes and Western paternalism in aid delivery, strengthening transparency and humanitarian accountability, and the defragmentation of relief efforts (Schweer, 2011). Emphasis on development and the growing role of social media has become a part of the debates about future of humanitarianism.

The development modality in contemporary humanitarianism has been indicative for the moving away from focusing on immediate relief to attending to the long-term problems and the investment in sustainable solutions, prevention, and building resilience (Anderson & Woodrow, 1989; Mackintosh, 2000).

Finding a right balance between prioritizing immediate needs or focusing on the long-term benefits of systems development has always been a challenge for humanitarian action (ICVA, 2016). The GMH field that primarily focuses on the relief activities, works on developing strategies for integrating the sustainable solutions into the immediate response.

Globalization of Humanitarianism and the Growing Role of Social Media

The severity and complexity of current humanitarian crises have global impacts, necessitating a rapid and globally and locally coordinated response including the international flow of money, resources, logistics, and ideas.

At some point, many were hopeful about the globalization of humanitarian action, which was seen in the consolidation of investments and the workforce, as well as the emergence of transnational institutions. The globalization trend has created extraordinary humanitarian power along with increased attention to humanitarian norms and the moral consensus around humanitarian goals (Slim, 2015b).

Globalization has blurred the boundaries between distant parts of the world and changed their perception, bringing them closer.

The failed hopes for global stability and the world order have also affected the humanitarian sector's capacity to respond, which heavily relies on international collaborations and funds. The emergence of non-Western relief agencies (Islamic NGOs, new donors from the Gulf, etc.) (Donini, 2012; Rueda-Sabater et al., 2009) challenged the absolute benefits of globalization of the humanitarian agenda.

Media and technology allow the instantaneous dissemination of information and narratives about events. The media plays an essential role in advocating for humanitarian causes and generating donations. Nearly one fourth of humanitarian aid is generated through private donations motivated by media attention to specific crises (Schweer, 2011). On the one hand, media remains an essential tool for advocacy; on the other hand, it has produced multiple ethical dilemmas because of the risk of exposure of the beneficiaries, violation of privacy, and potential for retraumatizing.

> To address these concerns, the International Red Cross and Red Crescent Movement have issued guidelines against portraying victims in an undignified way that focuses on their misery and helplessness. Instead, they encourage highlighting their resilience, capability, and strength despite very difficult circumstances. (IFRC & ICRC, 1994)

The polarized world can now watch disasters unfold in real time, creating the effect of presence, and the public media creates "on-the-go" narratives, often without the necessary verification of facts.

Seeing such images captures attention, elicits strong and polarized emotions, and radicalizes people to one side or another.

To a large degree, social media shapes the public perception of disasters, bringing awareness of humanitarian needs and informing the world about injustices. This also leads to the strange situation of agencies competing for public attention instead of focusing on the needs of affected populations, especially when the suffering is "not photogenic" enough.

Professionalization

Walker et al. (2010) argued that the size of humanitarian operations has elevated it to an industry: The global humanitarian response engages 210,000 individuals and entails an annual expenditure of nearly $15 billion. Furthermore, they have proposed that we should no longer view humanitarian efforts solely as motivated by good intentions, particularly in fields related to medicine or healthcare. Instead, we should consider this an industry that demands professionalism from all participants.

The pressure to increase professionalism in humanitarian action is a part of a commitment to high standards, as well as integrity of practice. Humanitarian competencies are part of the knowledge and skills that all responders require when responding to humanitarian emergencies and other forms of humanitarian work.

The professionalization of humanitarian sector includes the development and adoption of professional and humanitarian competencies, increase in transparency and accountability in the agencies, and strengthening governance and enforcement of codes and regulations.

Transparency and Accountability

The reputation of humanitarian relief agencies is the biggest asset they have. Reputation is essential for building the trust of beneficiaries and donors and assuring the safety of personnel, and humanitarian agencies must change in response to problematic feedback.

Due to the public visibility of the humanitarian response, humanitarian organizations are often scrutinized about how they develop their budget, where the money comes from and how they are allocated and monitored, and the cost of fundraising and management.

Humanitarian relief takes place in the remote or hard to reach places where it may be difficult to track discretionary spending or monitor everything that happens on the ground. An abundance of unpredictable situations makes it challenging to micromanage, plan finances or predict costs, which understandably creates potential for the misuse of funds. These concerns are the reason for placing transparency and accountability at the forefront of any humanitarian operation.

The most significant concerns about the integrity of humanitarian aid agencies come with the revelation of the misuse of humanitarian aid funds, and of exploitation and systemic sexual abuses involving humanitarian and development aid workers. These reports hit the humanitarian action very hard, making many agencies

In response to the calls for strengthened accountability in operations, humanitarian aid organizations began the UN Transparency and Accountability Initiative (UNTAI). UNTAI has identified areas where humanitarian entities can exercise greater oversight and tighten financial control over funds to ensure that resources are used efficiently and effectively for their intended purposes. (UN Transparency and Accountability Initiative, 2023)

reconsider their policies and strengthen their oversight. Various humanitarian organizations and NGOs have instituted the whistleblower policy and adopted binding guidelines that have become a part of the Code of Conduct for humanitarians, which is further described in Chap. 6.

Addressing Neocolonial Attitudes and Inequalities in Aid Delivery

The neocolonial mentality is the internalized attitude of ethnic or cultural superiority felt by people from Western countries who aid low-income countries (Nunning, 2015). It corresponds with the belief that Western cultural values are inherently superior to those of the people they try to help. Such an attitude includes making assumptions about what is best for the populations being serviced and how they need to live their lives.

Recognizing and confronting Western paternalism has been a driving force in transforming the humanitarian movement and led to the emergence of GMH. These changes resulted in acknowledging and confronting privileges, discrimination, inequality, and insensitivity to other cultures in humanitarian action (Otegui, 2022). The changing attitudes toward national staff, the establishment of anti-discriminatory institutional policies, and the practice of engaging beneficiaries has consistently become a part in the decision-making process (Davey et al., 2013).

Diversity and Inclusion

An environment where many different racial, ethnic, national, and cultural identities are present allows for diverse agendas and different perspectives that become instrumental in reconciling humanitarian priorities. And humanitarian agencies have been reevaluating their policies in order to increase diversity and inclusion in humanitarian action.

Diversity is associated with the representation of diverse groups in humanitarian agency administration, human resources, and aid workers. *Inclusion* refers to the degree to which diverse groups of individuals are represented, appreciated, and engaged into governance and decision-making processes.

The attention to diversity and inclusion in the humanitarian sector underscores the importance of having beneficiaries represented on multiple levels of an organization's functioning and aid delivery.

Humanitarian assistance can be successful only with active participation of those to whom the aid is designated and who must be a part of the decision-making. Or "nothing about us without us."

Donations Fatigue

Increased volatility and financial slowdown in the world have caused humanitarian organizations to increasingly rely on public funds, where they face the donation fatigue, which has already led to a marked reduction in donations. This combination of the increased need for assistance and shrinking resources has forced agencies to make difficult and sometimes unpopular decisions about prioritizing and allocating shrinking funds. Such situations have received negative public attention, leading to further reduced donations and efforts to increase fiscal oversight. Unfortunately, every scandal attributed to a lack of transparency in an agency's operations reduces the opportunities for future aid.

According to a report released by Iowa senator Grassley, the American Red Cross spent 25% or nearly $125 million of donations sent to Haiti after the 2016 earthquake on fundraising, management, and contingency funds (Sullivan & Elliott, 2016), which damaged public opinion and caused a reduction in donations.

That said, humanitarian agencies may find themselves in a challenging situation when donations are collected for a single, often highly publicized disaster, when the agency may receive a short-lived outpouring of targeted donations that they cannot process and capitalize. At the same time, there may be other emergencies that are not on the front pages of the newspapers, but which urgently need funding.

Vulnerable and Marginalized Groups in Humanitarian Emergencies

Humanitarian emergencies tend to amplify preexisting health disparities and the stigma surrounding MH treatment. Vulnerable and marginalized groups endure additional stresses and trauma and are exposed to further discrimination and victimization (Goodwin & Zaman, 2023). And these groups are prioritized in humanitarian aid and GMH interventions.

Vulnerability refers to people with less access to resources and those with diminished capacity to cope, problem-solve, and make sense of what is happening.

Regardless of the type of emergency and the extent of the needs, the humanitarian aid and GMH providers play a pivotal role in identifying, prioritizing, and protecting vulnerable and marginalized groups and individuals. These are children, single women, medically compromised people, those with limited mobility or who are unable to care for themselves, elderly people, and people with serious MH issues.

Children separated from their parents and single women can easily be taken advantage of: exploited, forced into the sex trade, or involved in trafficking. Women can become victims of gender-based violence. So can men.

UNICEF (2020) has voiced grave concerns about the impact of humanitarian crises on children. The international humanitarian community considers children a highly vulnerable group who are partially or totally dependent on adults.

Adolescents, when exposed to traumatic events, may resort to violence and substance abuse, and may struggle with self-esteem issues, health problems, poor school performance, self-harm, and even suicidal ideation.

During humanitarian crises, *parents and caregivers* often experience significant mental and psychosocial stress, which can hinder their ability to parent and offer essential support, protection, stability, and nurturing care to their children. Caregiver support, community interventions such as creating child-friendly spaces, school-based initiatives, and teaching parents and teachers about psychological first aid (PFA) for children are effective and well-received in post-conflict settings (UNICEF, 2020).

Medically compromised people, *people with mobility limitations*, and others with special needs (e.g., those with vision or hearing impairments) may find it difficult to navigate the situation and advocate for their needs.

Elders who depend on their children may have difficulty accessing resources, relocating, and meeting their basic needs. Often, they refuse to relocate to a safer environment because they fear uncertainty and separation from family (Cherepanov, 2022).

People who are addicted to drugs or alcohol, *unable to care for themselves* or engage in self-injurious or suicidal behavior are deemed vulnerable and prioritized for GMH assistance.

People who have *preexisting or current MH illnesses, who are emotionally fragile or have difficulties coping* must be the focus of attention by GMH providers.

People with *physical and mental disabilities and cognitive limitations* can be extremely vulnerable during a humanitarian crisis. The stresses of the humanitarian emergency and the ensuing chaos put persons with disabilities at higher risk for harm and further complicate access to resources and supports.

During the war against Ukraine, persons with limited abilities have faced greater difficulties accessing resources, medicine, and care in general. They often could not evacuate or go to a shelter and were becoming the first victims during the bombing. (Cherepanov, personal communication, 2023)

All too often, people with MH conditions face stigma and discrimination. They may be excluded from their community or subjected to violence. Individuals with such conditions face a heightened risk of neglect, abandonment, abuse, disruption in maintenance medication, and limited access to healthcare services. Furthermore, the stress from adversity can potentially lead to relapse, or worsening of symptoms in people with a history of severe mental disorders (Jones et al., 2009).

Ethnic, religious, or sexual identity minorities, displaced people and refugees, and those coming from disadvantaged socioeconomic backgrounds frequently experience disproportionate effects of humanitarian crises. They often have less support and more barriers to accessing health and MH services and other resources. They may have been subjected to discrimination, poverty, and violence. In a humanitarian crisis, previously disenfranchised groups that had fewer resources to begin with will likely have less access to recovery resources after the crisis.

Diversification of Humanitarian Practice

In addition to humanitarian relief (i.e., response to disasters) and development (addressing chronic issues), several newer areas of practice are now associated with humanitarian action. They are medical humanitarianism, digital humanitarianism, and military humanitarian interventions.

Medical Humanitarianism

Medical humanitarian organizations, such as Medicine Sans Frontiers (MSF), respond to public health crises produced by humanitarian emergencies.

> *Medical humanitarianism* involves medical and other health-related services for underserved populations, refugees, and victims of conflict, war, or disaster. The sector has established itself at the intersection of public and global health, emergency medicine, epidemiology, and medical anthropology. (Abramowitz & Panter-Brick, 2016)

Although there is no clear consensus among medical humanitarian organizations about the exact scope of medical humanitarian service, most of them treat underserved people in humanitarian crisis situations where no other medical services are available or accessible. In recent times, there have been discussions about expanding these services to provide healthcare to underserved populations in high-resource countries, such as treating undocumented refugees (Hoekstra, 2021). For example, such medical humanitarian organizations have established free clinics at borders where refugees are crossing or treated refugees in immigration detention camps.

However, such practices have created several points of contention, especially concerning the humanitarian agenda and political contexts (Castañeda, 2011, 2013; Gottlieb et al., 2012; Ticktin, 2006; Tiedje & Plevak, 2014). For example, in the United States, providing healthcare to migrants raised the following concerns (List, 2011; Pellegrino, 1999; Smith-Carrier, 2020):

- Amid the surge of migrants, free medical care can encourage more migrants to continue crossing the border to receive that care.
- It has created professional ethics issues for health professionals who are often not allowed to practice outside of the borders of the state where their license was issued.
- It can create tensions between undocumented migrants who can receive free care and people living locally who must pay for their healthcare.
- It was unclear how the agency would decide who could receive service and who was not eligible.
- Providing medical and MH care for these oppressed and disadvantaged populations relieves politicians of the responsibility to do something about it.

Digital Humanitarianism

During a humanitarian crisis, people increasingly rely on digital technology such as mobile phones or the internet to share information about their whereabouts and well-being. This technology is used to search for loved ones, to be warned of danger, and to learn about safe places, resources, and essential services.

The rise of digital humanitarianism dates to 2010 when, after the Haiti earthquake, humanitarian agencies collected and mapped social media messages to locate people in need (Meier, 2015). Since then, digital technology, including the use of cell phones and computers, has demonstrated many advantages. It helps people to access services and stay connected to their families and friends. Humanitarian organizations deploy new technologies that they can use for recordkeeping, data collection, data-intensive systems of monitoring, and quality assurance in their programs.

Humanitarian organizations use social media to engage with people in need. During crises, they might employ social media to convey information about secure locations, aid distribution, and services. Additionally, they may use social media to promote awareness of health activities and support or to encourage affected people to exchange information during an emergency (Kuner & Marelli, 2020). Social media can also be used for health education and promotion during epidemics.

Mass media can be used both for fact-checking and propaganda. It can project an image of the humanitarian organization as a helping or an adversary agency, which can undermine aid provision and the safety of aid workers.

That said, digitalization in humanitarian action allows us to collect data and gather the most current information necessary for assessing needs, facilitating efficient communication, and fostering collaboration and cooperation.

> The MH response to the war in Ukraine demonstrated the benefits of telemedicine and remote MH intervention. Remote MH counseling and training were often the only options to reach out to people in the war zone and connect to those fleeing to other countries. The lessons learned from the SARS pandemic accelerated the transition to digital interventions, when people did not have funds or reliable transportation to visit health and MH providers in person, and virtual connection was the only option. This is in addition to the chatbots and Telegram support groups that started during the political unrest in Belarus in 2020. (Cherepanov, 2022)

Like with any other innovation, digitalization has a flip side: the potential for the misuse of sensitive information that can exponentially elevate the risks to the victims. For example, confidential information about the agency's operations, location, or protected data about individuals' health may be leaked to strangers. The humanitarian sector constantly evaluates and manages these risks and takes health data protection very seriously (Kuner & Marelli, 2020; Aarvik, 2020).

Humanitarian Military Interventions: "Responsibility to Protect (R2P)" Doctrine

Although the military origins of humanitarianism can be recognized in terminology such as "humanitarian mission," "deployment," "chain of command," "reentry," and more, humanitarian action has been actively distancing itself from military interventions.

When assisting victims of conflicts, state-sponsored violence, or genocide, humanitarians are often asked why the international community, which proclaims a commitment to human rights, does not do more to stop the bloodshed. This issue is more complicated than it appears and speaks to the controversies surrounding the limits of humanitarian interventions.

> *Military humanitarianism* is the use of military force to further a humanitarian cause. Its origins coincided with tragic events like the genocides in Rwanda in 1994 and the Srebrenica in 1995, when the international community failed to respond effectively. (Gusterson, 2019)

Using military force "for humanitarian purposes" is formally justified by the "responsibility to protect doctrine" (or R2P), which means the responsibility to protect populations from genocide, war crimes, crimes against humanity, and ethnic cleansing. In 2005, the UN World Summit Outcome Document adopted the R2P doctrine. It is an unenforceable principle that dictates that outside powers should intervene to protect a population from mass atrocities such as genocide, even when this violates the local government's sovereignty. The R2P principle remains highly controversial, and its implementation remains inconsistent (World101, 2023).

In addition to questionable effectiveness, military interventions in humanitarian emergencies remain highly contentious. De Torrente (2004) expressed disdain for politicizing humanitarianism and calling military interventions "humanitarian." Such confusion, although beneficial for the military agenda, increases distrust of the humanitarian agenda, puts humanitarian aid providers at greater risk, and affects aid delivery. Chomsky (as quoted in Jayakumar, 2012) noted that virtually every use of military force is described as humanitarian intervention.

Safety and the Well-Being of Humanitarian Aid Workers

The well-being of aid workers has been gaining more attention, and MH professionals have been increasingly involved in providing training and psychological support to these humanitarians.

The Global Development Professionals Network estimates that 79% of aid workers reported that they have experienced mental health issues related to their work. (Young, 2015)

In the politically charged and criminalized contexts of modern conflicts, humanitarian actors are increasingly subjected to acts of violence. The surge in attacks against aid workers and health provides over the last decade has prompted numerous international agencies to implement new strategies to minimize their staffs' vulnerability to such threats. One such approach is "remote-control programming," where the providers operate from a distance (Schweer, 2011). However, it is often not possible.

Aiding disaster victims can take an emotional toll on humanitarian relief workers, impacting their MH, personal life, and work. In the process of their work, humanitarians are often exposed to the same risk factors as beneficiaries, which puts them at risk for trauma, compassion fatigue, burnout, and vicarious traumatization (McCann & Pearlman, 1990). Amid increased security threats to humanitarians, modern humanitarianism actively implements the measures to improve security.

Many humanitarian aid agencies that have been dealing with worker's burnout have realized the importance of supporting their personnel both during fieldwork and after the mission. For these reasons, many such agencies now routinely employ peer support modules, crisis response for employees and volunteers, and sometimes referral and payment for long-term services.

Misuse of Humanitarian Aid and Other Concerns

Despite undisputable achievements in the humanitarian sector, troubling developments have plagued the humanitarian community. Rysaback-Smith (2016) described this environment as being fraught with controversy, political battles, and multiple international organizations, and Cherepanov (2018) has underscored the role of professionalism in ensuring that interventions are implemented in ways that are consistent with both humanitarian and professional values.

The mounting concerns about integrity of practices have prompted self-reflection, leading to theoretical questions about the overall impact of humanitarian assistance, including how to avoid creating dependency on external aid and how the presence of NGOs can compromise the establishment of social and cultural orders to reduce self-reliance (De Waal, 1998; Rieff, 2002). These questions indicate the need for reconceptualizing some underlying assumptions in humanitarian interventions.

Volunteer Convergence or "Flocking"

There is a specific group of concerns relating to managing the situations where people's impulsive acts of goodwill and best intentions collide with strict demands for coordination and planning of relief activities.

Mass disasters such as earthquakes, tsunamis, and flooding sometimes activate extreme acts of helping activities, which, when not coordinated, can become problematic.

Humanitarians are well aware of the *convergence phenomenon*, when unaffiliated and often unprepared volunteers spontaneously travel to disaster sites (Barton, 1970; Cone et al., 2003). Inadequate, scattered, and sometimes competing movements of volunteers rushing (or "flocking") to a disaster site with little regard for security protocols or already established services can burden the professional relief providers and be confusing and damaging to the survivors.

Convergence has been associated with increased risk for both volunteers and beneficiaries, and it takes valuable time and resources away from the relief effort to accommodate and coordinate volunteers, e.g., providing security, food, and shelter. The local administration, police, and the first responders often impose restriction on entering the disaster zone to keep away strangers with unknown identity or unverified skills, questionable qualifications, or unchecked criminal backgrounds who are trying to gain access to highly vulnerable populations. The unorganized "volunteers," however, sometimes can travel long distances or ignore proper protocol in attempting to enter the restricted areas of the disaster site or the active war zone.

This collective behavior of convergence has long puzzled scholars, who have found it to be profoundly disruptive to disaster response (Cone et al., 2003). Auf der Heide (2003) identified several benign explanations for the rise of this phenomenon. Thanks to public media, a relatively minor disaster can swiftly transform into a national or international event. The initial reports of such incidents are frequently sensationalized, exaggerated, and inclusive of a direct appeal for help. From a distance, it is difficult to know how much help is needed, what has already been provided, and who is coordinating the aid delivery, leading to the erroneous presumption that helping more is better than helping less.

Another fuel for convergence behavior is the erroneous belief that disasters create mass panic or that most people are left in shock, immobilized and unable to act rationally, and cannot survive without external directions (the so-called "disaster syndrome").

(definition)

The term *disaster syndrome* has been used to describe a stunned, shocked mental state allegedly common in response to disaster (Wallace, 1957), but this assumption has long been disputed. Panic and disaster syndrome are rarely reported (Glass, 2001). More often, disasters tend to evoke community resilience rather than social breakdown (Auf der Heide, 2004; Jacob et al., 2008).

Cone et al. (2003) have proposed several solutions that relief organizations can implement to manage volunteer convergent behavior.

Table 3.2 Instructions for those who want to donate goods or items (Golubitskaya, 2023)

Unsolicited goods rarely reach the destination. You can send assistance to the agency which oversees relief.
Donate only what was specifically requested.
Trying to deliver donations independently only creates traffic congestion. It is better to coordinate donations with official agencies that oversee this work.
Donating funds is always better than bringing the goods so that the officials buy what they need and send it to disaster zones.
The list of what victims need can change quickly. It is vital to have up-to-date information.

- Limiting access to the disaster site. Disaster sites are often restricted for good reasons, such as to reduce crimes, looting, and trafficking.
- Educating volunteers about the potentially disruptive nature of unorganized and uncoordinated actions (which is one of the purposes of this book).
- Staffing humanitarian organizations with volunteer coordinators who screen, check credentials, organize, and support professional volunteers.

Humanitarian competencies help to prevent the convergence in MH professionals and use other forms of collective helping behavior that is organized and coordinated.

It is possible and may be beneficial for professional volunteers to self-organize and begin assisting those in need without waiting for official endorsement. In the wake of Russia's invasion of Ukraine, Ukrainian MH professionals self-organized and provided the essential bulk of MH crisis support activities. (Cherepanov, 2023)

Politicization and Misuse of Humanitarian Aid

In this era of increased political tensions, the politicization of humanitarianism has been a growing concern. Douzinas (2003) has asserted that governments can manipulate and distort information or use aid as a tool of conflict or corruption. Many efforts have been made to differentiate aid from political agendas, but these issues persist.

The CIA's use of a vaccination campaign to eradicate Bin Laden was met with much outrage by medical humanitarian organizations. As a result of disguising spies as vaccination providers, many healthcare workers were suspected of being US spies. The attacks forced organizations such as the UN to suspend polio vaccination efforts in Pakistan and have severely hampered anti-polio efforts, with parents refusing to have their children vaccinated. (Lancet, 2014)

Other concerning developments relate to the potential misuse of humanitarian aid and diversion of supplies, mainly by the government, militants, or gangs, when humanitarian assistance is diverted or is used to smuggle weapons or promote political agendas.

> A UN investigation into three Somali NGOs hinted that millions in UN Somalia aid were diverted or stolen, and some went to terrorists (Russell, 2015). More recently, the UN and the US halted food aid to Ethiopia, where 20 million people rely on aid, to investigate the "diversion" of supplies. (Harter, 2023)

"Misguided Goodwill" or Unsolicited Donations

Solicited donations often include nonperishable food, medical supplies, clothing, funds, and blood. When donations are unregulated, they can overwhelm and clog the processing system, which in turn can slow and disorganize the aid delivery infrastructure. This happened with the 2004 tsunami, when material donations created a so-called "tsunami of misguided goodwill," which hindered relief efforts and led to mountains of pricey pharmaceuticals being "dumped outside to rot under the monsoons and tropical sun" (Schweer, 2011).

Officials and news outlets might assume shortages exist and suggest that donations are needed without first checking with relief agencies. However, unsolicited donations can cause more problems for both the relief workers and the affected communities. They may be inappropriate or unneeded, and they take the time and efforts of the rescue and relief workers to manage or dispose of. They can also be plain humiliating, offensive, and undignifying for the survivors.

> Following the earthquake in Turkey in 2023, donations poured in. Local volunteers reported that people sent used dirty clothes, used night gowns, and women's stilettos, and the volunteers had to spend time sorting out and disposing of these goods. At the same time, people needed food and blankets. (Golubitskaya, 2023)

Sometimes, friends or colleagues ask MH providers engaged in helping activities about the best ways to donate. To assist in such instances, Golubitskaya (2023) and her team created special instructions for those who want to donate goods (Table 3.2).
Takeaways

- Humanitarianism is an active universal belief that has deep spiritual and cultural roots.

- When responding to humanitarian emergencies, MH providers become humanitarian actors and a part of the interdisciplinary action.
- The history of humanitarianism allows us to better understand how the humanitarian systems were formed. It carries direct relevance to the emergence of GMH work that shares priorities and trends.
- The landscape of humanitarianism is constantly changing and diversifies in response to changing needs and the demands of the global situation.
- The main priorities of humanitarian actions are professionalization, accountability, and partnering with people who receive humanitarian aid.
- When responding to humanitarian emergencies, all humanitarian actors, including MH providers, must have a working knowledge of humanitarian systems, as well as the awareness of vulnerable groups.
- Politicization and misuse of humanitarian aid exponentially increase risks for humanitarian workers, compromises aid delivery, and underscore the importance of humanitarian ethics.
- There is an increased attention to the aid workers' security, health, and the well-being.

References

Aarvik, P. (2020). Digital humanitarianism. In *Humanitarianism: Keywords* (pp. 43–44). Brill. https://doi.org/10.1163/9789004431140_021

Abramowitz, S., & Panter-Brick, C. (2016). Bringing life into relief: Comparative ethnographies of humanitarian practice. In S. A. Abramowitz & C. Panter-Brick (Eds.), *Medical humanitarianism: Ethnographies of practice* (pp. 1–20). University of Pennsylvania Press. https://doi.org/10.9783/9780812291698-002

Alnap. (2017). *Data Story: What's the Shape and Size of the Humanitarian System?* From https://sohs.alnap.org/blogs/data-story-whats-the-shape-and-size-of-the-humanitarian-system

Anderson, M. B., & Woodrow, P. J. (1989). *Rising from the ashes: Development strategies in times of disaster*. Routledge. https://doi.org/10.4324/9780429304859

Auf der Heide, E. (2003). Convergence behavior in disasters. *Annals of Emergency Medicine, 41*(4), 463–466. https://doi.org/10.1067/mem.2003.126

Auf der Heide, E. (2004). Common misconceptions about disasters: Panic, the "disaster syndrome" and looting. In M. R. O'Leary (Ed.), *The first 72 hours: A community approach to disaster preparedness* (pp. 340–380). iUniverse Publishing.

Barrett, P. (2022, May 20). *Social unrest is rising, adding to risks for global economy*. International Monetary Fund Blog. Retrieved from https://www.imf.org/en/Blogs/Articles/2022/05/20/social-unrest-is-rising-adding-to-risks-for-global-economy

Barton, A. (1970). *Communities in disaster: A sociological analysis of collective stress situations*. Anchor.

Batson, C. (2011). *Altruism in humans*. Oxford University Press.

Batson, C. D. (2012). A history of prosocial behavior research. In A. W. Kruglanski & W. Stroebe (Eds.), *Handbook of the history of social psychology* (pp. 243–264). Psychology Press.

Castañeda, H. (2011). Medical humanitarianism and physicians' organized efforts to provide aid to unauthorized migrants in Germany. *Human Organization, 70*(1), 1–10. https://doi.org/10.17730/humo.70.1.a16566172p238244

Castañeda, H. (2013). Medical aid as protest: Acts of citizenship for unauthorized im/migrants and refugees. *Citizenship Studies, 17*(2), 227–240. https://doi.org/10.1080/13621025.2013.780744

Cherepanov, E. (2018). *Ethics for global mental health: From good intentions to humanitarian accountability*. Routledge. https://doi.org/10.4324/9781351175746

Cherepanov, E. (2022). Mental health providers in Ukraine need support but they are not helpless: Professional self-organization and innovative practices. *Frontiers in Public Health, 10*, 1009431. https://doi.org/10.3389/fpubh.2022.1009431

Cherepanov, E. (2023). Refugees from countries with complex political contexts: Politically informed approach to health and mental health services. *Frontiers in Public Health, 11*, 1323259. https://doi.org/10.3389/fpubh.2023.1323259

China Famine Relief Fund Shanghai Committee. (1879). *The great famine: Report of the committee of the Chine famine relief fund*. American Presbyterian Mission Press. https://openlibrary.org/books/OL25495777M/The_great_famine

Church, C. (2007). Corruption and peacebuilding: How they may collide? In *The Nexus: Corruption, conflict and peacebuilding*. The Fletcher School, Tufts University 12–13 April. The Institute for Human Security. Retrieved from http://fletcher.tufts.edu/corruptionconf/pdf/Church.pdf

Cone, D. C., Weir, S. D., & Bogucki, S. (2003). Convergent volunteerism. *Annals of Emergency Medicine, 41*, 457–462.

Davey, E., Borton, J., & Foley, M. (2013). *A history of the humanitarian system: Western origins and foundations* (HPG Working Paper). Overseas Development Institute. http://www.odi.org/publications/7535-global-history-humanitarian-action

De Torrente, N. (2004). Humanitarian action under attack: Reflections on the Iraq war. *Harvard Human Rights Journal, 17*(1), 21–29.

De Waal, A. (1998). *Famine crimes: Politics and the disaster relief industry in Africa*. Indiana University Press.

Dodds, P. (2017, April 12). *More than 100 UN peacekeepers ran a child sex ring in Haiti. None were ever jailed*. Associated Press Online. https://www.thestar.com/news/world/2017/04/12/un-peacekeepers-child-sex-ring-leftvictims-but-no-arrests.html

Donini, A. (2012). *Sovereignty, globalization, and the future of humanitarian action*. Tufts University: Feinstein International Center (FIC). http://fic.tufts.edu/research-item/sovereignty-globalization-and-the-future-ofhumanitarian/

Douzinas, C. (2003). Humanity, military humanism and the new moral order. *Economy and Society, 32*(2), 159–183. https://doi.org/10.1080/0308514032000073383

Frennesson, L. J., Kembro, H., de Vries, M. J., & Van Wassenhove, L. (2022). International humanitarian organizations' perspectives on localization efforts, *International Journal of Disaster Risk Reduction, 8*, 103410. From https://www.sciencedirect.com/science/article/pii/S221242092200629X.

Glass, T. A. (2001). Understanding public response to disasters. *Public Health Reports, 116*(Suppl. 2), 69–73. https://doi.org/10.1016/S0033-3549(04)50146-2

Golubitskaya, Z. (2023, February 11). Volontery zhaluyutsa na "medvezhyu" pomosch zhertvam zemljatrjasenija v Turcii. [Volunteers complain about "bearish" assistance to earthquake victims in Turkey]. *MK.ru Moskow Komsomolec*. https://www.mk.ru/social/2023/02/11/volontery-zhaluyutsya-na-medvezhyu-pomoshh-zhertvam-zemletryaseniya-v-turcii.html

Goodwin, J., & Zaman, U. (2023). Editorial: Mental health stigma and UN Sustainable Development Goals. *Frontiers in Psychiatry, 14*, 1190406. https://doi.org/10.3389/fpsyt.2023.1190406

Gottlieb, N., Filc, D., & Davidovitch, N. (2012). Medical humanitarianism, human rights and political advocacy: The case of the Israeli Open Clinic. *Social Science & Medicine, 74*(6), 839–845. https://doi.org/10.1016/j.socscimed.2011.07.018

Grenfell, D. (2017). Humanitarian interventions and globalization. In A. Farazmand (Ed.), *Global encyclopedia of public administration, public policy, and governance*. Springer. https://doi.org/10.1007/978-3-319-31816-5_1236-1

Gusterson, H. (2019). Drone warfare in Waziristan and the new military humanism. *Current Anthropology, 60*(S19), S77–S86. https://doi.org/10.1086/701022
Harter, F. (2023, June 9). *Food aid suspended in Ethiopia after "widespread and coordinated" thievery*. Retrieved from https://www.theguardian.com/global-development/2023/jun/09/food-aid-suspended-in-ethiopia-after-widespread-and-coordinated-thievery
Hoekstra, E. (2021). "Not a free version of a broken system": Medical humanitarianism and immigrant health justice in the United States. *Social Science and Medicine, 285*, 114287. https://doi.org/10.1016/j.socscimed.2021.114287
International Committee of the Red Cross (ICRC). (1949). *Geneva Convention of 12 August 1949.*
International Council of Voluntary Agencies (ICVA). (2016). *World Humanitarian Summit 2016.* https://web.archive.org/web/20211019043731/https:/www.icvanetwork.org/world-humanitarian-summit-0
International Federation of Red Cross (IFRC). (2004). *The Sphere Project. Humanitarian charter and minimum standards in disaster response*. Oxfam Publishing.
International Federation of Red Cross and Red Crescent Societies (IFRC and ICRC). (1994). *Code of conduct for the International Red Cross and Red Crescent Movement and NGOs in disaster relief.* https://www.ifrc.org/document/code-conduct-international-red-cross-and-red-crescent-movement-and-ngos-disaster-relief
International Red Cross and Red Crescent Movement (IFRC). (1965). *The fundamental principles of the International Red Cross and Red Crescent Movement.* www.ifrc.org/en/publications-and-reports
Jacob, B., Mawson, A. R., Payton, M., & Guignard, J. C. (2008). Disaster mythology and fact: Hurricane Katrina and social attachment. *Public Health Reports, 123*(5), 555–566. https://doi.org/10.1177/003335490812300505
Jayakumar, K. (2012). *Humanitarian intervention: A legal analysis*. E-International Relations. https://doi.org/10.2139/ssrn.2121008
Jones, L., Asare, J. B., El Masri, M., Mohanraj, A., Sherief, H., & van Ommeren, M. (2009). Severe mental disorders in complex emergencies. *Lancet, 374*(9690), 654–661. https://doi.org/10.1016/s0140-6736(09)61253-8
Jordan, M. J. (2004, November 26). Sex charges haunt UN forces: In places like Congo and Kosovo, peacekeepers have been accused of abusing the people they're protecting. *Christian Science Monitor Online*. https://www.csmonitor.com/2004/1126/p06s02-wogi.html
Kuner, C., & Marelli, M. (Eds.). (2020). *Handbook on data protection in humanitarian action*. Vrije Universiteit Brussel, International Committee of the Red Cross (ICRC).
Lancet. (2014). Polio eradication: The CIA and their unintended victims. *Lancet, 383*(9932), 1862. https://doi.org/10.1016/S0140-6736(14)60900-4
Lasco, G. (2022, June 6). Did Margaret Mead think a healed femur was the earliest sign of civilization? *SAPIENS*. https://www.sapiens.org/culture/margaret-mead-femur/
List, J. M. (2011). Beyond charity: Social justice and health care. *Medicine & Society, 13*(8), 565–568. https://doi.org/10.1001/virtualmentor.2011.13.8.msoc1-1108
Mackintosh, K. (2000). *The principles of humanitarian action in international humanitarian law* (Humanitarian Policy Group Report 5). https://www.cmi.no/file/1865-The-Principles-of-Humanitarian-Action-in-International-Humanitarian-Law.pdf
McCann, I. L., & Pearlman, L. (1990). Vicarious traumatization: A framework for understanding the psychological effects of working with victims. *Journal of Traumatic Stress, 3*(1), 131–149.
Médecins Sans Frontières (MSF). (2011). *Founding of MSF*. http://www.doctorswithoutborders.org/founding-msf
Meier, P. (2015). *Digital humanitarians: How big data is changing the face of humanitarian response*. Routledge.
Ministerio de Asuntos Exteriores. (2023). *Humanitarian action and diplomacy*. Unión Europea y Cooperación. https://www.exteriores.gob.es/en/PoliticaExterior/Paginas/AccionHumanitaria.aspx

Nichols, M. (2016, December 5). U.N. identifies 41 Burundi, Gabon troops accused of abuse in Central Africa. Reuters. Retrieved from http://www.reuters.com/article/us-centralafricaun-crime-idUSKBN13U28H

Nunning, V. (2015). Fictions of empire and the un-making of imperialist mentalities: Colonial discourse and post-colonial criticism revisited. *Forum for World Literature Studies, 7*(2), 171–198.

Okasha, S. (2020). Biological altruism. In E. N. Zalta (Ed.), *Stanford encyclopedia of philosophy* (Summer 2020 ed.). Stanford University. https://plato.stanford.edu/archives/sum2020/entries/altruism-biological

Otegui, D. (2021). Understanding the cognitive gap between humanitarians and survivors during humanitarian operations. *International Journal of Disaster Risk Reduction, 63*(1), 102427. https://doi.org/10.1016/j.ijdrr.2021.102427

Otegui, D. F. (2022). *Symbolic approach to humanitarian action: It takes one to know one*. Springer International Publishing.

Pellegrino, E. D. (1999). The commodification of medical and health care: The moral consequences of a paradigm shift from a professional to a market ethic. *Journal of Medicine and Philosophy, 24*(3), 243–266.

Post, S. G. (2005). Altruism, happiness, and health: It's good to be good. *International Journal of Behavioral Medicine, 12*(2), 66–77.

Rieff, D. (2002). *A bed for the night: Humanitarianism in crisis*. Simon and Schuster.

Rueda-Sabater, E., Ramachandran, V., & Kraft, R. (2009). *A fresh look at global governance: Exploring objective criteria for representation* (CGD Working Paper 160). Center for Global Development. http://www.cgdev.org/content/publications/detail/1421065/

Russell, G. (2015, Jan 20). "Millions in UN Somalia Aid Diverted; Hints that Some Went to Terrorists", Fox News. From www.foxnews.com/world/2015/01/20/millions-inun-somalia-aid-diverted-hints-that-some-went-to-terrorists

Rysaback-Smith, H. (2016). History and principles of humanitarian action. *Turkish Journal of Emergency Medicine, 15*(Suppl 1), 5–7. https://doi.org/10.5505/1304.7361.2015.52207

Schmitt, E., & Shanker, T. (2005, July 26). U.S. officials retool slogan for terror war. *New York Times*. http://www.nytimes.com/2005/07/26/politics/us-officials-retoolslogan-for-terror-war.html

Schwartz, C., Meisenhelder, J., Ma, Y., & Reed, G. (2003). Altruistic social interest behaviors are associated with better mental health. *Psychosomatic Medicine, 65*(5), 778–785. https://doi.org/10.1097/01.psy.0000079378.39062.d4

Schweer, C. (2011, June 30). *The changing landscape of humanitarian aid*. Center for Security Studies. https://css.ethz.ch/en/services/digital-library/articles/article.html/130108

Six Emerging Trends Impacting the Future of Humanitarian Action. Global Humanitarian Policy Forum. (2020). *The changing global landscape: What's next for humanitarian action?* United Nations Foundations and OCHA. Retrieved from www.unocha.org/sites/unocha/files/GHPF%20Summary%20Report_Digital%20Distribution.pdf

Slim, H. (2015a). *Humanitarian ethics: A guide to the morality of aid in war and disaster*. Oxford University Press.

Slim, H. (2015b). Wonderful work: Globalizing the ethics of humanitarian action. In R. Mac Ginty & J. H. Peterson (Eds.), *Routledge companion to humanitarian action* (pp. 13–25). Routledge. https://hdl.handle.net/1814/61326

Smith-Carrier, T. (2020). Charity isn't just, or always charitable: Exploring charitable and justice models of social support. *Journal of Human Rights and Social Work, 5*, 157–163. https://doi.org/10.1007/s41134-020-00124-2

Storey, A. (1997). Non-neutral humanitarianism: NGOs and the Rwanda crisis. *Development in Practice, 7*(4), 384–394. http://www.jstor.org/stable/4029004

Sullivan, L., & Elliott, J. (2016, June 16). *Report: Red Cross spent 25 percent of Haiti donations on internal expenses, heard on morning edition*. NPR. Retrieved from https://www.npr.org/2016/06/16/482020436/senators-report-finds-fundamental-concerns-about-red-cross-finances#:~:text=The%20American%20Red%20Cross%20spent,Chuck%20Grassley

Ticktin, M. (2006). Between ethics and politics: The violence of humanitarianism in France. *American Ethnologist, 33*(1), 33–49.

Tiedje, K., & Plevak, D. J. (2014). Medical humanitarianism in the United States: Alternative healthcare, spirituality and political advocacy in the case of Our Lady Guadalupe Free Clinic. *Social Science & Medicine, 120*, 360–367. https://doi.org/10.1016/j.socscimed.2014.05.018

UN Transparency and Accountability Initiative. (2023). *United States mission to the United Nations*. https://usun.usmission.gov/mission/management-and-reform-section/un-transparency-and-accountability-initiative/

UNICEF. (2020). *Mental health and psychosocial support for children in humanitarian settings: An updated review of evidence and practice (November 2020)*. https://reliefweb.int/report/world/mental-health-and-psychosocial-support-children-humanitarian-settings-updated-review

Walker, P., Hein, K., Russ, K., Bertleff, G., & Caspers, D. (2010). A blueprint for professionalizing humanitarian assistance. *Health Affairs, 29*(12), 2223–2230. https://doi.org/10.1377/hlthaff.2010.1023

Wallace, A. F. C. (1957). Mazeway disintegration: The individual's perception of socio-cultural disorganization. *Human Organization, 16*, 23–27.

Walzer, M. (2011, July 1). On humanitarianism: Is helping others charity, or duty, or both? *Foreign Affairs*. https://www.foreignaffairs.com/articles/2011-07-01/humanitarianism

World101. (2023, April 10). The rise and fall of the responsibility to protect. *World101*. https://world101.cfr.org/understanding-international-system/building-blocks/rise-and-fall-responsibility-protect

Young, H. (2015, November 23). Guardian research suggests mental health crisis among aid workers. *The Guardian*. https://www.theguardian.com/global-development-professionals-network/2015/nov/23/guardian-research-suggests-mental-health-crisis-among-aid-workers

Chapter 4
The State of Global Mental Health: Reflecting on Achievements and Moving Forward

Global Mental Health Is a Field of Study and Practice

Defining Global Mental Health

As a professional specialization, global mental health (GMH) has branched out from mainstream Western mental health (MH) and is in the process of defining its scope of service, concepts, and developing a professional toolbox.

> *Global Mental Health (GMH)* is defined as a field of study and practice that is concerned with providing psychological aid and mental health (MH) support to people affected by humanitarian emergencies caused by disaster, war, political violence, famine, epidemic, or severe poverty. Typically, GMH work takes place in an international setting, but it can also include care for refugees at the locations of their resettlement. (Cherepanov, 2018, 2019)
> It is important to note that the word *global* in global and mental health usually refers to the problem's scope, not its location. (Koplan et al., 2009)

As a profession that originated in the high-resourced Western healthcare setting, MH professionals have enjoyed being a part of a highly regulated healthcare system with multiple levels of care, professional support, security, stability, and established referral systems.

The introduction of a global perspective made the MH discipline reevaluate its underlying concepts, theory and practice, open it up to the real world, and learn from it instead of molding it to our likeness. Not surprisingly, this approach has challenged many tenets of the MH profession, such as the idea of the transferability

E. Cherepanov, *Humanitarian Competencies for Global Mental Health Professionals*, Contemporary Humanitarian Action and Emergency Management,
https://doi.org/10.1007/978-3-031-74268-2_4

of evidence-based practices and other protocol-based interventions to a humanitarian context.

The emergence of GMH specialization in the professional arena has already created a great deal of interest, which is reflected in the growing number of graduate programs in GMH. This expanding frontier has made people more aware of the diversity and complexity of human functioning, especially in humanitarian crises that test human endurance.

The three factors that characterize GMH as a specialization are the GMH's dual professional identity, the humanitarian setting where this work occurs, and the global significance of the problems it works with.

Dual Professional Identity: Mental Health and Humanitarian Specialization

GMH has emerged at the intersection of MH practice and humanitarian relief, as a discipline with a dual professional identity, which means it is accountable to both professions.

The humanitarian identity underscores the GMH commitment to humanitarian missions. The humanitarian relief activities which include the GMH work, are guided by humanitarian principles and regulated by professional and humanitarian ethics. The GMH shares these values and regulations with other multidisciplinary humanitarian actors.

The Goals of Interventions

The overarching goals of GMH interventions in humanitarian emergencies are:

- Alleviation of suffering caused by extreme and traumatic stresses.
- Restoration of a person's or community's capacity to cope with mounting challenges.
- Strengthening resilience, coping mechanisms, and supports.
- Ensuring access to treatment for people with serious MH struggles.
- Prevention of further psychological breakdowns and dysfunctions, including concerns for sustainability, violence prevention, and facilitation of community-based support.
- Restoring individual and community functioning, reducing barriers affecting access to treatment, and empowering self-reliance.
- Promoting human rights, protection, support, advocacy for vulnerable groups, and anti-violence initiatives.
- "*Temoignage*," from the French verb "*temoigner*," which translates as "to witness." For humanitarians, this means a willingness to speak on behalf of the

people we serve and to bring abuses and intolerable situations to the public eye (MSF, n.d.).

History of GMH and Current Trends

The historical perspective on GMH helps better understand how it has become what it is now. For this book, the previously introduced historical periodization (Cherepanov, 2018) has been revised and updated to reflect the most current developments.

Brief but full of controversies, the history of GMH reflects overcoming the theoretical and practical challenges typically associated with emergence of interdisciplinary approaches in highly regulated professions.

In a short time, GMH, which started as voluntaristic efforts by globally minded MH professionals traveling to disaster sites, has emerged as a fully formed professional specialization and a recognized actor in humanitarian response.

For the sake of clarity, the history of GMH is divided into four phases: (1) fragmentation, (2) integrated approaches to complex needs, (3) toward best practices and standards of care, (4) gaining an edge and future directions, and (5) confronting "cargo cult."

This periodization is approximate and is consistent more with the "spirit of the time" than with designating any precise dates.

1980s. Fragmentation and Best Intentions: "The Wild West of Mental Health"

The origins of GMH can be traced to the 1980s, when interest in the cultural dimensions of trauma and the impact of large-scale disasters exploded and led professionals to explore the global frontiers of MH. Around that time, globally minded professionals with good intentions started traveling to places affected by humanitarian disasters to help survivors. At that time, no regulations or guidance were in place, and the providers have been using trial and error when defining their work.

In 1980, the American Psychiatric Association introduced the diagnosis of posttraumatic stress disorder (PTSD). The PTSD construct brought attention to the concept of trauma and the psychological impact of large-scale disasters and catastrophes, genocides, and armed conflicts. Studies of the prevalence of PTSD symptoms both nationally and internationally allowed us to compare the severity of trauma and justify the need for trauma treatment.

In almost a parallel development, international nongovernmental organizations (NGOs) started empirically implementing MH modules aiming to support survivors of gender-based violence (GBV), war trauma, and disasters.

This disconnect between practical advances and lagging theory and research worried the humanitarian community, which had already been concerned about unregulated interventions in humanitarian action. And there are many poignant examples of these ethically questionable practices.

> After the earthquake in Haiti, there were many psychological organizations. They were coming, taking pictures together with us, and quickly disappearing without a trace. Sometimes, they brought students who were using us as guinea pigs. It didn't feel right. They did not coordinate with each other, and every organization was doing whatever they wanted. Sometimes, they gave us the opposite advice. We did not take them seriously! We wanted to be nice to them but felt like they were doing this for themselves and not us. We felt used, and ended up going there only if they were giving something to us or children. (Cherepanov, personal communication with a Haitian earthquake survivor, March 18, 2016)

At that time, fragmented and often competing MH interventions lacked consistency and coordination and frequently were more confusing than helpful to the beneficiaries in a crisis. These efforts demonstrated how the best intentions can become problematic, unethical, risky, and even harmful if professional regulations do not support them.

> The combination of increased public visibility of MH and concerns about ethically questionable practices made it clear that if GMH were to exist, it must get organized, develop regulations, and work on developing concepts, standards of practice, and professional ethics.

Despite all the controversies, these pilot MH projects provided a basis for the consistent future development of GMH.

1990s. Integration

Medical, MH, and social needs assessments conducted in emergency settings have consistently pointed to the complexity of survivors' needs, where the integration of MH services into primary healthcare, education, social services, and the criminal justice system has demonstrated effectiveness.

The 1990s were marked by the emergence of integrated models where MH providers worked alongside primary care providers (integrated primary care) and social services providers (Mental Health and Psychosocial Support, aka MHPSS) (IASC, 2007). For many survivors of trauma and violence, the stigma associated with MH made receiving primary care and social assistance the only safe settings to talk about their experiences.

Empirically identified best practices and integrative models became widely accepted and have not only benefited global practices but also influenced the development of new models in Western health and human services.

To support these models, MH specialists started training healthcare providers, social workers, community outreach workers, and other human service providers on how to recognize signs of emotional distress, how to respond to crises, and when to refer at-risk individuals with intensive care needs to specialized colocated MH services.

2000s. Diversification: Quest for Consistency, Best Practices, and Standards of Care

By this time, the diversification of GMH services had led to the emergence of a variety of new models and interventions. Some of them are:

- Immediate disaster response, war trauma treatment, support to humanitarian interventions during famines, and health promotion during disease outbreaks.
- Behavioral health aspects of managing chronic disease or health conditions, including HIV, TB, neurological conditions, and epilepsy.
- Integrated primary care and maternal and reproductive health.
- Programs for victims of gender-based and sexual violence.
- Targeted programs for special needs groups such as children or persons with physical or MH disabilities.
- Participation in community development, prevention, health education, policy development, and training of local providers.

Concurrently, the professional MH community started expressing concerns about the lack of evidence-based best practices, standards of care, and effectiveness indicators. Some of these concerns were answered in the operational guidelines for Mental Health and Psychosocial Supports in Emergency (MHPSS), a manual developed by the Interagency Standing Committee (IASC, 2007). These guidelines became a milestone in the forming of GMH operations, establishing the framework and structure for psychosocial interventions based on the level of MH needs. The IASC's operational guidelines will be further explored in Chap. 8.

2010s. Gaining an Edge Through Policy Development

Major advances in global policy development characterized this period, beginning with the World Health Organization (WHO) issuing the Mental Health Global Action Plan (mhGAP, 2010), which outlined strategic and tactical priorities for GMH. The WHO has launched numerous GMH initiatives, including the Global Campaign for Suicide Prevention, which primarily aims to expand services for mental, neurological, and substance use disorders services, with a particular emphasis on low- and middle-income nations. To execute this plan, the WHO established a broad framework for developing MH policies, mainly focusing on distinctive challenges posed by complex emergencies and their systemic impacts.

In 2010, the Grand Challenges in Global Mental Health initiative identified top challenges, outlined strategic directions, and called for urgent action and investment in GMH. It underscores the importance of international collaboration in research, emphasizing the necessity to share access to data, expertise, and opportunities for capacity-building (NIMH, 2010).

In 2011, the War Trauma Foundation issued an essential guide for field workers in complex emergencies on providing Psychological First Aid (PFA) (World Health Organization et al., 2011). Since then, PFA has become a leading intervention in humanitarian crises.

Around the same time, several experts voiced their concerns and confronted emerging GMH developments. They heavily criticized the mechanical extrapolation of Western concepts to different contexts, which they saw as a continuation of colonial attitudes. The most prominent publications with self-explanatory titles were *Crazy Like Us* by Watters (2011), "Against 'Global Mental Health'" by Summerfield (2012), and *Decolonizing Global Mental Health* by Mills (2014).

2020 to Present: Professionalization of GMH and Confronting "Cargo Cults"

The development of GMH-friendly interventions and assessments marks this period. GMH has emerged as a truly multidisciplinary discipline, attracting a lot of interest from scholars and practitioners who want to expand the horizons of their work, and at that time we already see a growing number of graduate programs in GMH. Meanwhile, GMH continues to reinvent itself as a distinct yet integrated specialization and advance its professionalization.

GMH has been taking the lead in promoting novel transcultural concepts that allow overcoming the outdated norm-pathology dichotomy in understanding MH.

The adoption of Psychological First Aid (PFA) and MHPSS interventions, and GMH-friendly assessments (e.g., the International Trauma Questionnaire) has become routine part of practice for GMH professionals, paraprofessionals, community members, medical personnel, teachers, and social workers. The response to the Ebola epidemic highlighted the importance of community-based interventions in health promotion (Abramowitz, 2017; Bemme et al., 2023). It later helped with the SARS response and advancing a social justice component in GMH work.

Another major development in GMH has been its association with proxy specialties that enrich the multidimensional understanding of MH phenomena. For example, medical anthropology, an interdisciplinary subfield of anthropology, relies on an ecological approach that includes cultural influence. It aims to overcome the conflicts between medical and sociocultural perspectives and serves as a cultural broker to ensure the appropriateness of research and MH treatment at the community level and among health workers (Kohrt & Mendenhall, 2016). Transcultural psychiatry, on the other hand, focuses on the universality of human experience and the universal psychological and psychopathological mechanisms shared across cultures (Antić, 2021).

Although most Western MH interventions do not do actual cause harm in the humanitarian context, they can still contribute to the perpetuation of "cargo cults" in MH. This means reliance on replicating a "miracle cure" offered by Western doctors with little understanding of what such interventions encompass and how they work. The alternative would be studying and incorporating cultural traditions, capitalizing on culture- and family-bound sources of resilience, and taking responsibility for their recovery.

The term "*cargo cult*" refers to an incident observed in the indigenous people of Melanesia, who reportedly were profoundly impressed by the arrival of aircraft on their islands during World War II carrying various supplies. Lacking a comprehension of what airplanes were or their origin, they resorted to magical thinking, crafting bamboo models of planes and control towers in a superstitious hope that it would lure aircraft to deliver more material goods. In psychology, "cargo cult mentality" references fraudulent and unsubstantiated practices that people accept without understanding how they work (Feynman, 1974; Hall, 2016). In the humanitarian context of GMH, this can occur due to magical thinking, power differential, or just out of respect for foreign providers.

Recognizing and addressing the cargo cult mentality means abandoning preconceived assumptions about what is best for beneficiaries. The emphasis shifts from delivering "ready-to-go" and presumably "one-size-fits-all" approaches to the collaborative development of interventions through a dialog with the people served, building upon their strength and resilience, and learning from survivors.

The Need for Global Mental Health Specialization: A Changing Role of GMH Professionals

In response to global challenges and the changing humanitarian landscape, humanitarian organizations now more than ever recognize the role of MH providers in humanitarian emergencies and include MH modules in their programs. Subsequently, GMH providers have expanded their presence and their repertoire of interventions in these six areas:

- MH interventions and emotional support.
- Humanitarian research and needs assessment.
- Health promotion and psychoeducation to people affected by humanitarian crises.
- Facilitation or development of systems of support and resilience.
- Psychological support to humanitarian aid workers.
- Advocacy, violence prevention, and peacebuilding.

A lot has already been accomplished. The GMH movement, which first emerged as an informal professional initiative of MH professionals, has united globally minded researchers, clinicians, educators, global and public health professionals, anthropologists, advocates, and policymakers from various healthcare and social disciplines.

Global perspective places MH profession at the forefront of developing innovative models, research, best practices, and recommendations that have enriched both humanitarian action and mainstream MH. This work's humanitarian and collaborative nature is driven by the shared goal of alleviating suffering and establishing social justice and equity.

Designating GMH as a professional specialization allows us to further strengthen its contribution to the humanitarian sector and MH. Such designation facilitates establishing and maintaining priorities, outlining professional competencies and standards, and ensuring the quality and ethical integrity of the work. It calls for specialized training, supervision, and continuing education requirements, all essential components of humanitarian accountability.

Formal and recognized by professional bodies designation of GMH as a professional specialization allows for

- Reflecting upon achievements and identifying priorities for moving forward.
- Creating a professional community by bringing together the multidisciplinary MH and social support professionals who respond to the humanitarian needs of populations affected by crisis.
- Facilitating the exchange of ideas, outlining minimal professional competencies, and providing education, peer supervision, and peer support. These directions align with the push toward professionalizing all actors within the humanitarian sector.
- Developing context-appropriate practices and establishing professional standards.

- Conducting research, disseminating findings, and sharing best practices.
- Bringing attention to the needs of populations affected by humanitarian crises and advocating for global priorities, influencing legislation, and developing collaborations.

What Is a Humanitarian Setting?

GMH work often takes place in settings where multidisciplinary actors respond to systemic challenges posed by humanitarian emergencies. While maintaining separate professional identities, they are driven by a shared humanitarian mission.

Humanitarian Settings

(*Definition*)

> *Humanitarian setting* is the umbrella term used to designate situations of humanitarian emergencies caused by disasters, armed conflicts, epidemics, or severe poverty (Tol et al., 2011). Such settings are characterized by pressing humanitarian needs where the interactions between humanitarian actors and aid recipients shape everyday realities. (Hilhorst & Jansen, 2010)

Despite all the diversity of situations that can be branded as humanitarian settings, they all are marked by a power differential between aid providers and recipients, limited resources, and high social and political visibility. Humanitarian settings are affected by interplay between current, chronic, and preexisting problems such as community violence, which can reach catastrophic proportions and result in social breakdown and collapse.

Pressing needs, limited resources, uncertainty, and at times unpredictable and dangerous environment determine objectives, priorities, and limitations of GMH interventions.

Power Differential

Working with vulnerable populations in humanitarian emergencies means that aid providers carry tremendous power over the lives and well-being of those who depend on this aid. With this power comes responsibility.

A power differential is deeply imbedded in any helping activity but it becomes especially pronounced in humanitarian settings where aid providers control the access to scarce resources or benefits. The providers must be cognizant of their undue influence, which is inherently built into their role and relates to the resources to which they have access. The power difference highlights the importance of high standards of practice, accountability, professional competencies, personal integrity, and fidelity to professional and humanitarian ethics (Cherepanov, 2018, 2019).

Unfortunately, the history of humanitarianism is fraught with instances of abuse of power, and the GMH community is perfectly positioned to address inequalities and prevent taking advantage of beneficiaries.

A part of the problem is the legacy of colonial or paternalistic attitudes endemic to Western MH and, if not reflected upon, can be internalized by providers. Such attitudes are recognized in the implicit imposition of Western values, the expert bias ("We better know what you need"), a belief in the superiority of Western values, and interventions and denying people the ability to decide what they need. Some of these attitudes, sometimes explicit but mostly covert, can be recognized in the trauma approaches currently employed in Western MH (see section "Professional Mythology in GMH Work" below).

Limited Resources and Professional Support

Human resources are often scarce in humanitarian contexts, a referral system or professional support may be unavailable or not accessible, and GMH providers cannot rely on established child protection or psychiatric services.

When the situation becomes complicated, MH professionals seek out peer or professional support and supervision, which may also not be readily available, leaving the providers to their own professional expertise. Such situations underscore the capacity for independent decision-making and taking responsibility for complex decisions, which is a part of special professional expertise and the experience.

Global Significance and Public Visibility of Global Mental Health Work

Any humanitarian emergency and the subsequent interventions carry political significance (Redfield, 2013), and GMH responses often gain traction and gain high visibility due to media and public interest.

GMH providers meaningfully contribute to humanitarian causes and human rights and prevent future cycles of violence. The authors of the Grand Challenges (Bajbouj et al., 2022) emphasized the global relevance of GMH in promoting MH, health, and wellness in emergencies. However, the true impact of this work goes far beyond assisting the people served—GMH interventions carry the potential to influence global processes and politics.

The public attention to GMH work puts high expectations of the conduct of the providers because in their activities they represent not only themselves but also their profession and humanitarian action.

The Scope of Service

Areas of Practice

GMH work aims to mitigate the MH impact of humanitarian crises. They provide MH support, raise awareness of pressing MH needs and the effects of violence, and engage in advocacy on local and international levels. They attest to injustices and share their observations and conclusions to influence political and policy changes.

Although GMH continues defining and reevaluating its services, concepts, and tools, it has already established its professional distinctiveness and interdisciplinary recognition.

The humanitarian context primarily determines the GMH's framework, scope of service, theory and practice and distinguishes it from proxy disciplines such as international and cross-cultural psychology, global, anthropological and cultural psychiatry, global health, and disaster MH, where the latter focuses on supporting already existing disaster management systems.

Many question the difference between "GMH" and "international psychology." While these terms are often used interchangeably and some practice areas do correspond, they employ different frameworks. International psychology works toward establishing equal collaborations and networking, building partner relationships between national psychological associations, developing compatible professional standards, and credentialing psychologists from different countries (Leach et al., 2015; Amstutz, 2013). GMH does not exclude any of these activities, but its priority is to provide relief to vulnerable populations affected by humanitarian emergencies who need help.

What does GMH *not* do?
GMH does not attempt to interfere with the natural and culturally rooted systems of healing and recovery.
GMH does not impose norms and expectations onto different contexts and countries.
And GMH doesn't decide what is best for the people affected by the emergency, how they are supposed to feel or live their lives, or what the "good way to suffer" is.

The context of GMH work determines its other characteristics. Among them there are the focus on populations, balancing Relief and Development agenda, and the collaborative and integrated nature of this work.

Focus on Populations

In some ways, the emergence of the GMH specialization parallels the development in global health, which branched out from public health and has now become an established, recognized, and rapidly developing discipline that attracts much interest from health professionals.

The global health and GMH fields share other characteristics: They concentrate on populations, preventions, and fostering resilience, and less on individual afflictions. They rely on multidisciplinary and integrated approaches to focus on vulnerable and underserved groups, emphasize making sustainable changes, and recognize the significance of developing systems, health promotion, and the participation of stakeholders in decision-making.

Like global health specialists, GMH prioritizes populations' needs, specifically the needs of vulnerable groups in humanitarian settings. GMH shares this focus with public health and disaster mental health frameworks. Having to balance the populational and the individual needs requires some adjustment in the mindset of the GMH professionals who traditionally focus on individuals only (i.e., person-centered approach) and can lose the populational perspective.

> The community's coping with adversity is measured by how well cope the most vulnerable groups.

The improvement in vulnerable groups' well-being becomes the focus for the GMH needs assessment, upon which a decision is made as to whether the community is coping sufficiently, or it requires external assistance and what kind of assistance. In addition to the needs, this assessment identifies the population' blocks of resilience such as community-based and mutual support.

Balancing Emergency Relief and Development Agenda

As part of humanitarian systems, GMH navigates the same dilemmas as other humanitarians face. A big dichotomy is the prioritizing emergency relief goals versus the development agenda.

GMH services generally gear toward the emergency Relief modality of interventions, but lately, there have been many debates about whether this agenda must expand to serve Development and other long-term goals.

In general, humanitarian Relief is about meeting immediate needs, while Development agenda seeks to improve systems' functioning. Both goals are vital components of enhancing health and wellness, but each has its preferred modality of interventions used.

Examples of development aid can include building capacities such as setting up or supporting health centers, training MH providers, participating in policy development, addressing social determinants of health, and building MH referral systems. Using GMH interventions to change the systems is important for the sustainability of the efforts. Still, it triggers concerns about overreaching and using these interventions to change people's way of living, which comes dangerously close to interfering from the position of power or what we call the modern-day neocolonial attitudes (Cherepanov, 2019).

Currently, more efforts are made to identify intervention models that would combine the advantages of both modalities: responding to a crisis while ensuring sustainable changes. One solution can be incorporating components for sustainability, capacity, and resilience-building, training local providers, and fostering mutual support as part of short-term interventions. Another strategy can be assisting with coping with extreme stress while improving management of chronic health and MH conditions. For instance, a person who can better manage stress will be able to improve diabetes management or increase compliance with HIV treatment regimen.

In another example, a crisis response to survivors of gender-based violence is the relief work, while development tasks can be fighting stigma, challenging norms in the society, and developing community-based support for survivors. Both modalities of intervention are important, but when resources are scarce, having to make this choice can create a conflict of priorities and resources' allocations.

Relief and Development sectors have benefits and disadvantages. They have different priorities and goals and employ different groups of interventions.

Collaborative and Integrative Nature of GMH Work

GMH's mission is to support health and well-being, strengthen the resilience of people affected by humanitarian emergencies, and relieve suffering. This agenda can be accomplished only through collaborative efforts.

Providing MH support to people affected by disasters, wars, famines, and other humanitarian crises always means working with other relief providers across disciplines and sectors. For example, there is a growing recognition of the relevance of GMH's work to other services such as primary care, malnutrition relief, maternal and women's health, managing chronic and noncommunicable diseases, and violence prevention.

Interdisciplinary collaboration brings together multidisciplinary and humanitarian actors who must be able to work together and understand what others are doing to develop integrative approaches and other models that allow actors to work collaboratively in cross-sectoral teams (Tol et al., 2011). Such collaborative formats result in the most cutting-edge interdisciplinary research in fields such as transcultural and anthropological psychiatry and medical anthropology.

GMH Interventions as Preventions: Transition from Relief to Development

Public Health Preventions

Sometimes, the needs produced by a humanitarian situation are so complex that providers struggle to identify the most appropriate interventions, or resort to randomly choose them. The strategic priorities and demands of the situation determine the goals and modalities of the interventions that can best be described in terms of preventions, a public health concept of multilayered approaches to reducing mortality and morbidity in response to various health challenges.

In the suggested preventions-based classification of MH interventions, there are groups of interventions that are most appropriate for primary, secondary, and tertiary preventions. Thinking in terms of preventions simplifies the planning of MH interventions. For example, primary prevention goals can include psychoeducation and addressing social determinants of health; the crisis intervention modality is best to address the acute needs that emerge during a crisis; and tertiary prevention goals better suit situations where damage has already been done and treatment is indicated. Each prevention has specific objectives and the corresponding set of interventions to meet these objectives.

The next two tables (Tables 4.1 and 4.2) use the example of trauma-specific interventions to demonstrate how a GMH provider can use the model of preventions to decide on the choice of interventions that are most appropriated to the strategic objectives in a specific situation. In addition to three types of preventions used in public health, I added quaternary prevention envisioned as mitigation of the iatrogenic harm inflicted by faulty or unethical approaches.

Table 4.2 pairs the public health preventions (Kisling & Das, 2024) with the preferred modality of MH interventions.

Table 4.3 demonstrates how the preventions' strategic objectives translate into the choice of trauma interventions.

Table 4.1 Side-by-side comparison between the humanitarian Relief and Development agenda

	Relief	Development
Examples	Earthquake Armed conflict	Fragile or failed state Protracted conflicts
Needs	Acute and pressing	Long-term and chronic needs
Goals of Interventions	Immediate relief. Alleviation of suffering Improving survival odds	Systemic and structural changes Sustainable social transformation Infrastructure and services development and capacity building Reintegration of the child solders into the communities MH support to people infected by HIV
Agenda	Acute emergency. Short-term solutions	Chronic crisis. Long-term solutions Sustainability and capacity building
Examples of interventions	Psychological First Aid (Brymer et al., 2006)	Skills for psychological recovery (Berkowtz et al., 2010)
Potential concerns	When responding to emergency, concerns for the sustainability of the recovery efforts may not be a priority	Delay in meeting immediate needs can cost lives. Systemic changes and social transformation create a risk for perpetuating the neocolonial agenda

Table 4.2 Public health preventions and corresponding modality of MH interventions

Prevention	Public health definitions	Corresponding modality of mental health interventions
Primary prevention	Interventions intended to avoid the development of disease	Stress management and trauma prevention
Secondary prevention	Strategies that attempt to diagnose and treat an existing disease in its early stages before it results in significant morbidity	Crisis intervention, which is not a treatment
Tertiary prevention	Treatment aims to reduce the negative impact of already established disease by restoring function and reducing disease-related complications	MH treatment and supporting recovery for those who have serious or chronic MH conditions, such as serious mental illness, PTSD, or substance use disorders
Quaternary prevention (mitigating Iatrogenic harm)	Actions to mitigate iatrogenic harm. These actions taken to identify patients at risk of over-pathologizing and over-medicalization, to protect them from new medical invasion, and to suggest interventions, which are ethically acceptable (Martins et al., 2018)	De-pathologizing reactions to extreme stress

Transition from Relief to Development Agenda

The second way to look at the choice of interventions is to determine whether they belong to one of two main modalities of aid operations. They are Relief and Development, where GMH work and humanitarian aid are traditionally associated

Table 4.3 Preventions' strategic objectives and trauma-specific interventions

Prevention	Strategic objectives	Interventions
Primary	Improving stress management	Psycho- and health education Addressing social determinants of health (SDOH) Capacity building Training local providers and community workers to respond to mental distress
Secondary	Relief, stabilization, return to the previous level of functioning	Psychological First Aid Disaster mental health Debriefings
Tertiary	Treatment of serious disfunction, transitioning to higher level of services, if needed Establishing a new routine, symptoms management, tools for sustainable recovery	Skills for psychological recovery MH counseling and therapy Medications management
Quaternary (mitigating Iatrogenic harm)	Normalizing the reactions to extreme stress, enhancing coping, and strengthening resilience	Promoting self-reliance in healing and coping Mobilizing community support Assisting with accessing internal (personal) and external (social and cultural or) resources for overcoming

with Relief. However, there is also a third sector, which is Transition mode. Transition occurs after the Relief phase is over and the long-term programming has not been implemented yet. The quality of the Transition phase will in many ways determine the needs that must be addressed during the Development work.

As previously mentioned, Relief activities are most concerned with meeting immediate and emergency needs, which includes saving people's lives and bringing immediate relief. In the recent decade, however, the international humanitarian agencies have been putting more emphasis on the Development agenda and investing into improving health and MH outcomes, such as strengthening prevention in disasters or improving the social determinants of health.

Prioritizing one agenda over another in humanitarian action has been a point of contention, which has been affecting programs' priorities and resources and funding allocation. The special challenges occur during the transition from Relief to Development, which means moving from crisis response mode to facilitating systemic and structural changes in the community or region in the areas of poverty or violence reduction.

Both sectors are important. After an acute phase of crisis is over, the chronic dysfunction often lingers, and the providers who supported people through most difficult times must walk a thin line between maintaining the momentum of aiding and avoiding taking over and interfering with natural recovery.

The transition between Relief and Development agenda creates specific needs and different roles of GMH providers who often continue "chasing fires" while pondering about sustaining the achieved gains in the community. The special considerations for GMH providers during the transition phase are:

- Changing post-emergency phase creates different needs and different role of MH providers: From "chasing fires to systems development."
- The need for psychological and psychosocial relief will remain even in the comparatively more stable context.
- There is more focus on environmental (housing, nutrition) and psychosocial interventions, facilitating the life style changes and teaching self-help skills.
- More attention is given to supporting people with preexisting or chronic conditions such as depression, or other mental and neurological conditions.
- Other interventions can involve development of referral systems, organizing professional peer support, facilitating mutual support groups, and training and supervising local providers.
- Psychoeducation for the community can involve information about managing anxiety, depression, and trauma reactions and self-help recommendations.
- Part of psychoeducation must be information about when to seek further help.
- A special part of GMH assistance can be assisting the local MH and psychosocial providers with organizing and, at the same time, securing funding for their future work.

Challenges and Priorities for the Future

Challenges

The GMH field is rapidly developing but also faces growing pains in an increasingly complex environment fraught with controversy and political clashes.

Some challenges come from the interdisciplinary and cross-sectional junctions and having to reconcile different professional paradigms and agenda (which will be further discussed in Chap. 5). However, the most significant challenges come from inside the field. Since its origins, GMH has exposed many implicit biases and shortcomings in mainstream MH. The Western bubble has created a self-serving echo chamber in which practitioners are able to avoid "reality checks" by employing concepts that have never been validated in different situations. In addition to the questionable cross-cultural validity of psychiatric and psychological practice, there are other challenges impeding the future development of GMH. Other remaining challenges are as follows:

The non-critical translation of Western national MH theory and practice into implementation programs where local contexts, social, and economic aspects are often not considered is fraught with pitfalls (Barbui & Albanese, 2020).

The long legacy of the biomedical paradigm in Western MH has resulted in pathologizing and treating reactions to extreme stress, which are part of the normal human experience, rather than exploring culturally appropriate practices (Barbui & Albanese, 2020).

Many Western MH interventions *disregard individual and culturally specific strength and resilience*, which disempowers people, denies them the ability to cope with adversity themselves and heal, threatens indigenous healing practices (Bemme & Kirmayer, 2020).

There is *a scarcity of GMH-specific concepts, assessments, and intervention tools*, and there is still a limited number of trained GMH providers who see beyond treatment protocols to make informed decisions about the nature and choice of interventions appropriate to the context.

Future Directions

GMH priorities revolve around better understanding MH needs and finding the best strategies for meeting them in different situations. Other priorities are:

- Strengthening humanitarian accountability, professionalization, and quality assurance by prioritizing humanitarian research (Lambert, 2015; Chiumento et al., 2016).
- Moving away from biomedical models and diagnostic categories in favor of developing holistic models.
- De-pathologizing the psychological response to severe adversity and assisting affected persons to connect with their strengths and resources.
- Depoliticizing GMH assistance to emphasize neutrality and human rights instead of aligning with politically correct views.
- Defragmenting interventions to facilitate the development of collaborative and integrative approaches.
- Focusing on resilience and solutions instead of deficits and problems to facilitate recovery instead of trying to fix MH issues.
- Relying on community support to facilitate changes through dialog instead of seeking solutions from the external experts.
- Increasing self-reliance and flexibility in professional decision-making instead of relying on predetermined practices and protocols.
- Engaging in critical self-inspection and learning from experiences instead of replication of previously successful projects without examination.
- Developing a training curriculum and core training requirements and working with professional associations to establish the GMH formal designation, professional standards, and quality assurance systems.
- Expanding gender-based violence (GBV) and suicide prevention initiatives to challenge social and cultural norms, prevent violence, and foster resilience.
- Bringing attention to MH needs and strengthening advocacy, so GMH professionals can fight for policies that foster justice, respect human rights and dignity.

- Strengthening MH research to identify the needs, prevalence, and causes of MH problems to inform GMH work and advocacy.

Professional Mythology in GMH Work

Common misconceptions about humanitarian work illustrate the importance for MH professionals to understand their role within humanitarian systems, the scope of their service, and the nature of their professional contribution. Like many rapidly developing specializations, the GMH field has quickly developed pervasive misconceptions, which can interfere with work and challenge boundaries. Many myths have emerged that must be critically examined:

Myths about the invariance of culture, unconditional precedence of the cultural wisdom of elders, and indigenous healing practices:

> As much as we respect cultural differences and local cultures, there are multiple instances when cultural beliefs can go against human rights, as when victims of gender-based violence are treated as pariahs (Cherepanov, 2020) or when traditional healing practices involve torture.

Myths about the universality of diagnosable mental disorders, such as depression and PTSD, and the role of antidepressants:

> In fact, there is plenty of disagreement concerning the diagnoses of depression and PTSD, let alone treatments for these mental disorders. Many diagnostic categories are culture- or situation-bound and have different significances in different circumstances. In addition, Western MH concepts tend to overly pathologize stress reactions and treat them as mental disorders.

Myth about evidence-based practices:

> This myth suggests that perceived advances in Western MH directly translate to different cultures and contexts. Although some practices have good cross-cultural recognition, many are incongruent with local cultures and create rejection. Using practices not validated in other cultures, or even within the same culture but in different contexts, also means disregard for coping and stress management strategies that have been accumulated by local culture.

Most people in distress cannot overcome trauma without professional help:

> Most people who are affected by traumatic events will be able to cope independently; only a few will need help to survive. Thus, those who are not coping should be a priority in GMH interventions. The other role of GMH assistance is to facilitate recovery and foster strength and resilience.

The myth of helpless victims:

> The tendency to see beneficiaries as helpless victims or to stereotype people in need (Otegui, 2022) reflects neocolonial attitudes. Most victims exhibit remarkable strength and resilience despite challenging circumstances.

The myth about victims presenting as needy, humble, and grateful:

Most people take pride in their independence and try to preserve dignity and project strength, even during hard times. Their self-confidence does not mean that they do not need or appreciate help. If this myth is not recognized, providers may even experience frustration with beneficiaries who don't fit this expected image.

The myth that GMH providers must trust the community to support its members:

In many instances, communities will provide all possible supports. However, in some cultures, people believe that drawing attention to a suffering person is disrespectful and can be perceived as violating their privacy. (Cherepanov, "personal communication")

On other occasions, the community can turn against victims, particularly where domestic violence, sexual violence, or LGBTQ persons are involved, and continue victimization by making them social pariahs.

The myth that GMH experts know how people feel and what they need, and must help them whether they want it or not:

An example of such erroneous assumptions is the belief in the universal benefits of trauma processing, an approach commonly used for trauma treatment. On many occasions, the author observed GMH providers encouraging people to share their trauma experience, assuring them that they would feel better because this is what the evidence says. Some ended up retraumatized.

The myth that "Everyone knows about mental health. There is no need to explain what we do.":

Not only the people served but also many humanitarian actors know remarkably little about GMH and what to expect from practitioners. What is obvious to GMH professionals about their work may not be evident to others. At the same time, MH providers may not be aware of the image they inadvertently project on the people they assist and on their fellow relief workers.

The myth that "The coping skills that help me are going to help others.":

Before making recommendations, recognize conceptual, cultural, practical, and situational limitations of coping skills developed in different cultures and situations. For example, not all typically recommended stress management tools can realistically be used in humanitarian emergencies, e.g., taking a bath, lighting a candle, or taking a nature walk. In another example, recommending yoga practice in countries with totalitarian regimes may not be safe because of competing ideologies.

The myth that "If I don't do it, no one will.":

The illusion of centrality, common in first responders, can develop when they respond to an emergency. This misperception comes with feeling that their work is central to overcoming the crisis and losing sight of other actors. Such an attitude undermines the spirit of collaboration and finding joint solutions. This illusion signifies an erroneous belief that an MH provider is the only one who can help, and others are doing nothing or doing it too slowly.

Takeaways

- GMH is an interdisciplinary specialization that focuses on providing psychological relief and MH support to people affected by humanitarian emergencies.
- Typically, such activities take place in an international setting, but they can also include care for refugees at the locations of their resettlement.

- The GMH specialization is defined by its dual identity as a humanitarian and MH discipline, the humanitarian settings where the work takes place, and its global significance.
- The history of GMH is indicative of the pathways leading to its professional self-determination.
- The global perspective and humanitarian settings have challenged many professional assumptions in MH.
- The development of concepts, context-appropriate assessments, and best practices are currently the main priorities in the GMH field.
- The overall focus of GMH is shifting from treating individuals to implementing community-based interventions and strengthening coping and resilience.

References

Abramowitz, S. (2017). Epidemics (especially Ebola). *Annual Review of Anthropology, 46*, 421–445. https://doi.org/10.1146/annurev-anthro-102116-041616

Amstutz, M. R. (2013). *International ethics: Concepts, theories, and cases in global politics* (4th ed.). Lanham, MD: Rowman & Littlefield Publishers.

Antić, A. (2021). Transcultural psychiatry: Cultural difference, universalism and social psychiatry in the age of decolonisation. *Culture, Medicine, and Psychiatry, 45*(3), 359–384. https://doi.org/10.1007/s11013-021-09719-4

Bajbouj, M., Ta, T. M. T., Hassan, G., & Hahn, E. (2022). Editorial: The nine grand challenges in global mental health. *Frontiers in Psychiatry, 12*, 822299. https://doi.org/10.3389/fpsyt.2021.822299

Barbui, C., & Albanese, E. (2020). Global mental health: Good news, bad news and responsibilities for the future. *Epidemiology and Psychiatric Sciences, 29*, E76. https://doi.org/10.1017/S2045796019000738

Bemme, D., & Kirmayer, L. J. (2020). Global mental health: Interdisciplinary challenges for a field in motion. *Transcultural Psychiatry, 57*(1), 3–18. https://doi.org/10.1177/1363461519898035

Bemme, D., Roberts, T., Ae-Ngibise, K. A., Gumbonzvanda, N., Joag, K., Kagee, A., Machisa, M., can der Westhuizen, C., van Rensburg, A., Willan, S., Wuerth, M., Aoun, M., Jain, S., Lund, C., Mathias, K., Read, U., Salisbury, T. T., & Burgess, R. A. (2023). Mutuality as a method: Advancing a social paradigm for global mental health through mutual learning. *Social Psychiatry and Psychiatric Epidemiology, 59*, 545–553. https://doi.org/10.1007/s00127-023-02493-1

Berkowitz, S., Bryant, R., Brymer, M., Hamblen, J., Jacobs, A., Layne, C., Macy, R., Osofsky, H., Pynoos, R., Ruzek, J., Steinberg, A., Vernberg, E., Watson, P.; National Center for PTSD, National Child Traumatic Stress Network. (2010). Skills for psychological recovery: Field operations guide. https://www.ptsd.va.gov/professional/treat/type/skills_psych_recovery_manual.asp.

Brymer, M., Jacobs, A., Layne, C., Pynoos, R., Ruzek, J., Steinberg, A., Vernberg, E., & Watson, P. (2006). *Psychological first aid (PFA) field operations guide* (2nd ed.). National Child Traumatic Stress Network & National Center for PTSD. https://www.nctsn.org/

Cherepanov, E. (2018). *Ethics for global mental health: From good intentions to humanitarian accountability*. Routledge. https://doi.org/10.4324/9781351175746

Cherepanov, E. (2019). Ethical dilemmas in global mental health. *BJPsych International, 16*(4), 81–83. https://doi.org/10.1192/bji.2019.10

Cherepanov, E. (2020). Sexual and gender-based violence as warfare. In R. Geffner, V. Vieth, V. Vaughan, A. Rosenbaum, L. Hamberger, & J. White (Eds.), *Handbook of interpersonal violence across the lifespan*. Springer. https://doi.org/10.1007/978-3-319-62122-7_106-1

Chiumento, A., Khan, M. N., Rahman, A., & Frith, L. (2016). Managing ethical challenges to mental health research in post-conflict settings. *Developing World Bioethics, 16*(10), 15–28.
Feynman, R. P. (1974). Cargo cult science. *Engineering and Science, 37*(7), 10–13. https://calteches.library.caltech.edu/51/2/CargoCult.pdf
Hall, H. (2016, March 15). Cargo cult psychology. *Science-Based Medicine*. https://sciencebased-medicine.org/cargo-cult-psychology/
Hilhorst, D. J. M., & Jansen, B. J. (2010). Humanitarian Space as Arena: A Perspective on the Everyday Politics of Aid. Development and Change, 41(6), 1117–1139. https://doi.org/10.1111/j.1467-7660.2010.01673.x
IASC. (2007). *Guidelines on mental health and psychosocial support in emergency settings*. Interagency Standing Committee.
Kisling, L. A., & Das, J. M. (2024). Prevention strategies. [Updated 2023 Aug 1]. In *StatPearls* [Internet]. StatPearls Publishing. Available from: https://www.ncbi.nlm.nih.gov/books/NBK537222/
Kohrt, B., & Mendenhall, E. (2016). Anthropological perspectives on global mental health. In *Global mental health: Anthropological perspectives* (pp. 341–361). Left Coast Press.
Koplan, J. P., Bond, T. C., Merson, M. H., Reddy, K. S., Rodriguez, M. H., Sewankambo, N. K., Wasserheit, J. N., & Consortium of Universities for Global Health Executive Board. (2009). Towards a common definition of global health. *Lancet, 373*(9679), 1993–1995. https://doi.org/10.1016/S0140-6736(09)60332-9. Epub 2009 Jun 1. PMID: 19493564; PMCID: PMC9905260.
Leach, A. (2015, Feb 5). Exporting trauma: can the talking cure do more harm than good? The Guardian. Retrieved from https://www.theguardian.com/global-development-professionalsnetwork/2015/feb/05/mental-health-aid-western-talking-cure-harm-good-humanitarian-anthropologist
Lambert, J. (2015, January 27). Ethical considerations for research with victims of political violence and human rights violations. *StressPoints*. https://www.istss.org/education-research/traumatic-stresspoints/2015-january/ethical-considerations-for-research-with-victims-o.aspx
Martins, C., Godycki-Cwirko, M., Heleno, B., & Brodersen, J. (2018). Quaternary prevention: Reviewing the concept. *The European Journal of General Practice, 24*(1), 106–111. https://doi.org/10.1080/13814788.2017.1422177. PMID: 29384397; PMCID: PMC5795741.
Médecins Sans Frontières (MSF). (n.d.). *Advocacy and Temoignage*. https://msf.org.au/advocacy-and-t%C3%A9moignage
mhGAP Intervention guide for mental, neurological and substance use disorders for non-specialist health settings. (2010). World Health Organization.
Mills, C. (2014). *Decolonizing global mental health: The psychiatrization of the majority world*. Routledge.
National Institutes of Health (NIMH). (2010). *The grand challenges in global mental health initiative*. Office for Research on Disparities and Global Mental Health (ORDGMH). https://www.nimh.nih.gov/about/organization/cgmhr/grandchallenges
Otegui, D. F. (2022). Symbolic approach to humanitarian action: It takes one to know one. Springer International Publishing.
Redfield, P. (2013). *Life in crisis: The ethical journey of Doctors Without Borders*. University of California Press.
Summerfield, D. (2012). Afterword: Against "global mental health". *Transcultural Psychiatry, 49*(3–4), 519–530. https://doi.org/10.1177/1363461512454701
Tol, W. A., Barbui, C., Galappatti, A., Silove, D., Betancourt, T. S., Souza, R., Golaz, A., & van Ommeren, M. (2011). Mental health and psychosocial support in humanitarian settings: Linking practice and research. *Lancet, 378*(9802), 1581–1591. https://doi.org/10.1016/s0140-6736(11)61094-5
Watters, E. (2011). *Crazy like us: The globalization of the Western mind*. Robinson.
World Health Organization, War Trauma Foundation, & World Vision International. (2011). *Psychological first aid: Guide for field workers*. WHO.

Chapter 5
Challenges When Responding to Humanitarian Emergencies

Professional and Interdisciplinary Challenges

When global mental health (GMH) professionals respond to humanitarian emergencies, they must be prepared to encounter various challenges. Some professional and interdisciplinary challenges relate to the unreadiness of the profession to work in humanitarian situations. Other challenges are due to the scarcity of concepts and the unavailability of tools that can be adapted to the humanitarian context or are driven the interdisciplinary and cross-sectional disciplinary and multicultural nature of humanitarian action. Personal challenges are further discussed in Chap. 13.

Professional Idiosyncrasies

Work in humanitarian settings highlights the strength of the profession and also tests the viability of implicit beliefs and exposes shortcomings. The GMH experience of responding to emergencies, building community resilience, advocating for refugees, and supporting victims of violence has questioned many tenets of how Western mental health (MH) professionals conduct their work. Some of these concerns revolve around the cross-cultural transferability of clinical assessments and evidence-based practices as they apply to a humanitarian context.

The global perspective has opened the multiple opportunities for MH professionals to expand this professional framework, to incorporate the contextuality of everything we do (Wessells, 2009), and then learn from people we service. The global experiences in a powerful way challenge the "original sin" of the MH profession, which is the sense of professional omnipotence, the naïve conviction that the beneficiaries cannot cope without our help and a belief that experts know better what others need.

E. Cherepanov, *Humanitarian Competencies for Global Mental Health Professionals*, Contemporary Humanitarian Action and Emergency Management,
https://doi.org/10.1007/978-3-031-74268-2_5

Conceptual Challenges: "The Glove Doesn't Fit"

For many MH professionals trained in traditional Western approaches, GMH work becomes an eye-opening experience and exposes the limitations of the standard professional training. It also brings a realization about the limitlessness of human resilience and the imperative of understanding mental distress in relation to adversity and within a cultural context.

Historically, MH originated as a single-siloed module attempting to capture a narrow area of mental dysfunction. To prove its relevance, it indiscriminately extrapolated findings on the complex reality of human life in humanitarian settings. To everyone's surprise, the outdated concepts did not fit the challenges of newly discovered GMH findings. The professional echo chamber has produced self-serving assumptions, and the not always warranted pathology-oriented terminology, a sort of a secret knowledge insulating the field against laymen questioning some of its assumptions. Only a global perspective has allowed professionals to test these assumptions by placing them within a broader context. Contextual competencies and normalizing attitudes or even language have yet to be fully adopted despite all the efforts toward increasing cultural competencies. Bemme and D'Souza (2014) believe that underappreciation for individual and cultural strengths can further exacerbate stigma, discouraging people from reaching out and receiving MH support when needed.

There has been a growing discontent in the professional community with what mainstream MH has to offer, along with a greater understanding of the importance of holistic approaches, social integration, and recovery. Despite many efforts, the old lens through which MH professionals view problems remains a barrier to incorporating local healing practices and other non-Western perspectives on resilience (Mascayano et al., 2020).

This norm–pathology discourse continues affecting the choice of interventions or even understanding when interventions are needed. For example, not every mental distress requires treatment: In many instances, supporting natural recovery and healing, identifying personal strengths, and providing access to the resources and supports are the most effective ways to facilitate a sustainable recovery.

The conceptual changes reflecting cultural diversity have already started in the MH field and there is no way back. The MH professionals have accepted that some extreme psychological reactions are culturally bound and congruent to problematic situations, and cultural competency has been incorporated into all health and MH practices.

At the same time, the fascination with cultural sensitivity and collecting the so-called "idioms of distress" has created an overreliance on formalized cultural attributes to guide MH communications and interventions. Using these idioms of distress as a cultural thesaurus of clinical terminology has proven problematic. First, these idioms may have different meanings in different regions, and second, researchers have questioned whether the connotations of clinical terminology and the idioms are indeed identical (Wessells, 2009; Lambert, 2015). MH providers cannot completely trust "the wisdom" of traditional cultures, which values at times can appear judgmental, stigmatizing, prejudiced, and discriminatory against certain vulnerable groups and not consistent with the values of human rights.

Already in 2002, Dyregrov et al. (2002) has cautioned against over-reliance on the local culture for sources of coping and support and suggested that resilience plays a bigger role in preventing long-term traumatic stress on a disaster site.

Interdisciplinary Challenges

The GMH work is not confided to one discipline only. The aid workers coming from different disciplines participate in the disaster relief, where GMH providers must first define their role and then lead collaborative interventions that would amplify the benefits for the affected people.

The demands of humanitarian settings call for models that are comprehensive enough to reflect the complex reality of people functioning in situations of extreme stress and uncertainty. They also must be specific enough to reflect the uniqueness of each crisis, and flexible enough to adapt to evolving circumstances and incorporate newly emerging innovations.

Psychoeducation on the effects of trauma, as well as its coping and mutual support, has always been recognized as advantageous. It can be used across disciplines and sectors and remains an important interdisciplinary tool for addressing MH issues and for destigmatizing and de-pathologizing MH conditions. It is also used preventatively to address barriers to receiving services. In multidisciplinary and multicultural environments, psychoeducation can offer alternative labels to psychiatric conditions. For example, instead of "treating depression," MH providers can assist with "stress management" or "improving sleep." Other options can be relabeling MH symptoms to use locally accepted idioms such as "thinking too much."

The preventative benefits of public trauma education have become very clear in Ukraine. After the war broke out, many sought MH and trauma care, and stigmatization has not played a significant role is accepting services. (Cherepanov, 2022)

The biggest challenge for interventions, health promotion, and prevention comes from a shortage of interdisciplinary models of human functioning that would allow us to overcome the traditionally siloed frameworks of different disciplines.

Overcoming the interdisciplinary challenges in GMH can provide the path to reconciling concepts coming from different disciplines and sectors when the situation requires an orchestrated response.

The GMH-Friendly Tools

Humanitarian settings place special expectations on MH assessment tools and interventions, which are still critically unavailable to GMH providers. The development of such assessments and interventions is a current priority in GMH because only good assessments produce high-quality data and allow for developing evidence-based practices.

GMH-friendly and reliable assessments and interventions that can be comfortably used in a humanitarian emergency share specific characteristics.

Simplicity. The instructions must be simple enough to be used by nonspecialists and providers from different professions. These sentences must be easy to translate to avoid ambiguity, long questions, and use of cultural idioms or items that do not have parallel concepts in that culture (Hoeft et al., 2018; Bemme & Kirmayer, 2020). One example is the difficult-to-translate item 2 in the Refugee Health Screener-15 (RHS-15) questionnaire, which is phrased as "Feeling down, sad, or blue most of the time" (Hollifield et al., 2013). Very few cultures have the same understanding of "feeling blue" even with professional translation.

Brevity is a highly desirable characteristic of GMH-friendly tools because this work unfolds in a rapidly changing environment where time commitments are difficult to obtain. Most people are busy with survival tasks. In the meantime, many conventional trauma questionnaires can be excruciatingly long, and available interventions are structured in ways that require attending multiple sessions, which is not realistic to expect in a chaotic environment.

Portability means that the assessment tools and interventions can be easily adapted to different situations and languages if needed. They should allow use as a whole or in parts without sacrificing their therapeutic value, or have parts that can be used interchangeably.

Cross-cultural universality. A good GMH tool can remain culturally appropriate across various cultures. For example, the idiom of "thinking too much" is an equivalent of having excessive worries and has the same meaning in most cultures.

Good face-validity of interventions (i.e., not looking like a magic trick) is important for the people being serviced to understand what and why they are asked to do certain things and so they can make informed decisions about participating. Good face validity is an excellent way to combat the "cargo cult" mentality.

Cultural appropriateness. Implementing MH's innovative practice works best when they are congruent with the already existing local practices and appear culturally appropriate. To be sustainable, interventions must not conflict with local cultural beliefs.

For instance, the tradition of sharing one's positive and negative experiences in a group setting exists in many cultures. In the countries of West Africa, for one, this is called the "Palava" tradition. In other cultures, such as the Northern Caucasus, the ritual of personal sharing of misfortunate experiences happens while drinking coffee with a group of friends and serves a similar purpose. (Cherepanov, "personal conversation")

Appropriateness to the situation. There is an abundance of broadly publicized yet notoriously inappropriate recommendations for tools for effective communication or coping with stress, such as taking a warm bath, lighting candles, listening to calming music, or singing out loud.

The International Trauma Questionnaire (ITQ) and Psychological First Aid (PFA) are examples of tools that are friendly for use in humanitarian settings.

The main advantage of the ITQ is that this tool is brief, simply worded, and easy to administer for both MH professionals and paraprofessionals (Cloitre et al., 2021). The brevity comes at a price—to maximize its utility, this abbreviated version omits complex PTSD items. The questionnaire is translated into several common languages. The ITQ items can be retrieved from https://www.traumameasuresglobal.com/itq.

PFA is a versatile intervention aimed at providing immediate MH relief, support, and practical assistance to people affected by a disaster. It is well suited for humanitarian emergencies. The intervention consists of several modules that can easily be adapted to different situations and are filled with contents from other cultures (Brymer et al., 2006). PFA's objectives are restoring a sense of self-efficacy, connectedness, and hope by assisting a person to recognize and connect to their internal and external strength and resources and linking them to support systems. PFA offers a set of practical recommendations on coping with trauma reactions, anxiety, depression, and sleep problems as well as reducing social isolation. These skills can be used as an MH intervention, self-help, or for teaching volunteers, community workers, and other aid workers.

The structure of PFA allows the front-line responders, trainers, facilitators, and service recipients to use phone applications translated into different languages. For example, PFA-based iOS mobile applications assist those who provide MH relief to adults, families, and children. The World Health Organization, War Trauma Foundation, and World Vision International (2011) have recommended PFA for conflict-affected areas. Retrieved from https://apps.apple.com/us/app/pfa-mobile/id551079424/

Preference of nonverbal approaches in some humanitarian emergencies. When many people are affected, there may not be enough interpreters proficient in local or tribal languages, which can present a barrier to using talk therapy such as cognitive-behavioral approaches. In these cases, nonverbal interventions, such as expressive arts, dance therapy, tapping, body orientation, and holistic approaches, can be a better alternative.

Collaborative and Integrated Models

Meeting complex needs requires complex approaches. In humanitarian crises where basic, psychological, medical, and social needs often are intertwined and cannot be separated, integrated approaches have become the gold standard for MH relief.

Studies have consistently demonstrated that collaborative approaches and integrated service models have better outcomes and cost-effectiveness in treating depression, anxiety, and other mental disorders than treating these conditions separately (Hay et al., 2012; Archer et al., 2012). Integrated practices include psychosocial models (MHPSS), integrated primary care, and community-based interventions. All these models have advantages and limitations, but their benefits clearly outweigh their shortcomings.

Mental Health and Psychosocial Support (MHPSS) Interventions in Emergencies

The central premise of MHPSS is that MH and social well-being depend on each other, so addressing them concurrently promotes overall well-being. This assumption is rooted in the belief that helping people to access social resources and deal more effectively with stresses, personal challenges, or solving practical problems can greatly reduce their distress and suffering and strengthen their coping.

In 2007, the Interagency Standing Committee (IASC) issued operational guidance for systems of planning and implementing psychosocial interventions in a humanitarian emergency. These guidelines have become a major milestone in forming standards for GMH work (IASC, 2007). Currently, many leading NGOs employ the MHPSS module as their approach of choice.

Meta-analyses of MHPSS intervention outcomes have demonstrated some improved functioning and reduced PTSD when supporting victims of gender-based violence, sex trafficking, and refugees (Bangpan et al., 2019; Kamali et al., 2020). These studies were not able to determine whether MHPSS model was more effective than interventions targeting specific issues such as assisting victims of violence. They also suggested that more focused research is is needed to establish the effectiveness of MHPSS interventions in conflict settings (Tol et al., 2011).

On another occasion, the data analysis revealed a cautionary story that confirmed the importance of gathering the research evidence before implementing GMH interventions in humanitarian context.

> Rokhideh (2017) used data to provide an extreme example of the fallout of inadequately planned psychosocial interventions in northern Uganda, recovering from 22 years of civil war. The outpour of MHPSS interventions devoted to post-conflict recovery coincided with increased rates of suicide, increased domestic violence, and increased substance abuse. While the link between these developments might have other explanations, the data draws attention to the importance of thoroughly planning interventions.

Another concern has been that MHPSS programs often operate without collaborating with the existing health care infrastructure or coordinating their activities with humanitarian systems.

MHPSS has also drawn criticism because of the declared universality of this approach across settings and the seeming underappreciation of already established community- and culture-rooted practices in building systems of response and resilience. Positioning beneficiaries as passive recipients of services can do a disservice to the sustainability of a community's recovery (McCormack & Joseph, 2013).

This said, the MHPSS remains the most recognized and widely used approach, which has provided many vital benefits to the affected communities and regarded as the first standardized practice in GMH.

Integrated Primary Care

The integrated primary care is yet another integrated model that has gained broad acceptance among multidisciplinary healthcare practitioners. This model, places MH providers within primary care medical settings and medical providers make referrals for stress, trauma, and/or behavioral health issues such as substance misuse (Souza et al., 2009). The integrated care models have shown that treating people for medical and MH conditions concurrently is more cost-effective and has many benefits: Trauma survivors often have coexisting medical conditions and social needs, and it is more socially acceptable to receive services in a medical facility than in a standalone MH program.

The limitation of this model lies in its reliance on aftercare and social support infrastructure, which may become problematic to organize in humanitarian emergencies. For instance, assisting a survivor of intimate partner violence can only be truly effective if there is a concurrent availability of legal and psychosocial support, shelter, financial assistance, and employment opportunities. Similarly, the successful treatment of depression related to chronic health conditions depends on the quality of social and community support and access to medications.

Community-Based Interventions

Complex emergencies destabilize or destroy the fabric of social life in a community. They overwhelm the capacity for coping and heighten systemic vulnerabilities, which have broader implications for the perpetuation of victimization in the future. Community-based interventions play a role in restoring community function, strengthening resilience and self-determination, and facilitating mutual and community support (Abramowitz & Panter-Brick, 2016; Cherepanov, 2015; Bunn et al., 2023). Cherepanov (2015) proposed the Community-Based Recovery in Complex Emergency model, which includes interventions to empower the community and formal and informal leaders to assume an active role and responsibility for the safety, protection, and well-being of its members.

Community workers have been increasingly involved in a multitude of public health and MH activities, including health, MH and trauma education and outreach, infectious disease management, and disaster response and prevention. The latter has been particularly important with the expected increase in natural disasters due to climate change. The community workers are trained in scalable psychological interventions to increase the availability of psychological services.

Nonspecific Interventions

There is a group of interventions that are neither clinical nor psychological by nature, yet carry therapeutic value. Some aim to reestablish routines and daily structures in the community and organize activities that allow children and adults to informally learn about stress management, sleep hygiene techniques, or the harmful effects of substance use.

Group interventions can take the form of painting, singing, dancing, engaging in volunteer activities, joint prayers, and sports, and engaging the survivors in rebuilding their community (Math et al., 2015). For children, these can be educational or sport activities, storytelling, drawing, arts and crafts, and playing games, all of which can help them to practice social and mutual support skills and increase the mastery over their lives.

External or Contextual Challenges

This group of objective challenges stems from the nature of the humanitarian situation and refers to security risks as well as political, social, and logistical issues that MH professionals have little control over but which impact their work. A high degree of volatility and rapid changes in security in a humanitarian setting mean that the situation can change rapidly. There is never assurance that one will be able to continue with the work or of how long this client will be available to continue receiving services. Other challenges include compromised infrastructure, inconsistent funding, and undue political influence.

Security Concerns

Violence against humanitarians is on the rise. Aid workers have been targets of threats, kidnapping, and violence for political reasons, due to criminal activities or for ransom. Reducing the impact of safety and security concerns on the MH of humanitarian aid workers remains a priority problem in humanitarian action.

An American Red Cross study showed that over 40% of aid workers perceived the humanitarian work experience as more stressful than initially anticipated, 10% encountered accidents or injuries, and 16% faced instances of violence (Kivlehan & Kayden, 2023). The same study pointed out that the risks vary across regions, and the list of safer and less safe regions changes daily. Many deploying organizations nowadays pay increased attention to the security situation on the ground and have instituted surveillance systems to monitor risks in real time.

Unavailable or Destroyed Infrastructure, Child Protection, and Referral Systems

When responding to humanitarian crises, GMH providers often work with limited resources, destroyed supporting infrastructure, unavailable referral systems, and nonfunctional child protection and law enforcement systems. In these cases, providers rely on their professional skills to problem-solve and reduce harm in a very challenging environment. When no support is available, other humanitarian organizations can step in to assist with some problem. Specialized professional expertise is essential when making incredibly complex decisions and finding alternative solutions that often involve weighing cost–benefits and minimizing harm.

Professional and humanitarian competencies, having access to peer and professional support, and supervision are important parts of GMH work but they are not always available. Even when there is remote access to supervision, the supervisors may not be aware of all the nuances of the situation on the ground. Yet, they can assist GMH providers with their decision-making and with identifying and addressing cognitive biases that can affect this process.

Funding and Politics

Humanitarians' relationship with donors sometimes can get complicated. Donors provide funding for MH programs, but they also can influence the goals, scope, or scale of programs, as well as their durations, sometimes much to the frustration of GMH providers.

Inconsistent funding limits offered services, complicates long-term planning, and creates the potential for aid diversion. Much has been done to increase transparency and accountability in the humanitarian sector. Still, these challenges and accusations of corruption or mishandling of funds persist amid the chaos of a humanitarian crisis where monitoring of discretionary spendings can be difficult (Safarpour et al., 2020).

National, local, and global politics can affect programming priorities, influence access to services and the scope of interventions, and make interventions less safe. Humanitarian agencies, as a rule, try to balance this pressure by having policies about allocation of donated funds.

Humanitarian Culture

Multicultural Environment

To be effective and efficient in aid delivery, multicultural and multidisciplinary providers must find ways to share the personal and professional space, work together, reconcile conceptual differences and priorities, and firmly stand by their convictions when needed.

In humanitarian work, multiculturalism is present on several levels. In addition to expected cultural differences between providers and service recipients, there are at least as many cultural differences among the providers themselves, who come from different countries, cultural and professional backgrounds, and walks of life, all united by the common mission of providing relief in humanitarian emergencies. There are also different professional cultures.

For example, public health providers, psychologists, counselors, social workers, and psychiatrists may view a problem and the consequent solutions from different perspectives and use different professional language. In addition, similar-sounding terms such as treatment could have different connotations in different disciplines, which may lead to miscommunication, confusion, and misunderstanding.

Humanitarianism is not just a practical action. It also is an idea that brings together individuals, organizations, governments, private enterprises, the media, local NGOs, faith-based groups, and other actors. In the face of a disaster, these entities synchronize their efforts, offering collaborative assistance aligned with their values, standards, and perspectives on their role in a dynamically evolving world. All these complex and intertwined actions create meaning for this work and form a unique humanitarian culture that incorporates the practical and symbolic relationship between the actors and beneficiaries (Otegui, 2022).

Humanitarian culture is roughly divided into two interconnected domains: the humanitarian agencies' organizational cultures and the broader professional culture, which has developed over decades of responding to crises and become ingrained in identity of a professional humanitarian.

Organizational Culture

Large international humanitarian organizations accumulate significant economic, technical, and material resources, which give such organizations a lot of power and the ability to shape the response to emergencies.

High-profile INGOs have political presence, visibility, and the capacity to influence political processes. As always, power comes with the responsibility to ensure honesty, morality, and integrity in humanitarian aid provision. The moral responsibility of the large humanitarian agencies for the decisions they make or the calls they chose to ignore has been a subject of discussions in the humanitarian sector.

Every organization has developed the unique organizational culture. The organizational culture of humanitarian agencies is linked to their patterns of functioning, priorities, attitudes toward their employees, and the quality of the interactions between humanitarian actors and beneficiaries. For many years, the humanitarian sector has consistently made efforts to implement changes in their corporate cultures to be more inclusive and less discriminatory. Part of this is establishing equitable work relationships between expats, national and local aid workers, and the partnership with beneficiaries. Much work is yet to be done (Obrecht et al., 2022).

> *The nondiscrimination and inclusiveness policies in humanitarian agencies have been receiving much attention.* In the history of the humanitarian movement, there have been instances when INGOs were accused of discriminating against local providers. This sets up a demand for policies changes and oversight. Treating peers, local workers, translators, other personnel, and the people served with dignity and respect is a matter of being mindful of the power differential. Violating these norms conflicts with proclaimed and projected humanitarian values, where every act of injustice and discrimination, whether real or perceived, receives public attention and may undermine the perception of aid.

It is never easy to define any culture, especially organizational or corporate culture. Most definitions refer to the institution's mission, institutional memory, norms, assumptions, beliefs, and values that guide its employees and assign meaning to their social reality (Chalmers & Brannan, 2023; Needle, 2004). However, culture is always larger than the sum of its components, especially in mission-driven humanitarian agencies. Their culture is shaped by the work they do, their interactions with beneficiaries, and in the symbolic image they project on beneficiaries or their public perception (Otegui, 2022).

Besides direct aid provision, humanitarian agencies balance multiple agendas and interests, coordinating programming and managing resources, governance, and fundraising. Their internal processes can become so complicated and focused on supporting their functioning and the public image that they risk disconnecting from the needs of the population they are supposed to serve (Otegui, 2021).

All these seemingly disjointed and often conflicting processes powerfully come together and synergize when the agency moves into the humanitarian mode. The so-called humanitarian mode activated by the disaster means the special way of thinking when everyone focuses on one task, and one task only—the one-way helping, sometimes at the cost of disregarding partnership with beneficiaries (Otegui, 2022). Such mode of thinking may not be conducive to navigating multilayered, complex realities of humanitarian emergencies.

Humanitarian agencies have long been criticized for their actions and inactions alike. Some decisions are not made linearly and are influenced by various factors such as organizational culture. Such understanding elevates the role of GMH providers in bringing attention to and advocating for inclusive and nondiscriminatory workspace and partnering relationships between humanitarian organizations and beneficiaries.

Thinking Like a Humanitarian

The same way we talk about military culture, there is also a humanitarian culture. In addition to balancing multidisciplinary actors' professional agendas and organizational cultures, humanitarian action has formed its own professional culture with its own terminology, meanings, and special way of thinking. When GMH professionals enter the humanitarian space, understanding humanitarian culture remains an essential block in building productive collaborations.

Like any other culture, the humanitarian culture is recognized in its values, beliefs, history, shared memories and traditions, unspoken rules, and group practices. It is reflected in professional lingo (a lot of acronyms!), a sense of camaraderie, professional humor, and historical references. Professional culture can also be recognized in communication styles and even in a strictly casual dress code. However, most of all, it influences the members' way of thinking.

> *Humanitarian professional culture* has emerged from decades of aid provision experience and is the amalgamation of organizational and professional cultures, attitudes, beliefs, and behaviors of actors. It can be both responsive and bureaucratic, idealistic and extremely pragmatic, compassionate and cynical, dysfunctional and highly efficient, always being criticized for doing too little or too late. Yet, humanitarian aid workers are recognized as the people who will come to help in the most hopeless circumstances.

Below is the list based on my observations on the attitudes, beliefs, and norms that the GMH provider routinely encounter when working in humanitarian space. Humanitarian action rapidly changes in response to newly emerging crises; it is expected that much of what is discussed below may not pertain to every experience, and its relevance will change with time.

Appearance of chaos may be deceiving. Although never ideal, relief efforts often have a structure and an internal logic that may not be visible to outsiders. Contrary to common belief about the chaos following humanitarian emergencies, there is a lot of coordination going on behind the scenes. After receiving information, many humanitarian agencies immediately start planning and executing aid activities.

Being a team player is important for fostering collaborations. Even with the increasing diversity of humanitarian actors, the success of humanitarian action is determined by collective effort. There cannot be any stars on a disaster site where everyone works collegially toward the shared goal. Humanitarian work can be successful only as a collective effort. We have heard about "brilliant" therapists or clinicians, but no one has ever heard of a "brilliant humanitarian."

The needs for self-reliance and interdependence must be balanced. Initiatives are essential, but to be effective, safe, and noncompetitive, they need to be coordinated with others. In a humanitarian context, self-reliance, initiative, and independence of actors are important. Self-reliance means that the relief agencies operate independently, determine their own interventions, and take responsibility for every action or inaction. However, the demands of the situation create interdependence among actors who must rely on each other for successful interventions.

Coordination is a must. Humanitarian relief requires ongoing communication and tight coordination. Coordination helps to prevent fragmentation, avoid duplication of services, and prevent other inefficient use of scarce resources. It is beneficial when all the actors are aware of all the available programs on the ground and coordinate their work and initiatives with each other as well as with local functioning health structures and agencies, including the governmental systems of public or mental health.

Being aware of the "humanitarian mode" helps to stay grounded and focused. Humanitarian mode is an overpowering state of mind that emerges when humanitarians hear of a new disaster. They disengage from routine life and become entirely different people who start perceiving reality through the lens of humanitarian needs (Otegui, 2022). This overfocus on aiding activity in humanitarians can create cognitive aberrations, fantasies (see Chap. 13), and professional boundaries issues.

Humanitarians must be ready for the "hurry up and wait" experiences. Volatility and unpredictability of humanitarian situations can mean difficulties in planning and frequent adjustments, including significant delays. Having to respond on short notice and having to adjust plans later is expected, which can be very frustrating for everyone involved. Learning to deal with uncertainty and cope with waiting is an essential professional skill.

Expectations often must be adjusted. Some who choose humanitarian work expect independence in decision-making and may be disappointed to encounter a heavy bureaucracy. The humanitarian sector often functions as a corporation with a rigid hierarchy, chain of command, and sets of rules and expectations, and many decisions take a painstakingly long time and must be coordinated with the deploying agency.

GMH providers must being mindful of who they represent. When responding to international events, the aid workers represent more than just themselves or their profession. They also represent the country of their origin, the agency they work with, the whole humanitarian sector, and humanitarian values. Any indiscretions may increase risks for others, have political impacts, and undermine the aid delivery.

Humanitarians use a lot of professional lingos. Humanitarians' speech is often heavily laced with abbreviations and acronyms, which can sometimes be frustrating for outsiders. In my personal experience, little can be done about this. An outsider needs to keep asking for clarification of used terms. The ability to understand acronyms comes with time and is sometimes recognized as an indicator of being an experienced humanitarian. Some of the terms are described in the Acronyms and Glossary sections of this book.

Mental health may not always be a priority. In an ideal world, humanitarian (i.e., basic) and MH needs would not compete, but when resources or funding are severely limited, there is a priority for safety, nutrition, sanitation, and medical assistance. For example, the decision whether to include a GMH module can be weighed against other populational priorities in determining the greatest benefits for the group. Accepting that MH may not be a priority at a particular time should not deter GMH specialists from continuing to advocate for the MH needs of the beneficiaries.

Populations and collective priorities can conflict. Humanitarians think in terms of populational needs. MH providers trained in the person-centered paradigm may have a hard time accepting the precedence of collective priorities over individual needs. Such conflict can be emotionally draining for MH professionals and lead to moral dilemmas (see Chap. 10).

Safety protocols are not negotiable and must be followed. Noncompliance with security recommendations and rules can be highly problematic and can put at risk the safety of many people. The security determination partially comes from regular meetings of representatives from different agencies coordinating actions on the ground and sharing information from various sources. This is yet another reason why the humanitarian community must be aware of the presence of GMH providers and the services they provide.

Humanitarian Etiquette: Dos and Don'ts

Awareness of the unwritten rules of etiquette in a humanitarian setting helps one to navigate the humanitarian culture with ease. Those included here are based on the author's experience and may not be applicable to every situation. Some can be found in corporate professional interactions; others are more specific to humanitarian settings. For clarity, they are organized around small practical suggestions (Table 5.1).

Table 5.1 Humanitarian etiquette: Dos and Don'ts

Dos
Always advocate for the needs of the people served.
Any proposal for actions, change, or initiative must start with the words: "This is what I can do!"
Be a good team player but advocate for the professional agenda.
Be mindful of cultural differences between the international aid workers.
Be sensitive to the power differential between international specialists, local providers, and beneficiaries, never discriminate against them, and be very careful in communicating recommendations that can be perceived as imperative.
Pay attention to good manners: In a high-stress situation, manners can appear less of a priority. However, bad manners and being rude are disrespectful and may distract people from focusing on serious problems.
Presume that everyone around you is doing everything they can unless proven otherwise.
Treat others with respect regardless of their position, role, or place of birth.
When unsure about the reasons for the decision, give managers the benefit of doubt before suspecting ulterior motives. There can be a bigger picture related to the information that may not be available for all or challenges balancing conflicting priorities.
Don'ts
Don't tell a humanitarian they don't care or are not committed to the cause.
Don't provide therapy to peers in the team. Be ready that the MH provider may be asked to help the peers or participate in conflict resolution. It is always a balancing act. Show genuine concern and empathic support instead.
Don't drop big names in conversation.
Don't use big titles and credentials like "doctors" in casual conversations—everyone is doing their best, and academic credentials are irrelevant. They can be used when representing the agency for public relations purposes.
Don't talk with peers about your high social or professional status or how much money you make. It is insensitive. Talk about professional experience directly relevant to work instead.
Don't overdress, wear expensive accessories, or expose the big brands' labels. Dress casually instead.
Don't offer personal money to beneficiaries or private gifts to the community. They can be donated centrally through the agency instead.
Don't offer to send gifts from the homeland or invitations for a visit.
Don't treat beneficiaries as helpless victims. Acknowledge and show respect for their strength instead.
GMH providers, such as any other humanitarians, do not wear weapons and do not participate in the fighting. Doing so is inconsisent with the professional role and can have long-term implications for the provider, humanitarian action, and the consumers.

And finally—never, ever say, "It is not my job!" Humanitarian actors must be ready to do what the situation requires and not limit their involvement only to professional duties.

Takeaways

- When navigating the multicultural humanitarian space, GMH professionals face various professional, interdisciplinary, and external challenges.

- The interdisciplinary environment of GMH work requires that providers overcome their professional idiosyncrasies and prioritize the integrated and collaborative approaches and interventions
- Contextual or external challenges stem from the demands of the situation and can include funding constraints, political pressure, and security concerns.
- Humanitarian organizations accumulate significant economic, technical, and human resources, and shape the response to complex emergencies on multiple levels. The GMH plays a role in advocating with the agencies for the needs of people they serve.
- Understanding humanitarian culture and etiquette in fieldwork facilitates productive collaborations and helps to minimize miscommunication.

References

Abramowitz, S., & Panter-Brick, C. (2016). Bringing life into relief: Comparative ethnographies of humanitarian practice. In S. A. Abramowitz & C. Panter-Brick (Eds.), *Medical humanitarianism: Ethnographies of practice* (pp. 1–20). University of Pennsylvania Press. https://doi.org/10.9783/9780812291698-002

Archer, J., Bower, P., Gilbody, S., Lovell, K., Richards, D., Gask, L., Dickens, C., & Coventry, P. (2012). Collaborative care for depression and anxiety problems. *Cochrane Database of Systematic Reviews, 17*(10), CD006525. https://doi.org/10.1002/14651858.cd006525.pub2

Bangpan, M., Felix, L., & Dickson, K. (2019). Mental health and psychosocial support programmes for adults in humanitarian emergencies: A systematic review and meta-analysis in low and middle-income countries. *BMJ Global Health, 4*(5), e001484. https://doi.org/10.1136/bmjgh-2019-001484

Bemme, D., & D'Souza, N. (2014). Global mental health and its discontents: An inquiry into the making of global and local scale. *Transcultural Psychiatry, 51*(6), 850–874.

Bemme, D., & Kirmayer, L. J. (2020). Global mental health: Interdisciplinary challenges for a field in motion. *Transcultural Psychiatry, 57*(1), 3–18. https://doi.org/10.1177/1363461519898035

Brymer, M., Jacobs, A., Layne, C., Pynoos, R., Ruzek, J., Steinberg, A., Vernberg, E., & Watson, P. (2006). *Psychological first aid (PFA) field operations guide* (2nd ed.). National Child Traumatic Stress Network & National Center for PTSD. https://www.nctsn.org/

Bunn, M., Samuels, G., & Higson-Smith, C. (2023). Ambiguous loss of home: Syrian refugees and the process of losing and remaking home. *Wellbeing, Space and Society, 4*, 100136. https://doi.org/10.1016/j.wss.2023.100136

Chalmers, R., & Brannan, G. D. (2023). Organizational culture. In *StatPearls [Internet]*. StatPearls Publishing. https://www.ncbi.nlm.nih.gov/books/NBK560543/

Cherepanov, E. (2015). It takes a village: Psychological recovery in complex emergencies. *International Journal of Psychology and Behavioral Sciences, 5*(1), 16–25.

Cherepanov, E. (2022). Mental health providers in Ukraine need support but they are not helpless: Professional self-organization and innovative practices. *Frontiers in Public Health, 10*, 1009431. https://doi.org/10.3389/fpubh.2022.1009431

Cloitre, M., Hyland, P., Prins, A., & Shevlin, M. (2021). The international trauma questionnaire (ITQ) measures reliable and clinically significant treatment-related change in PTSD and complex PTSD. *European Journal of Psychotraumatology, 12*(1), 1930961. https://doi.org/10.1080/20008198.2021.1930961

Dyregrov, A., Gupta, L., Gjestad, R., & Raundalen, M. (2002). Is the culture always right? *Traumatology, 8*(3), 135–145. https://doi.org/10.1177/153476560200800302

Hay, J. W., Katon, W. J., Ell, K., Lee, P.-J., & Guterman, J. J. (2012). Cost-effectiveness analysis of collaborative care management of major depression among low-income, predominantly Hispanics with diabetes. *Value in Health, 15*(2), 249–254. https://doi.org/10.1016/j.jval.2011.09.008

Hoeft, T. J., Fortney, J. C., Patel, V., & Unützer, J. (2018). Task-sharing approaches to improve mental health care in rural and other low-resource settings: A systematic review. *Journal of Rural Health, 34*(1), 48–62.

Hollifield, M., Verbillis-Kolp, S., Farmer, B., Toolson, E. C., Woldehaimanot, T., Yamazaki, J., Holland, A., St Clair, J., & SooHoo, J. (2013). The refugee health screener-15 (RHS-15): Development and validation of an instrument for anxiety, depression, and PTSD in refugees. *General Hospital Psychiatry, 35*(2), 202–209. https://doi.org/10.1016/j.genhosppsych.2012.12.002

IASC. (2007). *Guidelines on mental health and psychosocial support in emergency settings.* Interagency Standing Committee.

Kamali, M., Munyuzangabo, M., Siddiqui, F. J., Gaffey, M. F., Meteke, S., Als, D., Jain, R. P., Radhakrishnan, A., Shah, S., Ataullahjan, A., & Bhutta, Z. A. (2020). Delivering mental health and psychosocial support interventions to women and children in conflict settings: A systematic review. *BMJ Global Health, 5*(3), e002014. https://doi.org/10.1136/bmjgh-2019-002014

Kivlehan, S., & Kayden, S. (2023). Humanitarian aid workers. In *CDC Yellow Book 2024.* Centers for Disease Control and Prevention. https://wwwnc.cdc.gov/travel/yellowbook/2024/work-and-other-reasons/humanitarian-aid-workers

Lambert, J. (2015, January 27). Ethical considerations for research with victims of political violence and human rights violations. *StressPoints.* https://www.istss.org/education-research/traumatic-stresspoints/2015-january/ethical-considerations-for-research-with-victims-o.aspx

Mascayano, F., Toso-Salman, J., Ho, Y. C. S., Saloni, D., Tapia, T., Thornicroft, G., & Susser, E. (2020). Including culture in programs to reduce stigma toward people with mental disorders in low- and middle-income countries. *Transcultural Psychiatry, 57*(1), 140–160.

Math, S. B., Nirmala, M. C., Moirangthem, S., & Kumar, N. C. (2015). Disaster management: Mental health perspective. *Indian Journal of Psychological Medicine, 37*(3), 261–271. https://doi.org/10.4103/0253-7176.162915

McCormack, L., & Joseph, J. (2013). Psychological growth in humanitarian aid personnel: Reintegrating with family and community following exposure to war and genocide. *Community, Work & Family, 16*(2), 147–163. https://doi.org/10.1080/13668803.2012.735478

Needle, D. (2004). *Business in context: An introduction to business and its environment.* Cengage Learning Business Press. ISBN 978-1861529923.

Obrecht, A., Swithern, S., & Doherty, J. (2022). *The state of the humanitarian system (SOHS)—Full report.* ALNAP/ODI.

Otegui, D. (2021). Understanding the cognitive gap between humanitarians and survivors during humanitarian operations. *International Journal of Disaster Risk Reduction, 63*(1), 102427. https://doi.org/10.1016/j.ijdrr.2021.102427

Otegui, D. F. (2022). *Symbolic approach to humanitarian action: It takes one to know one*. Springer International Publishing.

Rokhideh, M. (2017). Peacebuilding and psychosocial intervention: The critical need to address everyday post conflict experiences in northern Uganda. *Intervention, 15*(3), 215–229.

Safarpour, H., Fooladlou, S., Safi-Keykaleh, M., Mousavipour, S., Pirani, D., Sahebi, A., Ghodsi, H., Farahi-Ashtiani, I., & Dehghani, A. (2020). Challenges and barriers of humanitarian aid management in 2017 Kermanshah earthquake: A qualitative study. *BMC Public Health, 20*, 563. https://doi.org/10.1186/s12889-020-08722-5

Souza, A., Yasuda, S., & Cristofani, S. (2009). Mental health treatment outcomes in a humanitarian emergency: A pilot model for the integration of mental health into primary care in Habilla, Darfur. *International Journal of Mental Health Systems, 3*(1), 17.

Tol, W. A., Barbui, C., Galappatti, A., Silove, D., Betancourt, T. S., Souza, R., Golaz, A., & van Ommeren, M. (2011). Mental health and psychosocial support in humanitarian settings: Linking practice and research. *Lancet, 378*(9802), 1581–1591. https://doi.org/10.1016/s0140-6736(11)61094-5

Wessells, M. G. (2009). Do no harm: Toward contextually appropriate psychosocial support in international emergencies. *American Psychologist, 64*(8), 842. https://doi.org/10.1037/0003-066X.64.8.842

World Health Organization, War Trauma Foundation, & World Vision International. (2011). *Psychological first aid: Guide for field workers*. WHO.

Chapter 6
The Guidance and Regulations in Global Mental Health Practice

Sources of Guidance

The guidance and regulations ensure that GMH workers conduct their interventions consistently and ethically. The guidelines become vital when aiding highly vulnerable populations in an increasingly complex environment where little is as it seems and there may not be any good solutions.

The dual identity of global mental health (GMH) as a mental health (MH) and humanitarian specialization and the interdisciplinary nature of this work means that there must be more than one source of professional guidance and regulations (Cherepanov, 2018). In a humanitarian emergency, four sets of interconnected, hierarchically organized, and partially overlapping systems of regulations guide GMH work.

The first guidance comes from the binding professional codes of ethics that are specific to the profession. The second set consists of aspirational values and humanitarian principles that outline expectations shared across humanitarian sectors, which are at the core of all humanitarian activities. The third group includes the Humanitarian Code of Conduct, which serves to ensure professional and personal integrity when working in a humanitarian situation (Sphere, 2018). The fourth group offers operational guidance for providing MH and psychosocial support in humanitarian emergencies. These are the recommendations issued by the Interagency Standing Committee (IASC, 2007) and other coordination groups responsible for setting and maintaining international standards for operations.

E. Cherepanov, *Humanitarian Competencies for Global Mental Health Professionals*, Contemporary Humanitarian Action and Emergency Management,
https://doi.org/10.1007/978-3-031-74268-2_6

Professional Codes of Ethics

Regardless of the role that GMH professionals play in humanitarian relief, the professional code of ethics primarily regulates everything they do in their professional capacity and must be a first consideration in any decision-making. Professional codes are binding and nonnegotiable for professionals. But are they sufficient?

The codes of ethics are often precedents-based, and they may not provide enough guidance to navigate the unique and unprecedented humanitarian situations. Then, the supplementary aspirational and operational guidance provides a broader frame of reference and points out the directionality of the complex decisions. More on ethics for GMH is in Chap. 10.

Humanitarian Principles

Humanitarian principles offer overarching aspirational guidance shared among all the actors of multidisciplinary humanitarian action. While the precise wording of the principles varies slightly across sectors, they are all built upon respect for human rights and strive for integrity, honesty, truth, and fairness to keep us true to the profession's ideals.

> *Aspirational values* are meant to ensure universal human rights in complex environments fraught with controversy and political battles. They designate the moral compass for such interventions.

To summarize, the role of humanitarian principles in GMH work is to:

- Provide aspirations and remind of humanistic ideals.
- Set the system of highest-level values to navigate conflicts of professional values.
- Establish a meta-level frame of reference shared across disciplines and sectors.
- Recognize practices that violate human rights.

Humanitarian principles reflect the core values of any helping profession. They communicate humanistic values that are at the basis of the most professional codes of ethics. However, as Hilhorst (2005) points out, they have limitations: they organize decision-making but do not ensure the results. It means that practitioners need additional guidance that is more practical and better translates into operations.

Humanitarian Principles and the Discussion

Let us examine the humanitarian principle many professionals accept without giving it much thought. The 1949 Geneva Conventions formulated four core principles of humanitarian law, reiterated by the International Federation of the Red Cross (IFRC, 1965). These principles aspire to make humanitarian aid impartial and based on need only, independent, and not prejudicial. Although the precise formulations of the principles may vary, they communicate a consistent message across disciplines and sectors. The formulations below come from the OCHA Humanitarian Principles (2011) and are followed by a discussion of challenges that emerge when using them as practical guidance.

Table 6.1 lists four core humanitarian principles, followed by a discussion about how these principles are used in practice.

Discussion of the Core Humanitarian Principles

1. Humanity
   The concept of humanity is a fundamental principle of humanitarianism that has priority over all other considerations. In humanitarian crises where the needs are massive, providers must make difficult decisions about whom to prioritize and who will be left behind. However, those who follow the letter of the principle of humanity over its spirit inevitably face moral dilemmas. In practice, choices about who to serve first are often influenced by external factors outside providers' control, such as the availability of human resources, donor expectations, institutional directives, and the political or security landscape.

Table 6.1 Humanitarian principles (OCHA Humanitarian Principles, 2011)

• *Humanity* Human suffering must be addressed whenever it is found. The purpose of humanitarian action is to protect life and health and ensure respect for all human beings.
Neutrality Humanitarian actors must not take sides in hostilities or engage in controversies of a political, racial, religious, or ideological nature.
Independence Humanitarian action must be autonomous from the political, economic, military, or other objectives that any actors may hold with regard to areas where humanitarian action is being implemented.
Impartiality Humanitarian action must be carried out on the basis of need alone, giving priority to the most urgent cases of distress and making no distinctions on the basis of nationality, race, gender, religious belief, class, or political opinions.

2. Neutrality
   The humanitarian principle of neutrality is probably the most ambiguous from a moral standpoint. It was formulated to assert the precedence of international humanitarian law during armed conflicts and support assisting everyone in need without taking sides. However, it has become a source of considerable debate because many have argued that the principle of neutrality contradicts the promotion for social or political change, as well as the advocacy of social justice.

   Destexhe (1996) asserted that maintaining neutrality in times of war is impossible, and Chomsky (1999) went on to state that neutrality in the face of murder is immoral.

   There are also proponents for neutrality in conflicts. The agencies and providers that uphold political neutrality often find it enables them to access and deliver aid to people in politically precarious situations. As a rule, both professional associations and humanitarian agencies can call for the cessation of violence while maintaining neutrality.

   (Key phrase)

   The neutrality principle requires that humanitarian agencies refrain from expressing solidarity with one side of a political conflict. However, they can make their opinions known by public and political advocacy for victims, bearing witness, and voicing their demands to stop the violence. Neutrality differentiates humanitarian entities from human rights organizations that openly take sides against human rights violators.

3. Impartiality
   Offering MH support to all parties involved in a conflict is consistent with humanistic values. Yet, during a conflict, such a position may undermine trust, create community resentment, complicate access to survivors, and increase risks to providers. Treating both presumed victims and perpetrators can put a moral burden on healthcare professionals and lead to burnout.
4. Independence
   The independence principle emphasizes that humanitarian agencies alone must decide who and when to help, independent of governments. In practice, however, such decisions are always a balancing act because the effectiveness of aid and the sustainability of recovery depends on fundings, available infrastructure and developing collaborations with local governments and public health establishments when possible. There may be political pressure on the agencies to increase their operations, and public opinion and moral judgment affect the public image.

Additional Principles: Humanitarian Accountability and Not Exploiting Beneficiaries

Humanitarian principles are a continual work in progress that responds to the positive and problematic experiences of the humanitarian community. In 1995, the list of principles expanded to add accountability, transparency, and not taking advantage of beneficiaries. Addressing the dynamics of power and control in MH fieldwork helps minimize the risks of purposely exploiting those we are trying to help.

Humanitarian accountability means that humanitarian actors must hold themselves accountable to both beneficiaries and those from whom we accept resources (IFRC/ICRC, 1994). The power differential between aid providers and aid recipients drives the imperative to use this power responsibly.

Humanitarian accountability implies that beneficiaries must be involved in the decision-making that is supposed to benefit them. Affected communities are the most qualified to assess the benefits of proposed solutions made on their behalf and should fully engaged as cocreators or "nothing about us without us."

In GMH work, accountability underscores the importance of professional competencies, commitment to humanitarian ideals, and the professional code of ethics. It signifies the dedication to the highest personal and professional integrity and responsibility for the intended and unintended consequences of helping interventions.

Accountability implies that the organization is accountable to beneficiaries, donors, and the staff. It accepts responsibility for their work and conduct and the proper use of resources (IASC, 2007). In the changed political and security situation, organizations must do everything they can to prevent the abandonment of local personnel and leaving them at greater risk due to their work.

In Afghanistan, after the Taliban took over, many NGOs we worked for left us without protection and at risk. The people we were trying to help were angry at us because no one asked them if they wanted or needed these services. We did not ask for it, nor did we want it. We had to do this work for money. And now we are in trouble ... (Cherepanov, "personal communication", September 15, 2021)

The last two principles, *Not to Engage in Sexual Exploitation* and *Not to Proselytize*, are not aspirational. They are imperative—and there are no circumstances where they can be waved or misunderstood. They prohibit humanitarian workers from taking advantage of the vulnerability of those affected by war, violence, or famine.

The principle *Not to Engage in Sexual Exploitation* proclaims that any sexual exploitation by aid workers is gross misconduct and will not be tolerated. Sexual exploitation and abuse are situations in which the aid workers misuse their position of power and the trust of those in need of aid and protection to obtain sexual relations or favors and benefits (UN, n.d.).

Humanitarian agencies have accepted responsibility for preventing the abuse of beneficiaries, and since then, multiple safeguards have been put in place and procedures instituted for filing confidential complaints.

In an emergency, survivors who lost everything become particularly vulnerable to exploitation (Wall, 2016). The "sex-for-aid" scandal broke out after Oxfam workers were accused of using aid to pay for sex while responding to the 2010 Haiti earthquake (Burke, 2021). Other alleged incidents of sexual exploitation by the UN and aid workers were reported in Liberia, Guinea, Sierra Leone, and the Democratic Republic of the Congo. (Thomson Reuters Foundation, n.d.; Mednick & Craze, 2022)

The fact that not all of these allegations could be later substantiated (Gillan & Moszynski, 2002) only emphasizes that humanitarians must not engage in unethical actions and must avoid any impressions of impropriety.

The massive fallout from the "sex-for-aid" scandal has compromised the agencies' reputations as well as trust in their humanitarian aid provision, affecting their ability to deliver humanitarian assistance.

The principle *Not to Proselytize* states that the provision of aid must not be used to further political or religious creeds.

Benefiting from people's vulnerabilities in any shape or form is not acceptable in a humanitarian context (Lynch & Schwarz, 2016). In the wake of a disaster, many regions are often inundated by faith-based charities and missions. Most of these honestly offer aid out of selfless and humanitarian intentions. Some, however, seize this opportunity to preach, proselytize, and convert. In a humanitarian context, such intent violates the humanitarian principle of not exploiting a desperate situation for selfish benefits.

Humanitarian Code of Conduct

Currently, much attention is given to the behavior of aid workers. Any misconduct attracts a lot of public attention and affects the whole sector. A tarnished image means increased risks for humanitarians and fewer donations for lifesaving aid.

The IFRC/ICRC Code of Conduct (1994) and the *Sphere Handbook* (Sphere, 2018, pp. 385–388) outline the minimum standards for humanitarian response and the ten code of conduct principles. These principles affirm the core humanitarian values in aid provision and emphasize personal and professional responsibility, integrity, and transparency (Table 6.2).

Table 6.2 Ten core principles of humanitarian conduct (The IFRC/ICRC Code of Conduct, 1994; The Sphere Association, 2018, pp. 385–388)

1.	The humanitarian imperative comes first.
2.	Aid is given regardless of the race, creed, or nationality of the recipients and without adverse distinction of any kind. Aid priorities are calculated on the basis of need alone.
3.	Aid will not be used to further a particular political or religious standpoint.
4.	We shall endeavor not to act as instruments of government foreign policy.
5.	We shall respect culture and customs.
6.	We shall attempt to build disaster response on local capacities.
7.	Ways shall be found to involve program beneficiaries in the management of relief aid.
8.	Relief aid must strive to reduce future vulnerabilities to disaster as well as meeting basic needs.
9.	We hold ourselves accountable to both those we seek to assist and those from whom we accept resources.
10.	In our information, publicity, and advertising activities, we shall recognize disaster victims as dignified human beings, not hopeless objects.

Operational Guidance: IASC Guidelines

> To paraphrase Candilis and Martinez (2006), where aspirational values honor ideals and moral presence, the operational guidelines acknowledge duty.

When designing and implementing interventions, operational guidance establishes strategic objectives and the means for intervention and ensures adherence to best practices, professional standards, and efficiency of interventions. The IASC Guidelines (IASC, 2007) lay out the operational framework for MH and Psychosocial Support in Emergency (MHPSS)

IASC Guidelines for MHPSS

In 2007, with input from UN agencies, NGOs, and universities, the Interagency Standing Committee (IASC) published comprehensive Mental Health and Psychosocial Support guidelines for emergency settings. The guidelines inform the planning, establishment, and coordination of responses to protect, support, and improve people's MH and psychosocial well-being. The guidelines offer strategic guidance on multisectoral responses and complementary interventions based on levels of needs, which is summarized in the IASC's famous Pyramid of Psychosocial Needs (IASC, 2007; García-Moreno & van Ommeren, 2012).

- Support should be multilayered, complementary, and targeted toward individuals and communities.

- The goals of interventions and the role of psychosocial providers are situation-specific.
- The nature of the emergency, level of need, and available resources determine the most appropriate intervention. The choice of interventions will be different whether they are conducted in a disaster, post-conflict setting, or in economically developed countries with sound healthcare systems.
- These interventions can include PFA, support groups, psychoeducation, linking survivors with other community services, integrated primary care, psychotherapy (such as expressive arts or trauma therapies), and, where indicated, psychotherapy or psychopharmacological treatment for those most seriously impaired.

The IASC has cautioned against using their guidelines "as a cookbook" (IASC, 2007, p. 9), emphasizing that they contain vital actions, but their practical implementation requires tailoring interventions to a context.

Operational Principles

The IASC Guidelines (pp. 9–13) offer six core principles of GMH MHPSS interventions: Human Rights and Equity, Participation, Do No Harm, Building on Available Resources and Capacities, Integrated Support Systems, and Multilayered Supports. The operational principles below are followed with a discussion about the challenges in their implementation.

1. Human rights and equity

   This principle echoes the humanitarian principles. Humanitarian organizations must promote equity and nondiscrimination, advocate for human rights, and offer protection for vulnerable individuals and groups.
2. Participation

   The principle promotes the survivors' active role in their psychological and social recovery. In humanitarian action, this principle means partnering with the affected communities that must become the cocreators of their recovery.
3. Do no harm

   The World Medical Association (WMA, 2015, p. 120) has defined this principle as "avoiding inflicting harm on patients and research subjects." This principle exists in most healthcare codes of ethics and is probably the most self-evident yet ambiguous (Sheather et al., 2016).

   In volatile and poorly predictable contexts, providers must resort to choosing the less harmful action but it may not be an easy choice.
4. Building on available resources and capacities

   This principle recognizes survivors' resilience and strength and cautions against fostering dependence.

   Assisting affected people to access internal and external resources aims at facilitating mutual support, independent problem-solving, and eventually becoming self-reliant in addressing their concerns.

5. Multilayered support

This principle emphasizes that the effectiveness of GMH work is associated with complementary and collaborative efforts. During emergencies, individuals are impacted in many ways that require different forms and levels of care. A multilayered and hierarchically organized system of complementary services must be tailored to the unique needs of diverse groups.

The IASC (2007, pp.12–13) introduced the Intervention Pyramid model to illustrate how multilayered support is used in an emergency response. A four-layer pyramid represents an MHPSS model, where levels of MH needs are paired with recommended levels of interventions. From the bottom up, these layers are basic psychosocial support, focused psychosocial support, psychological support, and specialized mental healthcare. The model is based on the idea that in emergencies, the majority of the population needs support that addresses basic needs. Only a few who are seriously affected require MH treatment in the moment (Picture 6.1).

6. Integrated support systems

Finally, this principle recommends that the activities and programming be as integrated as possible. Fragmented, uncoordinated standalone services undermine aid efficiency, resulting in the duplication of services and inefficient use of resources.

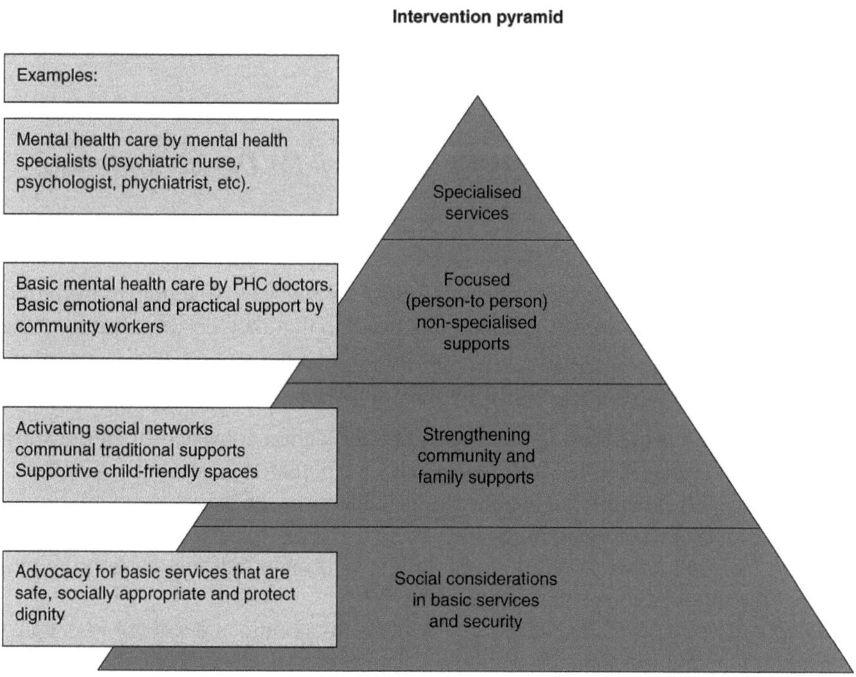

Picture 6.1 The IASC's Intervention Pyramid of MHPSS intervention (IASC, 2007, p.12–13)

What Will You Do? Suggested Protocols and Case Studies

The goal of the exercise is to provide an opportunity to practice incorporating humanitarian values and operational guidance for practical decision-making. The training protocols and scenarios are rooted in real-life examples drawn from the author's experience and peer conversations (Cherepanov, 2018).

The suggested protocols below include decision-guiding questions. They are followed by case scenarios that allow GMH providers to practice. These scenarios are strategically chosen to provide examples of common situations that GMH providers can encounter in their work and that require additional guidance. First, I focus on aspirational guidance and then discuss applying operational guidelines.

The Roadmap for Using Humanitarian Values

As previously demonstrated in this chapter, aspirations do not directly translate into operations, but rather set ideals and directionality. Because humanitarian values are a significant part of the professional identity and determine the profession's image, any interventions in humanitarian situation must not only be just, transparent, and fair but also appear as such to the stakeholders.

The proposed four-step roadmap can be instrumental to navigate programming decisions and to calibrate them to assure their contextuality and consistency with the spirit of humanitarianism.

Exercise 1: Using Aspirational Framework for Decision-Making

Instructions

Read the hypothetical case scenarios and follow the four-step roadmap to ask yourself the suggested questions to decide on actions so that they do not contradict the humanitarian principles. Justify how the proposed intervention is (in)consistent with humanitarian principles. Adjust the intervention if needed.

1. *Humanitarian principles.* Is the proposed intervention consistent with the spirit of humanitarian principles, and does it carry the potential for a conflict of values?
2. *Accountability.* Identify to whom the providers are primarily accountable. Is there a conflict of accountabilities?
3. *Safety or lesser harm.* Is safety at risk? What solution brings less harm: to implement the intervention or to decide against it?
4. *Justification and injustice reduction.* Are the interventions designed in a transparent, fair, and just manner, and do they appear as such? How can the intervention decision be justified for funders, stakeholders, and the community?

Walkthrough

Scenario: Art Therapy Program in a Refugee Camp

A provider has received a grant to set up an art therapy program for a group of children in a refugee camp. This intervention will definitely benefit children who are recovering from the trauma of the armed conflict. The program can accommodate 20 children. At the same time, many other children could benefit from this intervention. In addition, specialists brought snacks and colorful supplies that made participation in the group very attractive. Rumors swirl in the community that bribery is involved in selecting participants, and parents have started bringing food and valuables and asking to admit their children.

Discussion

1. *Humanitarian principles as aspiration.* Superficially, the suggested intervention appears to conflict with the "humanitarian imperative" because the target group is chosen based on targeted funding and resources, not on need alone. Although the providers may not have a full flexibility in designing the program, the criteria for selecting children must be clear, transparent, and objective and discussed with the community ahead of time, and the community must be informed of the process. Scores on a questionnaire, for example, can serve as an objective criterion.
2. *Accountability.* It appears that prioritizing accountability to donors has already produced negative psychological dynamics: The divided community has not been informed or consulted about the project and did not take part in designing it, nor was it consulted about prioritizing children in need.
3. *Safety or lesser harm.* A discussion with the community members about cost–benefits can help answer questions about what brings less harm—to provide an intervention that appears unjust or to decide against it. Yet, even if this limited intervention cannot help all the children, it will help some. However, the problematic project implementation may increase the risk to the participants and the providers.
4. *Justification and injustice reduction.* The criteria for selection of children must be justified. They must appear fair, just, and transparent to the community to avoid accusations of corruption and to reduce jealousy toward participating children. Community leaders should be involved in this communication. Providers can offer fun activities for the remaining community members and small gifts to children who are not selected to participate in the project.

Training Case Scenarios

Scenario 1. Advocacy vs No Harm

A GMH provider in a war-torn region hears accounts of torture and violence perpetrated by a government-sponsored militia group. They feel compelled to document these abuses and speak out against them to raise international awareness of the atrocities. However, survivors express fear that if their testimonies are brought to the attention of the government, they could face further persecution or retaliation. Moreover, there's a probability that the MH workers have their access to affected communities restricted or they themselves may be expelled from the country if they openly criticize the government or its allies.

Scenario 2. Potential for Exposure

A GMH provider works with rape survivors in a small town where incidents of sexual violence are often hushed up or dismissed. Seeing the recurring trauma experienced by survivors and the systemic barriers to justice, the therapist adopts a proactive approach. They want to organize support groups for survivors, providing them with a platform to share their experiences openly and develop strategies to challenge the culture of silence, impunity, and victim-blaming. Through empowerment workshops and community outreach programs, the therapist hopes to gather personal accounts, help survivors reclaim their agency, speak out against their assailants, and demand accountability from local authorities and institutions. Survivors express hesitation about participating in these programs.

Scenario 3. Disparities in Pay?

An international NGO has funded a GMH development project in a rural village. It employs local social workers who work alongside expat MH providers to implement various initiatives aimed at improving MH, healthcare, and education. However, it becomes evident that the local providers are being paid significantly less than their foreign counterparts for similar roles and responsibilities.

Recognizing the disparity in compensation, the community workers gather to discuss their concerns and collectively request equal pay for equal work. They highlight their dedication, expertise, risks they take, and contributions to the success of the projects, emphasizing that their lower salaries perpetuate economic inequality and undermine their sense of value and dignity.

Scenario 4. Sponsoring a Client

An MH counselor working in an underserved urban community where access to quality education is limited, develops a bond with a 14-year-old client, a girl named Maria who dreams of becoming a nurse, but cannot afford to attend high school due to financial hardships at home. Through their interactions, the provider becomes aware of the financial constraints preventing Maria from pursuing a high school education. Driven by a desire to support the teenager's academic aspirations and personal development, the MH worker decides to sponsor their education in high school. Maria is very happy and asks if the money will be given to her in cash.

Scenario 5. Romantic Relationship

A local aid worker shares their observation with the NGO administration that expat Alex, who is a GMH team member, is romantically involved and moved in with a local woman Rosa, who had never been an Alex' client. Rosa's family is unhappy about this relationship. Reportedly, Alex promised Rosa to take her to his home country and marry her there. Being concerned about the projected image of this relationship and the potential backlash from the community, the NGO leadership seeks guidance on how to approach such situation respectfully and responsibly.

Scenario 6. Sport Equipment

A village soccer team is preparing for a match against a neighboring community, which makes everybody excited. The upcoming game was not only a chance for the team to showcase their skills but also an opportunity for the community to come together and show their cohesion.

Seeing the enthusiasm surrounding the match, a health professional sees an opportunity to contribute positively to the community's morale. Wanting to foster community spirit, the provider decides to donate new equipment to the team. The hope is that this gesture will not only help the team prepare for the match but also promote mental well-being. The opposing team (which did not have such nice gears) questioned the sportsmanship in this gesture.

Scenario 7. Fundraising Photos

A journalist—specialist in fundraising—approaches an MH provider with a request to take photos of their clients who experience difficulties coping, emphasizing that these images would be instrumental in raising funds for the healthcare services for affected people. They argue that showcasing the raw realities of MH struggles can evoke empathy and encourage people to contribute to the cause.

Additional questions to ask:

What about taking photos of providers in the work environment?
What about MH providers taking selfies with the survivors?

Scenario 8. A Purchase

While passing by the stalls of the local street market, an MH provider notices a family selling their precious family jewelry for little money and ponders about making a purchase.

Choose one or more from the following options and justify the selection.

- Decide against purchase.
- Pay the asked price, which is much below the one they would have to pay for the same item in their homeland.
- Pays a fair price for the family, ensuring that the family receives adequate compensation for their possessions.
- Through dialogue, the provider learns about the family's challenges, including financial hardships. Recognizing the importance of preserving their cultural heritage and sentimental valuables, the provider connects the family with local support services and community resources that can offer ongoing assistance and empowerment.

Scenario 9. Payment for Access
In a small town where access to psychosocial and health services is limited, local administrations have implemented a system where they would allow the international medical NGO to operate within the community in exchange for "donations" to the administration representatives or militia. The GMH provider is concerned about transparency of the financial operations and the integrity of the project.

Additional question:

What if the government allows MH providers to access the survivors of sectarian violence only if they also treat the governmental armed forces?

Scenario 10. Financial Compensation
Community members ask to be financially compensated for participating in MH programs, research, or for attending the community health and psychoeducational event. In this scenario, a community leader also expresses an interest in being compensated for hosting a community educational event focused on destigmatizing MH issues.

Exercise 2: Operational Guidance

This exercise provides an opportunity to use operational guidance in designing ethical MH and psychosocial interventions. The vignettes describe practices that have the potential to become ethically problematic if not executed according to the guidelines.

"Affected areas" can be a disaster, armed conflict, or authoritarian state or any other humanitarian emergency that is more familiar or relevant to participants' experience. In practicing the scenarios, the reader can fill in the information about the nature of the crisis and the region where it occurs.

The objective is to alter interventions so that they are consistent with aspirational values, the code of conduct, and operational guidelines.

Instructions

Read the proposal for a mental health intervention. Answer the following questions and discuss the possible implications:

1. What is the intent or goal of the practice or intervention?
2. What may be the unintended consequences?
3. What can make these practices ethically problematic, and which guidelines do they challenge?
4. How can these practices or interventions be revised?

Walkthrough

An international NGO is interested in sponsoring a retreat for children to a safe region, away from the conflict zone and asked the GMH provider for suggestions.

Discussion

1. *Presumed goal.* This intervention aims to offer children a safe and therapeutic space to facilitate recovery.
2. *Unintended consequences.* The selection process can become contentious. The selected children may not be those who need it most: The local administration might object to the camp unless their children and relatives' children are part of the program. In addition, other children who are eligible may want to participate, but the program cannot accommodate them due to limited capacity. Another concern is that if the camp is located outside of the conflict zone, the children may have difficulties readjusting to their routine lives full of hardship after camp is over. In addition, there was one more possible issue that has emerged during the war in Ukraine: Some children evacuated to the safe zone had logistical difficulties reuniting with their parents who evacuated to the remote places (Cherepanov, "personal communication").
3. *Do no harm.* If poorly planned, this intervention could put participants and providers at risk because it can make them easy targets for the opposing force.
4. *Nothing about us without us.* Making the selection process more transparent helps reduce possible harm and negative dynamics by engaging the community in the decision process. Developing reentry and aftercare and alternative communication and reunification plans would allow this program to be successful, ethical, and beneficial for the involved children. Additionally, the selection of the participants must not only be transparent per se but also appear as such to the community.

Practice Scenarios

Use the protocol to discuss the following scenarios.

Case Study 1. Bringing Students to a Disaster Site
Professor Smith has designed an immersive learning experience for psychology students who are interested in GMH studies. With the recent international disaster, they see an opportunity for their students to not only learn about trauma psychology but also actively engage in helping those affected.

They arranged a field trip to the disaster area, ensuring safety measures are in place. Once there, the students work under supervision, applying their theoretical knowledge to real-life situations.

They engage with locals who have experienced trauma, offering support and counseling. Through this hands-on experience, the students not only gain a deeper understanding of the psychological impact of disasters but also develop practical skills in trauma counseling.

Case Study 2. Traveling Alone

Dr. Sarah, a seasoned MH professional specializing in trauma therapy, feels a strong call to action upon hearing about a recent natural disaster that has devastated a neighboring community. Witnessing the aftermath and recognizing the urgent need for psychological support, Dr. Sarah decides to take matters into their own hands.

Dr. Sarah devises a plan to travel alone to the affected area. Her goal is clear: to equip local mental health providers with the knowledge and skills necessary to implement exposure therapy techniques in their work with trauma survivors.

Before embarking on her journey, Dr. Sarah meticulously prepares a comprehensive training program tailored to the specific needs and resources of the local providers. Drawing on her expertise and the latest research in trauma psychology, she develops training materials, lesson plans, and interactive activities aimed at demystifying exposure therapy and guiding participants through its practical application.

Case Study 3. "A Beacon of Hope." Scaling up Services for Sexual Assault Survivors

Dr. Hernandez, a compassionate MH professional, has long been concerned about the lack of specialized support available for survivors of sexual assault in the rural community. Motivated by a desire to address this pressing need, and drawing on their extensive experience in trauma therapy and her background in evidence-based interventions, she embarks on a mission to create a standalone program, or as she calls it, a beacon of hope, specifically tailored to the unique needs of rape victims.

Case Study 4. "Holding them Accountable"

Mrs. Rodriguez, an MH provider specializing in trauma therapy, has been deeply moved by the stories of resilience and strength shared by survivors of gender-based violence in a small town where she lived as a child before moving to the United Staes. Recognizing the critical need for comprehensive support for survivors, Dr. Rodriguez explores innovative ways to address the issue beyond individual therapy sessions. She believes that holding perpetrators of gender-based violence accountable is essential for survivors' healing and for preventing future harm.

Motivated by this belief, Dr. Rodriguez initiates discussions with local law enforcement agencies to explore opportunities for collaboration. She recognizes that law enforcement plays a crucial role in responding to and preventing gender-based violence, and she sees potential in partnering with them to create a more coordinated and effective response.

Additional questions:

What if this activity involves the disclosure of the victim's identity?

What if the local authorities are known to have corroborated with traffickers and are siding with the perpetrators?

Case Study 5. Academic Research Conundrum

Dr. Johnson with his research team, comprised of graduate students and fellow academics, has long been interested in understanding the psychological impacts of natural disasters on affected communities. When the conflict breaks out, he recognizes the opportunity to contribute to their field of study. With extensive planning and a research protocol in hand, the team travels to the affected area to conduct a comprehensive assessment related to their research interests. They conduct surveys, interviews, and observations within the community to gather data on the prevalence of symptoms commonly associated with trauma, such as post-traumatic stress disorder (PTSD), anxiety, and depression.

The researchers believe that informed consent is necessary because signing it would have taken too much time. Also, confidentiality will be automatically ensured because participants will never read the paper they plan to publish.

With their findings in hand, Dr. Johnson and his team prepare a manuscript for submission to a scientific journal specializing in disaster MH.

The publication of their research not only advances Dr. Johnson's career and enhances the academic reputation of her institution but also contributes valuable knowledge to the broader scientific community.

The participants were never informed of the outcomes and findings.

Case Study 6. A T-Shirts Issue

An MH provider with a strong commitment to supporting marginalized populations and recognizing the unique challenges faced by LGBTQ individuals in times of crisis, organizes an initiative to distribute T-shirts with empowering messages to people belonging to the LGBTQ group.

As LGBTQ individuals come to receive support from MH providers, they are given a T-shirt with a message of empowerment that allows survivors to reclaim their dignity.

The provider was surprised to learn that most chose to decline this gift.

Takeaways

- GMH practice has several sources of guidance and regulations because it is both an MH and humanitarian discipline.
- The professional code of ethics is binding for healthcare professionals, but its guidance may not be sufficient in humanitarian situations.
- Humanitarian principles reflect the spirit of humanitarianism. They offer aspirations and directionality when navigating professional and moral dilemmas but have limited decision-making utility in operations.
- In the wake of "sex-for-aid" scandals, the Humanitarian Code of Conduct regulates the conduct of all humanitarians.
- The IASC's Mental Health and Psychosocial Support in Emergency (MHPSS) provides operational guidance for GMH professionals.

References

Burke, J. (2021, April 2). Oxfam to investigate misconduct claims against staff in DRC. *The Guardian*. https://www.theguardian.com/world/2021/apr/02/oxfam-to-investigate-misconduct-claims-against-staff-in-drc

Candilis, P. J., & Martinez, R. (2006). Commentary: The higher standards of aspirational ethics. *Journal of the American Academy of Psychiatry and the Law, 34*(2), 242–244.

Cherepanov, E. (2018). *Ethics for global mental health: From good intentions to humanitarian accountability*. Routledge. https://doi.org/10.4324/9781351175746

Chomsky, N. (1999). Stop U.S. intervention: Noam Chomsky, interviewed by Michael Lerner. Tikkun. Retrieved from https://chomsky.info/19990405/

Destexhe, A. (1996). Humanitarian neutrality: Myth or reality? in K. Cahill (Ed.), Preventive diplomacy. Basicbooks

García-Moreno, C., & van Ommeren, M. (2012). *Mental health and psychosocial support for conflict-related sexual violence: Principles and interventions*. World Health Organization. https://www.unicef.org/protection/files/Summary_EN_.pdf

Gillan, A., & Moszynski, P. (2002, February 28). Agencies hid scandal of aid workers who bought child sex with food. *The Guardian*. https://www.theguardian.com/world/2002/feb/28/immigration.uk

Hilhorst, D. (2005). Dead letter or living document? Ten years of the Code of Conduct for disaster relief. *Disasters, 29*(4), 351–369. https://doi.org/10.1111/j.0361-3666.2005.00297.x. PMID: 16277645.

IASC. (2007). *Guidelines on mental health and psychosocial support in emergency settings*. Interagency Standing Committee.

International Federation of Red Cross and Red Crescent Societies (IFRC and ICRC). (1994). *Code of conduct for the International Red Cross and Red Crescent Movement and NGOs in disaster relief*. https://www.ifrc.org/document/code-conduct-international-red-cross-and-red-crescent-movement-and-ngos-disaster-relief

International Red Cross and Red Crescent Movement (IFRC). (1965). *The fundamental principles of the International Red Cross and Red Crescent Movement*. www.ifrc.org/en/publications-and-reports

Lynch, C., & Schwarz, T. B. (2016). Humanitarianism's proselytism problem. *International Studies Quarterly, 60*(4), 636–646. https://doi.org/10.1093/isq/sqw024

Mednick, S., & Craze, J. (2022, September 22). Alleged sex abuse by aid workers unchecked for years in UN-run South Sudan camp. *New Humanitarian*. https://www.thenewhumanitarian.org/2022/09/22/exclusive-alleged-sex-abuse-aid-workers-unchecked-years-un-run-south-sudan-camp

OCHA. (2011). *OCHA on message: Humanitarian principles*. UN Office for the Coordination of Humanitarian Affairs (OCHA). https://reliefweb.int/report/world/ocha-message-humanitarian-principles-enar

Sheather, J., Jobanputra, K., Schopper, D., Pringle, J., Venis, S., Wong, S., & Vincent-Smith, R. (2016). A Médecins Sans Frontières ethics framework for humanitarian innovation. *PLoS Medicine, 13*(9), e1002111. https://doi.org/10.1371/journal.pmed.1002111

Sphere. (2018). *The Sphere handbook: Humanitarian charter and minimum standards in humanitarian response* (4th ed.). www.spherestandards.org/handbook

Thomson Reuters Foundation. (n.d.). *Sex abuse in the aid sector*. https://news.trust.org/packages/Sex-scandal-in-the-aid-sector/

UN. (n.d.). Preventing sexual exploitation and abuse. https://www.un.org/preventing-sexual-exploitation-and-abuse/content/agencies-funds-and-programmes

Wall, I. (2016, March 21). "We are demanding change": The Somali woman taking on international NGOs. *The Guardian*. https://www.theguardian.com/globaldevelopment-professionals-network/2016/mar/21/degan-ali-somali-woman-taking-onthe-humanitarian-system

World Medical Association (WMA). (2015). *Medical ethics manual* (3rd ed.). John R. Williams.

Chapter 7
Global Mental Health Interventions in Various Settings

Defining Humanitarian Crisis and Complex Emergency

Humanitarian crises pose an immediate and long-term threat to the population's lives, health, and security. They drastically alter people's lives, depriving them of basic needs such as water, food, shelter, and healthcare. Humanitarian emergencies can result in mass fatalities, injuries, displacements, and the destruction of property and infrastructure, affecting entire communities and potentially leading to social and economic collapse.

> *A humanitarian crisis or emergency* is an adverse situation where the impact of a disaster, an armed conflict, epidemic, or famine exceeds the ability of a country to cope with it, and external humanitarian aid is essential for survival. (Malteser International, 2024)

This chapter outlines the principles and assumptions of global mental health (GMH) interventions in different situations. It examines the MH impacts and interventions based on the nature of different humanitarian emergencies: disaster relief, assistance for survivors of gender-based violence, and refugees.

Chapter 8 discusses the GMH response to societal victimization caused by armed conflicts, genocide, political dysfunction, and complex political contexts (CPCs).

E. Cherepanov, *Humanitarian Competencies for Global Mental Health Professionals*, Contemporary Humanitarian Action and Emergency Management,
https://doi.org/10.1007/978-3-031-74268-2_7

Principles and Basic Assumptions of GMH Interventions

GMH interventions take place as a part of humanitarian relief and in response to humanitarian, health, and political crises. The interventions involve direct care, facilitating community support and recovery, supporting vulnerable groups (e.g., victims of gender-based violence and refugees), capacity-building, and designing trauma-informed healthcare and prevention systems of care.

Each kind of humanitarian emergency brings its own challenges and ethical dilemmas, which determine strategic priorities and the choice of the most appropriate interventions. The crisis nature of humanitarian situations, in many ways, defines core assumptions, basic principles, and intervention modalities across settings.

Basic Assumptions

GMH has emerged on the shoulders of its antecedents. Some of the GMH's basic assumptions are rooted in Disaster MH, secondary prevention, and crisis interventions modality (For reference, see Chap. 4) and are shared across different situations. Other assumptions are more specific to humanitarian settings in general. Here are these assumptions of GMH work.

- People are strong, healthy, competent, and adaptable. They are resilient and capable of change.
- Most individuals impacted by a crisis possess sufficient psychological resilience to recover adequately.
- Some individuals will require MH support, assistance, or treatment.
- MH interventions can prevent the development of more serious conditions and reduce self-destructive behaviors, substance misuse, violence, or suicide.
- The breadth and depth of the MH needs depend upon the severity of the incident and the extent of vulnerabilities. But most of all, the needs depend on the people's coping ability and the support they get.
- Most people respond to adversity, loss, and hardship with distress. Their response and presenting problems do not reflect an underlying mental disorder or illness but the need for assistance and support.
- Most trauma reactions are adaptive by nature. For example, hypervigilance can keep people aware of danger and, as a result, safer.
- In a crisis, MH providers facilitate and strengthen the individual's coping rather than working toward a permanent solution or cure.
- MH interventions can play an essential role in preventing future violence, including gender-based violence or escalation of retaliatory violence.

Principles of GMH Interventions in Humanitarian Emergencies

Any GMH interventions in a humanitarian emergency must be tailored to the crisis modality, culture, trauma history (i.e., trauma-informed care), and socioeconomic and political context of an emergency.

The crisis modality of humanitarian emergency primarily determines the goals of interventions that are to assist people in accessing external and internal resources and regaining functionality, strength, and self-efficacy. Most often, these interventions are not treatment.

Focusing on imminent and pressing needs in a crisis is more important than dwelling on the past or contemplating the distant future. The "one day at a time" formula is more conducive to an unpredictable humanitarian crisis than focusing on long-term goals.

Humanitarian emergencies affect not only individuals but the entire population and community. *Working with and through the affected community* is often the most effective way to support the individual's recovery.

During a crisis, there is *an emphasis on the quality of coping instead of attaching clinical diagnoses*. Needs assessments are done on a continual basis rather than with assumptions-based conclusions.

The volatility of humanitarian situations suggests that every professional encounter must be conducted as if it were the last one and that there be some kind of closure at the end of every session. It also means incorporating coping methods, self-help solutions for independent use, and directions for accessing support in the future.

In such situations, *preference is given to crisis or brief intervention over long-term treatment*. Intrusive trauma interventions such as trauma processing may leave a person feeling worse and more vulnerable if no support is readily available after the session.

Due to the systemic impact of humanitarian crises, *minimally invasive community-based interventions,* like empowering community leaders, can enable a large and sustainable impact (Cherepanov, 2016). In another example, changes in a community's attitude can reduce stigma and increase support for survivors.

Most MH support is provided in nonmedical, family, or community settings. Only a small percentage of the population will need targeted MH interventions in a treatment-specialized facility.

Community outreach needs to be a part of MH interventions because most who would benefit from clinical and/or preventative interventions do not self-refer.

GMH providers are *concerned with the safety of the people served* during and after the session, and provisions for their safety must be a routine part of treatment planning. For instance, relaxation techniques must be exercised with caution because they can decrease alertness and situational awareness which are important survival skills in a hostile environment.

Local providers, whenever possible, must lead the MH services with the support of GMH professionals. The national staff are expected to spearhead relief efforts due to their intrinsic familiarity with the prevailing situation and local culture. They are committed to the long-term well-being of their country and will remain present after external providers depart. International experts' involvement is best limited to educating, training, and supporting local mental health workers.

International organizations should step in to deliver MH treatment which is a higher level of care *only in critical situations when local resources are unavailabl*e. Compared to short-term crisis interventions, long-term individual treatment and psychotherapy necessitate prolonged engagement, proper terminations, follow-up, and aftercare support, which may not always be readily available in a crisis.

Disaster Mental Health (DMH)

GMH workers are often called to assist survivors in the aftermath of disasters.

Disasters cause significant disruptions in the community's functioning that exceed its capacity to cope using its resources. (See: https://www.ifrc.org/our-work/disasters-climate-and-crises/what-disaster, n.d.)

Based on their origins, disasters are roughly divided into natural and man-made.

Natural disasters result from natural causes and are considered the unpredictable "acts of God" (Ursano & Norwood, 2003). These include earthquakes, flooding, tsunamis, famines, and epidemics. With climate change, natural disasters are expected to become more frequent. Disasters often have a sudden onset, although famines and other ecological disasters may develop slowly over time while people try to adjust, sometimes losing valuable time to drastic survival efforts or inevitable relocation.

Man-made disasters are typically caused by technological accidents and human errors or malice and include acts of terrorism. People tend to react differently to man-made disasters than they do to natural disasters. The man-made and terrorist incidents make people feel targeted and are associated with a greater deal of anger (Kar, 2010). However, this distinction is not always so clear: even natural disasters or epidemics are often blamed on enemy forces.

After the earthquake in Spitak in Armenia on December 6, 1988, that measured 7.0 on the Richter scale and resulted in multiple casualties, there were multiple reports about the victims believing that Turkey deliberately caused the earthquake to continue the 1915 Armenian genocide. (Personal communication, 1989)

During the COVID-19 pandemic, conspiracy theories suggesting the sinister origins of SARS were rampant and became a significant barrier to containing the disease. Some suggested it was created as a bioweapon (Imhoff & Lamberty, 2020). Similar disinformation was earlier documented with the AIDS (Geissler & Sprinkle, 2013), Ebola (Feuer, 2014), and Zika viruses (Klofstad et al., 2019) and other epidemics of infectious diseases.

In addition to lost lives and destroyed homes, property, and livelihoods, disasters have wide-ranging economic and social impacts. They can sever family and community ties, disrupt life's social routine and fabric, and cause mass migration.

Mental Health Impact

The MH impact of disasters and wars is comparatively well studied, and disaster preparedness and recovery management have exponentially advanced in many high-resource countries. However, poverty, lack of resources, and the political context add complexity to the disaster MH response.

People react to disasters in various ways, but many reports have an initial transient state of shock, emotional numbness or over-activity, severe stress, anxiety, depression, despair, and hopelessness, along with worries about the future (Hackbarth et al., 2012). The individual reaction depends on the severity of the direct impact and predisposing factors (age, cognitive and physical abilities, and quality of support). Having access to support systems and recovery resources can exponentially increase resilience.

It was previously suggested that the community's reaction to a disaster changes with time and fits into predictable and consecutive phases. According to this model, the post-disaster recovery typically has four distinct phases: the heroic, honeymoon, and disillusionment phases, followed by restoration (Math et al., 2015). Each phase creates prioritized needs that determine strategic priorities in interventions and the corresponding role of MH providers.

For example, during *heroic* and *honeymoon phases*, when survivors participate in the relief efforts, there are high hopes that everything will get back to normal. In this phase, MH providers can join multidisciplinary relief and recovery teams to support first responders and volunteers. Other activities include evaluating the MH impact, available resources, and cultural specifics. GMH responders provide disaster MH support, promote resilience and mutual support, initiate collaborations with local organizations, and support public and community leaders in charge of the recovery.

In the *disillusionment phase*, when community's morale diminishes and the reality sets in, MH providers can attend to those with chronic or preexisting MH conditions and those severely impacted. They can support medical and social service providers and community workers, assist with building a referral system, and work with the community to develop a positive future vision. Eventually, the disillusionment phase turns into the *recovery phase*, signifying gradual improvement.

Although popular in disaster management, this four-phase model has been extensively criticized for its oversimplification (Neal, 1997). Questions revolve around the lack of conceptual clarity of the phases, their claimed linearity, and the need for more proof of the scientific and practical benefits of such periodization. The arbitrary duration of phases and attached fixed timing and meaning underappreciates the variability of people's reactions to different circumstances and that survivors can assume an active role and take responsibility in their and community's recovery. For example, when a disaster or terrorist attack strikes a disadvantaged and previously victimized community, survivors may not have any illusions and high expectations phases at all and go straight back to rebuilding their lives. Despite skepticism, this model continues to be considered in post-disaster recovery planning, and it prepares people for the long road to recovery before life gets back to normal. It also helps with the realization that media attention, public enthusiasm, and crowdfunding are more likely during the heroic phase but will probably be short-lived.

Strength and Resilience

Disasters often allow a community to recognize its strength and the value of caring, compassion and mutual support. The collective memory of survivorship and overcoming can become a source of future resilience.

During a disaster, the primary source of resilience often comes from personal, family, and communal sources of strength. They can be past experiences of endurance and overcoming, devotion to the well-being of the family, resourcefulness, and family and community support. It has long been noted that in a disaster, children sometimes demonstrate significant resilience if they have good support (Masten, 2020). However, during disasters, many children and teenagers become separated from their parents or caregivers and are at higher risk for physical or sexual exploitation.

Trauma aggregation is a phenomenon that emerges in the wake of some collective traumas. There, collective experience of survival tends to synergize and create a shared mental space where people can relate and support each other because they share similar experiences (Cherepanov, 2020). Aggregation adds to resilience.

The collective memory of surviving a disaster in the past helps people to prepare for and survive disasters in the future; these memories can pass down through the

generations and become a cultural heritage. In this way, survival tools, and hopes for the future can come from the memories of the past survivorship.
The vast difference in the death toll between two tsunamis (90% of the population in the 2004 Indian Ocean tsunami and less than 1% of the population in Papua New Guinea) made researchers seek answers. It was suggested that the oral traditions that preserved the memories from 1930 surviving tsunami transmitted this memory through generations which contributed to this difference: In Papua New Guinean culture, people were explicitly guided to seek higher ground promptly when the sea receded (Mercer et al., 2012). Or, in a more recent instance, the Chernobyl disaster survivors explained their resilience by survival skills they had accumulated during the World War II: "We survived the war, we can do it now!" (Pearson & Cherepanov, 2012)

Interventions

The MH response to a disaster concentrates on five areas:

1. Services for those most severely impacted and training outreach workers to identify those with MH special needs.
2. Supporting and protecting children and other vulnerable persons who cannot access resources in the community or who are at high risk of exploitation.
3. Targeted interventions for those with serious or chronic medical and MH conditions who have had their usual service delivery disrupted and/or may be experiencing worsened symptoms.
4. Facilitating mutual and community support.
5. Services for first responders and aid workers aimed at trauma support and burnout prevention.

The sheer volume of people affected by a disaster can be overwhelming. This calls for systems-based approaches like community-level interventions. As time goes by, there is even more need for a community's self-reliance, assuming responsibility for its members and leading recovery efforts because international involvement in disaster relief is time-limited.

The interventions that best fit this agenda are psychoeducation, Psychological First Aid (PFA), and training paraprofessionals in disaster MH. The services for aid and relief workers focus on psychological support and burnout management which is further discussed in Chap. 13.

Psychoeducation allows reaching out to more people throughout the community. Such an approach can be a preventative measure. It teaches about expected trauma reactions, coping, sources of strength, and when to seek further assistance. It normalizes reactions, reduces stigma, and emphasizes the importance of mutual support. In Ukraine, psychoeducation before the Russia–Ukraine war has proven to be a crucial factor for enabling people to reach out for help (Cherepanov, 2022).

PFA is the initial intervention of choice when responding to a disaster. It is used as a standalone intervention and as part of MHPSS or integrated primary care modules. PFA helps with normalizing stress reduction, assessing, transforming, and modifying maladaptive behaviors, linking to resources, and informing people on how to cope with a stressful or traumatic situation (Makwana, 2019; Wachinger et al., 2013).

Training paraprofessionals in core competencies of disaster MH response can include the locally adapted components of PFA (World Health Organization, War Trauma Foundation, & World Vision International, 2011) and the Tools for Psychological Recovery (Berkowitz et al., 2010). These modules offer practical and portable recommendations for managing trauma symptoms, depression, anxiety, problematic sleep, and self-care. Such interactive training can be provided to community members or leaders and champions involved in supporting other community members in various capacities or those interested in helping others. It can also facilitate the sharing of the acquired knowledge further within the community, for example, by community and faith leaders, healthcare workers, outreach community workers, educators, and other health and human service providers who routinely interact with traumatized populations.

Disaster response and MH practice in humanitarian settings have demonstrated the clear advantages of integrated, multidisciplinary, and collaborative practices over a single-service intervention module.

Special Considerations

The true impact of a disaster often extends far beyond the event itself: The disaster zone is often beset by increased poverty and lack of healthcare resources. Politicians may use looting and increased violence as bargaining chips, as happened after the earthquake in Turkey (Genc, 2023).

GMH work in a disaster requires the providers to be "systems savvy," which refers to the ability to quickly familiarize themselves with the situation on the ground—relief agencies and disaster resources that are already in place—and find a professional niche within those systems (Young et al., 1998). Finding consensus and coordinating priorities and resources between agencies and organizations can be a difficult but necessary task in a seemingly chaotic environment.

Sometimes, disaster relief becomes overwhelmed by unorganized help. Even without this effect, called convergence, disaster sites can appear chaotic, making it much more important to respond as part of the concerted efforts in order to avoid activities that increase disorganization and chaos.

Establishing professional connections on the ground is the most effective way to engage with local MH providers. This step is crucial for fostering collaboration and communication and developing peer support.

Sometimes, community members benefit from the simple encouragement to show compassion and empathy. In some cultures, offering emotional support is considered an intrusion into personal space, and ignoring emotional expression may be done out of respect.

From the beginning, BH providers need to incorporate provisions for sustainability and what will happen to the people served after the project runs its course. In case of a disaster, this can mean allocating donations to train local providers and community workers or investing in long-term community-based projects.

Disasters can become political events, and disaster relief organizations often face political pressure where politicians try to dictate who and how to help, which can interfere with the aid delivery and disaster response (Young et al., 1998).

GMH professionals must be aware that local MH providers have been exposed to the same crisis as the people they serve and often have been traumatized themselves. In this case, skills for self-care and burnout management must be a routine part of PFA training.

Due to public attention, relationships with media can become contentious, and every word carries great significance. The role of MH providers in communication with media involves advocacy but also protecting the identities and dignity of survivors from intrusive media by explaining to survivors their rights to consent or deny consent to be photographed or give interviews.

Disaster survivors often encounter stigmatization and discrimination even following their relocation. The survival experience brings victims together but also complicates the post-disaster recovery and reintegration. It underscores the importance of advocacy and ongoing support long after the disaster.

The survivors of the atomic bombing of Hiroshima and Nagasaki were labeled *hibakusha* (Simons, 1984). Similarly, the survivors of the explosion in Chernobyl were labeled "fireflies" (supposedly, due to glowing in the dark) (Pearson & Cherepanov, 2012), and the survivors of the earthquake in Armenia and Turkey were accused of "playing victims" to receive more benefits. (Cherepanov, personal communication)

GMH specialists are sometimes the first to become aware of rumors and conspiracy theories. While mythology is a way of making sense of an event, rumors and conspiracy theories are a form of informal communication. Without trustful information sources, they can have toxic and harmful impacts. For example, misinformation has been preventing people from getting vaccinated in case of polio or covid virus. MH providers can play a role in curbing the negative effects of rumors and providing accurate information.

One example of mythology is the pervasive idea emerging after the Chernobyl nuclear disaster in 1986 that the explosion allegedly had been predicted in the Book of Revelation (8:10–11) as a sign of the apocalypse: "After the third angel sounded, the star Wormwood fell from heaven and poisoned the water, and many men died." "Wormwood" translates as "Chernobyl" in the Ukrainian/Belarusian language (Pearson & Cherepanov, 2012). This mythology has provided survivors with a sense of centrality and significance to their experience.

In epidemics, conspiracy theories and rumors can undermine public health efforts to contain infectious diseases.

During the 2022–2023 Ebola epidemic in Uganda, common rumors claimed that Ebola was a result of powerful witchcraft, that Westerners were injecting the Ebola virus into Ugandan people because they wanted their resources, and that the government was earning money from Western people by exaggerating Ebola cases. These conspiracy theories led to a faster spread of infection and more deaths. (Cherepanov, personal communication)

Refugees and Internally Displaced People (IDPs)

At present, the world faces a global refugee crisis. As of June 2023, over 110 million people had been forcibly displaced. This is more than 1 in every 73 people on Earth. Almost 9 in 10 lived in low- and middle-income countries (UNHCR, 2023).

The 1951 Refugee Convention defined *a refugee* as "someone unable or unwilling to return to their country of origin owing to a well-founded fear of being persecuted based on race, religion, nationality, membership of a particular social group, or political opinion" (UN, 1954). Internally displaced people (IDPs) are people who were forced to relocate to a different region within the same country.

This convention and the 1967 protocol became the basis for forming the UN High Commission for Refugees (UNHCR).

This book uses the term "refugee" in a broader sense to designate a wide range of forcibly (externally or internally) displaced people and migrants, not only those who have obtained legal status.

The politics of migration have become contentious issues that impact the provision of humanitarian aid. In the meantime, studies have demonstrated that refugees enrich the social, cultural, and economic life of their host communities (Taylor et al., 2016). In the process of adjustment and integration, refugees must overcome many cultural and language barriers as well as trauma and depression while coping with multiple losses (Bunn et al., 2023).

GMH providers support refugees who have resettled in safer host countries as well as those who reside in refugee camps. They also reach out to refugees in transition or meet them at the borders and in deportation jails.

MH Impact of Refugee Experience

The severity of refugee trauma, barriers to accessing resources, and sensitive social and political realities of current migration trends make MH workers encounter issues that are unusual in routine clinical practice.

The refugee experience often involves severe trauma, exposure to violence in the country of origin or during fleeing, and stresses related to displacement and resettlement. Systematic reviews of refugee adults and children have consistently demonstrated high rates of depression, anxiety, PTSD, and sleep problems (Frounfelker et al., 2020; Kessler, 2022; Nesterko et al., 2020; Özdemir, 2020). Worries about the future, uncertainty, and unpredictability in refugees' lives add to the chronic stresses.

Losing loved ones, separating from family, and losing home are significant parts of any refugee experience (Kokou-Kpolou et al., 2020). Forced migration is also associated with loss of social status, loss of role, identity, and social networks, and broken community ties (Bunn et al., 2023; Wachter & Gulbas, 2018). Such experiences increase social isolation and worsen MH in adults and youth (Júnior et al., 2020).

Resettled refugees often deal with anti-immigrant sentiments and discrimination, language and cultural barriers, food, housing, financial insecurity, un- or underemployment, and social isolation, which lead to increased adjustment stresses and high rates of domestic violence (Butler & Sheriff, 2021; Weine, 2011).

Interventions

Refugee mental health (RMH) services aim at improving refugees'physical and psychological well-being and supporting their adjustment and integration. Today's RMH focuses on developing evidence-based and culturally informed practices, incorporating integrated paradigms of trauma-informed care, psychosocial support, and psychological recovery.

Refugees face numerous barriers to accessing health and MH services: they may lack health insurance, have difficulties navigating healthcare systems, be unable to communicate in local languages, and often lack transportation (Derr, 2016). Specialized MH care often remains out of reach (Schlechter et al., 2023).

There have been increased efforts to screen newly arriving refugees for MH conditions consistently. One such tool is the RHS-15 (Refugee Health Screening-15), a standardized refugee health screening administered in the United States as part of the immigration process (Hollifield et al., 2013; Magwood et al., 2022). Meaningful referrals, however, remain a problem due to limited cultural understanding of MH needs and symptoms in refugees and stigmatized perception of MH services (Backe et al., 2021). In addition, refugees may avoid requesting treatment because they seek relief in the traditional healing or religious practices of their homeland. This is why family focused and school-based MH programs have been shown to be more accessible and more effective in engaging refugees in MH services. Concurrently, building healthcare- and community service providers' cultural and trauma competencies and educating the host communities (e.g., creating neighborhoods) enhances refugees'adaptation and integration (Bunn et al., 2023).

Suggested treatment modalities in refugee MH include cognitive behavioral therapy for the treatment of PTSD, anxiety, and depression (Hinton et al., 2012), and narrative and exposure therapy to reduce the symptoms of trauma (Wright et al., 2020). There are also interesting emerging models. One of them proposes approaching the refugee experience of losing their home and community as an ambiguous loss and treating it accordingly (Bunn et al., 2023).

Boss (2006, p. 105, 2017) described ambiguous loss as "there, but not there."

I saw the burned Mariupol only in photographs, and in my dreams, I still go to places that no longer exist. I continue to live in the old reality. I cannot accept that there are no houses where my friends live. And there are no more friends. (Dmitry's recollections, in Ryzhova, 2023)

Bunn et al. (2023) argued that losing a home or homeland alters identity and social connections. A proposed intervention called "Remaking Home" envisions a process by which refugees reconcile with losses by preserving their memories and building new meanings and traditions to remake a sense of home.

Special Considerations

Undocumented refugees can be highly vulnerable socially and can be easily exploited, like not being paid for their work or subjected to sexual degradation.

Generalized distrust remains the most significant barrier for refugees, deterring them from seeking help and accessing health and MH services. It can present. Distrust to officials not only increases the risk of victimization for refugees but also can present a significant public health and humanitarian issue in the host community.

Fear of how the disclosed information will be used can prevent refugees from reporting a crime such as domestic violence to law enforcement, or substance misuse and communicable diseases to health authorities. Fear of exposure and subsequent deportation often deters refugees from seeking medical attention for urgent medical and MH conditions.

During the SARS pandemic, undocumented refugees were often reluctant to seek medical attention because it could attract the unwanted attention of public health authorities, resulting in deportation. (Cherepanov, Personal communication)

The refugees may also have concerns associated with the possible impact of disclosed health and MH issues on the immigration process. These partially substantiated fears are that this information will be used against them to deny residency (e.g., "public charge" provision), thus adding a layer of complexity to seeking health and MH help.

In the US, a "public charge" provision applies to refugees and immigrants primarily dependent on the US government for assistance who may become a "burden" to the country (See https://www.federalregister.gov/documents/1999/05/26/99-13202/field-guidance-on-deportability-and-inadmissibility-on-public-charge-grounds). The Public Charge provision has undergone several revisions, but the memory of it is still present in the minds of refugees.

The challenges of resettlement can intensify the internal dynamics in the family and within a community, increasing the potential for domestic violence and further marginalizing already vulnerable groups.

Many refugees are aware of the potential presence of former perpetrators (e.g., gang members or political rivals) or their friends in the community who may go to great lengths to hide their identities. This also makes them less inclined to seek services because a disclosure or public statement could put the refugees'families at risk in their homeland.

Health, MH, and psychosocial providers must be aware that refugee communities formed in places of resettlement or in the camps may reproduce the prejudices, stigmas, discrimination, and political divisiveness that existed in their homeland. This means that some marginalized people such as victims of domestic violence or LGBTQ persons, cannot count on community support. MH providers can assist by connecting them with specialized support groups and facilitating social connection and support outside of the community.

Refugee work experience reminds GMH professionals to stand by the most vulnerable people in the community, regardless of the political context or whether they are undocumented migrants or refugees.

Refugee Camps and Other Places of Compact Resettlement

GMH professionals sometimes work in camps or other areas of compact resettlement of the refugees.

Refugee camps are temporary facilities built to provide immediate protection and assistance to people who have been forced to flee their homes due to war, persecution, or violence. (https://www.unrefugees.org/refugee-facts/camps/?utm_medium=website_source=archdaily.com)

Mental Health Impact

Although living in a refugee camp provides basic protection and is considered a safer alternative to their homeland, life there can be very difficult. Refugee camps are often located in areas where the refugees'presence is tolerated but not necessarily welcomed. Due to security situation, residents are often unable to leave freely at their discretion due to high risks, which can be difficult psychologically and economically. In many instances, the residents have to rely on external aid for basic needs like food and shelter. Still, they cannot provide for themselves due to the scarcity of jobs, which can be a disempowering experience.

Lack of daily structure, powerlessness to change anything, lack of privacy, and the loss of hope for the future can be detrimental for refugee MH, and the impact is recognized in high rates of depression, substance use, and suicides (Araujo et al., 2019; Horyniak et al., 2016; Kane et al., 2014; Scharpf et al., 2023).

> Most of the research was conducted among refugees, internally displaced people (IDPs), and asylum seekers (n = 55, 87%), predominantly in high-income settings. The highest-quality prevalence estimates of hazardous/harmful alcohol use ranged from 17%–36% in camp settings and 4%–7% in community settings. (Horyniak et al., 2016)
> Among refugees living in camps, the prevalence of suicidal ideation and suicide attempts ranged from 1.2% to 32.3% and from 0.18% to 7.3%, respectively. (Cogo et al., 2022)

Interventions

When working in a refugee camp, GMH specialists identify, support, and treat people with depression, anxiety, trauma, and anyone else having a hard time coping with the demands of a difficult life situation. When life routine and community ties are broken, maintaining, preserving, and reintroducing a sense of communal identity and restoring rituals, routine, and daily structure gain great importance.

MH providers can assist refugees with normalizing feelings, stabilizing moods, and skills for self-regulation of emotions. Facilitating mutual support helps to restore social support and rebuild a sense of being in control of their life. An increase in the sense of self-efficacy can be achieved by helping to identify the small things they have control over, even if those are just daily life routines.

GMH providers can contribute by training and providing supervision for community champions to recognize those in distress or at behavioral health risk and refer them to the appropriate help, engaging spiritual and community leaders, and counteracting toxic rumors. Other nonspecialized interventions can include strengthening the family, making cultural and religious connections, providing information, and educating parents and teachers about stress management and crisis coping.

Support groups can facilitate the sharing of information about practical skills and resources. They provide the opportunity to receive community support and contribute to countering stigmatization. They can be psychoeducational groups that discuss coping with stress and can have elements engaging in shared activities such as cooking classes, yoga, expressive arts, theatre, or meditation. It is always better when these groups are co-facilitated by community members who eventually take over and become the group leaders. MH professionals can continue supporting them by providing supervision, at least initially.

According to disaster managers, other nonspecialized camp activities can be at least as effective as MH interventions. They include involving refugees in volunteer or camp maintenance activities like keeping a clean space. Engaging children, youth, and adults in regular educational activities, sports, arts and crafts, or culturally appropriate dancing and singing in the refugee camps brings daily structure and instills a sense of purpose in their everyday lives (Math et al., 2015).

Sporting team activities, football matches, and cheering for their teams are probably one the most powerful coping actions that unite the community and can significantly reduce the need for additional psychological support.

Special Considerations

Sometimes, refugees and migrants at their places of resettlement reproduce conflicts coming from their places of origin, which complicates and slows the recovery and community integration. At the same time, reconciliation within these communities can become a model for reconciliation processes in their homelands.

Refugee camps can become an enclave for many traumatized, scared, and sometimes angry people who have lost everything and have no other choice but to live together in a situation of total uncertainty and isolation. Understandably, such a situation can exacerbate group tensions and trigger violence and vigilantism. Spontaneously emerging self-defense structures in camps can improve the sense of safety, but creating parallel legal systems and vigilantism can turn problematic.

Despite presumed safety, some vulnerable people in refugee camps need additional protection and support. The high incident rates of sexual violence and exploitation have been well documented (Brito, 2020). Vulnerable people may voluntarily engage in sex work because it may be the only way to make money. High rates of sexual violence and exploitation highlight the vital importance of having available MH and medical services, as well as birth control options.

In refugee camps, people can stay for a short time or remain for a long time, sometimes for decades. Refugees who stay in camps for too long, sometimes for generations, may end up having limited vocational skills and encounter more challenges readjusting to the "free" life where they must advocate for themselves, provide for their families, and pursue employment opportunities. In such instances, they will benefit from support and life skills education.

Sexual and Gender-Based Violence (SGBV) in Refugees' Experience

Despite all efforts of the international community, sexual and gender-based violence (SGBC) remains a prevalent and underreported concern in humanitarian emergencies and among refugees (Araujo et al., 2019; Refugee Council, 2009; Freedman et al., 2022).

In 2015, the IASC issued the Guidelines for Integrating Gender-Based Violence Interventions in Humanitarian Action, which offer comprehensive guidance on reducing risk, promoting resilience, and aiding recovery. Acknowledging that stresses related to humanitarian situations disproportionally affect women and girls who have fewer resources and support for recovery, the Guidelines focus on intimate partner violence and other forms of domestic violence, forced and/or coerced prostitution, child and/or forced marriage, female genital mutilation/cutting, female infanticide, and trafficking for sexual exploitation and/or forced/domestic labor. Guidelines examine the detrimental impact of GBV on individuals and communities and contributing factors and draw attention to the responsibility of humanitarian actors to address GBV in their work. The resource recommends actions across thirteen domains on preventing and addressing GBV on the society, community, and individual levels. It introduces specific guidance for the implementation of GBV-related programming in the 1. Camp Coordination and Camp Management; 2. Child Protection; 3. Education; 4. Food Security and Agriculture; 5. Health; 6. Housing, Land and Property; 7. Humanitarian Mine Action; 8. Livelihoods; 9. Nutrition; 10. Protection; 11. Shelter, Settlement and Recovery; 12. Water, Sanitation and Hygiene; and 13. Humanitarian Operations Support Sectors.

Although GMH providers are not part of all the thematic areas, it is important for them to be aware of the prevailing issues to define their role in relation to the systems of strategic priorities.

Victims of rape face serious MH, health and social consequences. Child molestation is considered an Adverse Childhood Event that carries a heavy long-term impact on the health, MH, and the child's wellbeing.

The MH impact is associated with symptoms of PTSD, anxiety, depression, problems with sleep, and behavioral health problems such as difficulties forming relationships, eating disorders, substance abuse, and other self-destructive behavior. Child and adult victims of rape are more likely to attempt or commit suicide (van Egmond et al., 1993).

Rape carries a significant stigma, and victims (particularly those who were previously virgins) may be perceived by society as "damaged." They may face social isolation, be abandoned by friends and family, deemed not fit for marriage, get divorced if already married, or even be at risk of being killed by their partners. This type of additional suffering is known as secondary victimization (Jiloha, 2013). Jiloha goes on to outline multiple legal barriers the rape victims encounter seeking justice. The culture of impunity and the gender cultural stereotypes are blamed for the perpetuation of rape.

Rape, sexual assault and other forms of GBV are routine part of refugees' experience (Ward & Vann, 2002). During their journey, refugees—especially females and minors, but also men—encounter the risk of assaults and rape or being trafficked by bandits, "coyotes" (the smugglers of illegal immigrants), border guards, and pirates.

Refugees who are desperate and trying to survive can be coerced to engage in sex work or forced prostitution. They may experience intimate partner violence, exploitation, and sexual slavery (Marsh et al., 2006; Sheehy, 2016). By the time refugees arrive at their destination, there is a strong likelihood that they will have already experienced instances of sexual or other forms of gender-based violence.

After reaching their destination, physically or sexually assaulted refugee women and men may still face stigmatization, shame, and social isolation, being rejected by their own families and the community (Hagen & Yohani, 2010). This is why many refugees are reluctant to disclose this experience of victimization. To adequately meet refugees' needs, providers must recognize the direct and indirect indicators of sexual abuse, participate in educating the community, and build support systems around them.

Below is a list of indicators suggesting a history of intimate partner violence or SGBV victimization. The indicators reflect the author's empirical observations based on the extensive RMH work experience. Beside indicators, there are corresponding symptoms or personal statements that alert clinicians to a need to further explore the issue to ensure the safety of a client. Each of the indicators may have a benign explanation, but all together, they signal a higher probability of the experience of gender-based victimization.

Awareness of the history of sexual victimization and gender-based violence helps health and MH professionals to understand the complex needs of refugees and migrants and to tailor interventions accordingly. For medical providers serving refugees, it is important to conduct medical procedures in trauma-informed way. Recognizing the sexual and GBV indicators means that these refugees may not have a place of safety and are not able to access family and community support (Table 7.1).

In providing interventions with survivors of SGBV, MH providers choose integrated and psychosocial models because survivors often have concurrent MH, medical, and social needs. The strength-based approaches center around safety planning, empowering the individual, and validating that the experience was not their fault. Community-focused interventions and advocacy are also implemented to fight

Table 7.1 Indirect indicators of sexual gender-based victimization

Indicators	Symptoms and statements from the survivors
Coming from a particular conflict region with high prevalence of SGBV	Belonging to a particular group or tribe that is known to be subjected to war rape, or just being a refugee
Symptoms of PTSD and reluctance to disclose the nature of trauma	Avoidance Dissociation Flashbacks Nightmares Hypervigilance Isolates when in distress
Psychosomatic symptoms	Dizzy spells Pain (stomach, joints, headaches) Headaches
Intolerance of physical contact	Have a hard time and display extreme nervousness during medical exam
Self-neglect	(Despite availability of means) Poor self-care Disheveled Dirty clothes Poor hygiene
Social isolation	No friends they can talk to when in distress. No desire to socialize or to make new friends
Problematic family relationships	Being physically or emotionally abused or "put down" often
Reluctant to attend community religious services or no longer is a believer	"I pray at home alone"
Chronic depression, persistent suicidal ideations	"I feel that my life is not worth living." "Sometimes I want to fall asleep and never wake up"

stigma and mobilize family and community support systems for individuals experiencing social isolation (Cherepanov, 2016).

In designing interventions, providers must be aware that communities may not be supportive of victims of domestic and sexual violence. Victims' advocacy or organizing support groups can be misperceived or disapproved by the family or community and, subsequently, can increase the victims' risks. Developing measures for securing the confidentiality and safety of participants must be a part of programming.

Takeaways

- Many assumptions and principles of GMH interventions stem from the crisis nature of a humanitarian setting, which calls for time-limited interventions that assist people in reducing suffering and regaining their functioning and capacity for self-determination.
- Most people affected by humanitarian emergencies will be able to recover, but some need additional MH support.
- The impact of natural and man-made disasters often exceeds the community's capacity to cope and require external aid.

- Disasters allow community to recognize its strength and the value of mutual support, caring, and compassion. The collective memory of survivorship and overcoming become sources of resilience in the future.
- Refugees enrich host communities' cultural and economic life, but they first must overcome many barriers to access social and healthcare resources.
- Refugee camps and other places of compact resettlement provide basic protection but can amplify the divisions and replicate conflicts existing in the refugees' homeland.
- Persons marginalized in their homeland may remain socially excluded at the place of resettlement and need a higher level of social and MH support.
- Sexual and gender-based violence remains prevalent on a disaster site and a common part of the refugee experience.

References

Araujo, J. O., Souza, F. M., Proença, R., Bastos, M. L., Trajman, A., & Faerstein, E. (2019). Prevalence of sexual violence among refugees: A systematic review. *Revista de Saude Publica, 23*(53), 78. https://doi.org/10.11606/s1518-8787.2019053001081

Backe, E. L., Bosire, E. N., Kim, A. W., & Mendenhall, E. (2021). "Thinking too much": A systematic review of the idiom of distress in Sub-Saharan Africa. *Culture, Medicine and Psychiatry, 45*(4), 655–682. https://doi.org/10.1007/s11013-020-09697-z

Berkowitz, S., Bryant, R., Brymer, M., Hamblen, J., Jacobs, A., Layne, C., Macy, R., Osofsky, H., Pynoos, R., Ruzek, J., Steinberg, A., Vernberg, E., Watson, P., National Center for PTSD, & National Child Traumatic Stress Network. (2010). *Skills for psychological recovery: Field operations guide*. https://www.ptsd.va.gov/professional/treat/type/skills_psych_recovery_manual.asp

Boss, P. (2006). Loss, trauma, and resilience: Therapeutic work with ambiguous loss. W W Norton & Co.

Boss, P. (2017). Families of the missing: Psychosocial effects and therapeutic approaches. *International Review of the Red Cross, 99*(2), 519–534. https://doi.org/10.1017/S1816383118000140

Brito, I. (2020, November 4). Protecting female refugees from gender-based violence in camps. *International Affairs Review*. https://www.iar-gwu.org/blog/iar-web/protectingfemale-refugees

Bunn, M., Samuels, G., & Higson-Smith, C. (2023). Ambiguous loss of home: Syrian refugees and the process of losing and remaking home. *Wellbeing, Space and Society, 4*, 100136. https://doi.org/10.1016/j.wss.2023.100136

Butler, S., & Sheriff, N. (2021, October 14). *The challenges of addressing the health care needs of Afghan evacuees*. Brookings Institute. https://www.brookings.edu/blog/up-front/2021/10/14/the-challenge-of-addressing-the-healthcare-needs-of-afghan-evacuees

Cherepanov, E. (2016). Role of the international trauma specialist in settings with complex trauma needs. In B. Ghafoori, Y. Caspi, & F. S. Smith (Eds.), *International perspectives on traumatic stress: Theory, access, and mental health services* (pp. 116–131). Nova.

Cherepanov, E. (2020). *Understanding the transgenerational legacy of totalitarian regimes: Paradoxes of cultural learning*. Routledge. https://doi.org/10.4324/9780429030338

Cherepanov, E. (2022). Mental health providers in Ukraine need support but they are not helpless: Professional self-organization and innovative practices. *Frontiers in Public Health, 10*, 1009431. https://doi.org/10.3389/fpubh.2022.1009431

Cogo, E., Murray, M., Villanueva, G., Hamel, C., Garner, P., Senior, S. L., & Henschke, N. (2022). Suicide rates and suicidal behaviour in displaced people: A systematic review. *PLoS One, 17*(3), e026379. https://doi.org/10.1371/journal.pone.0263797

Derr, A. S. (2016). Mental health service use among immigrants in the United States: A systematic review. *Psychiatric Services, 67*(3), 265–274. https://doi.org/10.1176/appi.ps.201500004

Feuer, A. (2014, October 19). The Ebola conspiracy theories. *New York Times*. https://www.nytimes.com/2014/10/19/sunday-review/the-ebola-conspiracy-theories.html

Freedman, J., Tastsoglou, E., & Sahraoui, N. (Dir.). (2022). *Gender-based violence in migration: Interdisciplinary, feminist and intersectional approaches* (p. 271). Palgrave Macmillan, 978-3-031-07928-3. https://doi.org/10.1007/978-3-031-07929-0. hal-03982457

Frounfelker, R. L., Miconi, D., Farrar, J., Brooks, M. A., Rousseau, C., & Betancourt, T. S. (2020). Mental health of refugee children and youth: Epidemiology, interventions, and future directions. *Annual Review of Public Health, 2*(41), 159–176. https://doi.org/10.1146/annurev-publhealth-040119-094230

Geissler, E., & Sprinkle, R. H. (2013). Disinformation squared: Was the HIV-from-Fort-Detrick myth a Stasi success? *Politics and the Life Sciences, 32*, 2–99.

Genc, K. (2023, May 2). The political aftershock of Turkey's devastating earthquake. *The Nation*. https://www.thenation.com/article/world/turkey-earthquake-erdogan-election-akp/

Hackbarth, M., Pavkov, T., Wetchler, J., & Flannery, M. (2012). Natural disasters: An assessment of family resiliency following Hurricane Katrina. *Journal of Marital and Family Therapy, 38*(2), 340–351.

Hagen, K. T., & Yohani, S. Y. (2010). The nature and psychosocial consequences of war rape for individuals and communities. *International Journal of Psychological Studies, 2*(2), 14–25. https://doi.org/10.5539/ijps.v2n2p14

Hinton, D. E., Rivera, E. I., Hofmann, S. G., Barlow, D. H., & Otto, M. W. (2012). Adapting CBT for traumatized refugees and ethnic minority patients: Examples from culturally adapted CBT (CA-CBT). *Transcultural Psychiatry, 49*(2), 340–365. https://doi.org/10.1177/1363461512441595

Hollifield, M., Verbillis-Kolp, S., Farmer, B., Toolson, E. C., Woldehaimanot, T., Yamazaki, J., Holland, A., St Clair, J., & SooHoo, J. (2013). The refugee health screener-15 (RHS-15): Development and validation of an instrument for anxiety, depression, and PTSD in refugees. *General Hospital Psychiatry, 35*(2), 202–209. https://doi.org/10.1016/j.genhosppsych.2012.12.002

Horyniak, D., Melo, J. S., Farrell, R. M., Ojeda, V. D., & Strathdee, S. A. (2016). Epidemiology of substance use among forced migrants: A global systematic review. *PLoS One, 11*(7), e0159134. https://doi.org/10.1371/journal.pone.0159134

Imhoff, R., & Lamberty, P. (2020). A bioweapon or a hoax? The link between distinct conspiracy beliefs about the coronavirus disease (COVID-19) outbreak and pandemic behavior. *Social Psychology and Personality Science, 11*(8), 1110–1118. https://doi.org/10.1177/1948550620934692

Jiloha, R. C. (2013, July). Rape: Legal issues in mental health perspective. *Indian Journal of Psychiatry, 55*(3), 250–255. https://doi.org/10.4103/0019-5545.117141. PMID: 24082245; PMCID: PMC3777346.

Júnior, J. G., de Sales, J. P., Moreira, M. M., Pinheiro, W. R., Lima, C. K. T., & Neto, M. L. R. (2020). A crisis within the crisis: The mental health situation of refugees in the world during the 2019 coronavirus (2019-nCoV) outbreak. *Psychiatry Research, 288*, 113000. https://doi.org/10.1016/j.psychres.2020.113000

Kane, J. C., Ventevogel, P., Spiegel, P., Bass, J. K., van Ommeren, M., & Tol, W. A. (2014). Mental, neurological, and substance use problems among refugees in primary health care: Analysis of the health information system in 90 refugee camps. *BMC Medicine, 12*(1), 228. https://doi.org/10.1186/s12916-014-0228-9

Kar, N. (2010). Indian research on disaster and mental health. *Indian Journal of Psychiatry, 52*(Suppl 1), S286.

Kessler, G. (2022). Numbers behind Afghanistan evacuation come into focus. *The FactChecker*. https://www.washingtonpost.com/politics/2022/05/25/numbers-behind-afghan-evacuation-come-into-focus

Klofstad, C. A., Uscinski, J. E., Connolly, J. M., & West, J. P. (2019). What drives people to believe in Zika conspiracy theories? *Palgrave Communications, 5*, 1–8.

Kokou-Kpolou, C. K., Moukouta, C. S., Masson, J., Bernoussi, A., Cénat, J. M., & Bacqué, M.-F. (2020). Correlates of grief-related disorders and mental health outcomes among adult refugees exposed to trauma and bereavement: A systematic review and future research directions. *Journal of Affective Disorders, 267*, 171–184. https://doi.org/10.1016/j.jad.2020.02.026

Magwood, O., Kassam, A., Mavedatnia, D., Mendonca, O., Saad, A., Hasan, H., Madana, M., Ranger, D., Tan, Y., & Pottie, K. (2022). Mental health screening approaches for resettling refugees and asylum seekers: A scoping review. *International Journal of Environmental Research and Public Health, 19*(6), 3549. https://doi.org/10.3390/ijerph19063549

Makwana, N. (2019). Disaster and its impact on mental health: A narrative review. *Journal of Family Medicine and Primary Care, 8*(10), 3090–3095. https://doi.org/10.4103/jfmpc.jfmpc_893_19

Malteser International. (2024). *Humanitarian crises*. https://www.malteser-international.org/en/current-issues/humanitariancrises.html

Marsh, M., Purdin, S., & Navani, S. (2006). Addressing sexual violence in humanitarian emergencies. *Global Public Health, 1*(2), 133–146. https://doi.org/10.1080/17441690600652787

Masten, A. S. (2020). Resilience of children in disasters: A multisystem perspective. *International Journal of Psychology, 56*(1), 1–11. https://doi.org/10.1002/ijop.12737

Math, S. B., Nirmala, M. C., Moirangthem, S., & Kumar, N. C. (2015). Disaster management: Mental health perspective. *Indian Journal of Psychological Medicine, 37*(3), 261–271. https://doi.org/10.4103/0253-7176.162915

Mercer, J., Gaillard, J. C., Crowley, K., Shannon, R., Alexander, B., Day, S., & Becker, J. (2012). Culture and disaster risk reduction: Lessons and opportunities. *Environmental Hazards, 11*(2), 74–95. https://doi.org/10.1080/17477891.2011.609876

Neal, D. M. (1997). Reconsidering the phases of disaster. *International Journal of Mass Emergencies & Disasters, 15*(2), 239–264. https://doi.org/10.1177/028072709701500202

Nesterko, Y., Jäckle, D., Friedrich, M., Holzapfel, L., & Glaesmer, H. (2020). Prevalence of post-traumatic stress disorder, depression and somatisation in recently arrived refugees in Germany: An epidemiological study. *Epidemiology and Psychiatric Sciences, 29*, e40. https://doi.org/10.1017/s2045796019000325

Özdemir, G. S. (2020). Refugees in new destinations and small cities. In P. Bose (Ed.), *Resettlement in Vermont*. Springer Nature. https://doi.org/10.25071/1920-7336.41105

Pearson, A., & Cherepanov, E. (2012). Building a disaster behavioral health response to radiological nuclear disaster. *Journal of Emergency Management, 10*(6), 413–424.

Refugee Council Report. (2009). *The vulnerable women's project: Refugee and asylum seeking women affected by rape or sexual violence*. Refugee Council. https://www.bl.uk/britishlibrary/~/media/bl/global/social-welfare/pdfs/non-secure/v/u/l/vulnerable-womens-project-refugee-and-asylum-seeking-women-affected-by-rape-or-sexual-violence-literature-review.pdf

Ryzhova, A. (2023, July 10). Dom v kotorom. [House in which.] *Verstka*. https://verstka.media/mariupol-istorii-lyudey-chyi-doma-razbombili-i-snesli

Scharpf, F., Masath, F. B., Mkinga, G., Kyaruzi, E., Machumu, M., & Hecker, T. (2023). Prevalence of suicidality and associated factors of suicide risk in a representative community sample of families in three East African refugee camps. *Social Psychiatry and Psychiatric Epidemiology, 59*, 245–259. https://doi.org/10.1007/s00127-023-02506-z

Schlechter, P., Wagner, U., Morina, N., & Hellmann, J. H. (2023). Psychotherapy motivation in refugees: The role of alexithymia, stigmatization, self-esteem, and psycho-therapy expectations. *Psychological Trauma: Theory, Research, Practice, and Policy, 15*(2), 227–236. https://doi.org/10.1037/tra0001167

Sheehy, I. (2016, October 17). Sexual assault in refugee camps. *Havard Political Review*. http://harvardpolitics.com/hprgument-posts/sexual-assault-in-refugee-camps/

Simons, L. M. (1984, June 7). Children of Hiroshima, Nagasaki survivors facing prejudice, discrimination in Japan. *Ottawa Citizen*. https://news.google.com/newspapers?nid=2194&dat=19840607&id=Z6QyAAAAIBAJ&pg=1441,3702452&hl=en

Taylor, J. E., Filipski, M. J., Alloush, M., Gupta, A., Valdes, R. I. R., & Gonzalez-Estrada, E. (2016). Economic impact of refugees. *Proceedings of the National Academy of Sciences, 113*(27), 7449–7453.

UN. (1954). *Convention and protocol relating to the status of refugees* (189 U.N.T.S. 150). United Nations. https://www.unhcr.org/us/media/convention-and-protocol-relating-status-refugees

UNHCR. (2023). *Refugee Data Finder*. from https://www.unhcr.org/refugee-statistics/

Ursano, R. J., & Norwood, A. E. (Eds.). (2003). *Trauma and disaster: Responses and management* (Review of psychiatry series) (Vol. 22). American Psychiatric Publishing, Inc.

van Egmond, M., Garnefski, N., Jonker, D., & Kerkhof, A. (1993). The relationship between sexual abuse and female suicidal behavior. *Crisis, 14*(3), 129–139.

Wachinger, G., Renn, O., Begg, C., & Kuhlicke, C. (2013). The risk perception paradox—Implications for governance and communication of natural hazards. *Risk Analysis, 33*(6), 1049–1065.

Wachter, K., & Gulbas, L. E. (2018). Social support under siege: An analysis of forced migration among women from the Democratic Republic of Congo. *Social Science & Medicine, 208*, 107–116. https://doi.org/10.1016/j.socscimed.2018.04.056

Ward, J., & Vann, B. (2002). Gender-based violence in refugee settings. *Lancet, 360*(Suppl), 13–14.

Weine, S. M. (2011). Developing preventive mental health interventions for refugee families in resettlement. *Family Process, 50*(3), 410–430. https://doi.org/10.1111/j.1545-5300.2011.01366.x

World Health Organization, War Trauma Foundation, & World Vision International. (2011). *Psychological first aid: Guide for field workers*. WHO.

Wright, A., Reisig, A., & Cullen, B. (2020). Efficacy and cultural adaptations of narrative exposure therapy for trauma-related outcomes in refugees/asylum-seekers: A systematic review and meta-analysis. *Journal of Behavioral and Cognitive Therapy, 30*(4), 301–314. https://psycnet.apa.org/doi/10.1016/j.jbct.2020.10.003

Young, B. H., Ford, J. D., Ruzek, J. I., Friedman, M., & Gusman, F. D. (1998). *Disaster mental health services: A guidebook for clinicians and administrators*. National Center for Post-Traumatic Stress Disorder. http://www.ncptsd.va.gov/publications/disaster/index.html

Chapter 8
Political Emergency and Political Violence

Complex Political Emergency

A political emergency is a form of complex emergency (CE). Let us talk first about what means when a situation is designated as complex emergency, and what all these situations have in-common.

> *Complex political emergency* is a term used to describe acute or protracted political crises involving political upheaval, violent conflict, or war. (Duffield, 1994; Sondorp & Zwi, 2002)

A Complex emergency (CE) is a humanitarian crisis that typically involves Extensive violence and loss of life.

- Displacement of populations.
- Widespread damage to societies and economies.
- The need for large-scale, multifaceted humanitarian assistance.
- Political and military constraints that complicate the delivery of humanitarian aid.
- Significant security risks for humanitarian relief workers in some areas.

The social and psychological impacts of CEs are often extensive and severe and carry the potential for intergenerational transmission. Other examples of CE are conflicts, wars, especially civil wars, genocide, epidemics, and other events causing a high degree of devastation. A complex emergency caused by political dysfunction and politically motivated violence is called a complex political emergency.

The impact of political emergencies is usually multilayered—they affect not only individuals and groups but also the whole society and undermine the administration's ability to govern and control the situation, creating barriers to humanitarian assistance delivery. This chapter describes different humanitarian crises caused by

E. Cherepanov, *Humanitarian Competencies for Global Mental Health Professionals*, Contemporary Humanitarian Action and Emergency Management,
https://doi.org/10.1007/978-3-031-74268-2_8

political dysfunction and focuses on the impact of MH, the role of GMH providers, and context-specific interventions.

Examples of political emergencies are fragile or failed states, armed conflicts, genocide, and complex political contexts (CPCs), a newer term that is associated with tyranny and authoritarian and totalitarian regimes (Cherepanov, 2023a, b).

Despite all the diversity of complex political emergencies—their origins, triggers, and multiplicity of players—they all share several characteristics.

- The government is unable or unwilling to protect its citizens or deliberately instigates violence in violations of human rights, which creates massive humanitarian needs.
- Violence is politically motivated and people are targeted because of their collective identity.
- Political emergencies have political causes and can only be understood within the geopolitical and historical context.
- Every political emergency accentuates a particular facet of a humanitarian crisis and produces unique challenges, priorities, and dilemmas.
- These crises and conflicts carry political significance, and humanitarian interventions are often politicized.
- Providing humanitarian aid can become unsafe for the aid workers and sometimes the recipients.
- Political dysfunction results in compromised or destroyed economics and infrastructure and disrupts healthcare. It creates political, logistical, and security barriers to delivering humanitarian aid and difficulties in evaluating its impact.
- Ineffective political governance increases susceptibility to disasters, famines, and dictatorships. It weakens the nation's resilience and establishes the potential for recurring cycles of violence and victimization.
- The world is often unaware of the full impact of such situations until much later, but the international humanitarian community monitors such crises and gets involved when aid is needed.

Fragile or Failed States

Fragile or failed states can emerge in post-conflict or political transition situations or because of prolonged political or economic crisis or impasse. The difference between fragile and failed states is only approximate. The main attribute of a fragile state is economic instability and disorganization; and the failed state goes through a legitimacy crisis where the government fails to control crime and violence and loses the ability to govern effectively.

These states are characterized by extreme wealth gaps and inequality in accessing healthcare or education and other resources, as well as high rates of poverty, crime, and gang activity—all of which make the country susceptible to humanitarian crises. Ridden by local or transnational organized crime, cartels, and terrorism, the opaque and unpredictable governance creates rising humanitarian needs and produces economic refugees (Tyagi, 2012).

Armed conflicts leave behind a governmental dysfunction, increasing the likelihood of the conflict's recurrence. Peacebuilding and violence prevention measures are important in post-conflict settings (Fiedler et al., 2016). Post-conflict or post-dictatorship countries are often poor with disorganized and often corrupt administrations, so they have to rely on foreign aid. In the meantime, political volatility and sweeping corruption remain barriers to aid delivery, MH services, sustainable development goals, and economic recovery. Furthermore, weak or troubled governance is often unable to prevent or control future humanitarian crises, power struggles, criminal activities, social tensions, or the recurrence of violence.

Special Considerations and Interventions

Conflicts do not end with the signing of peace agreements. The post-conflict consequences can linger for a long time and create chronic volatility. Many post-conflict societies struggle with an increase in criminal activities, poverty, criminal violence, and corruption. The unfavorable economic and social aftermath is known to amplify the likelihood of renewed political violence.

When feasible, the international community assists with post-conflict transition, economic and social rehabilitation, and development project funding, including MH and psychosocial programs in the region.

In a fragile state, socially ignored, invisible, and forgotten groups carry a disproportional weight of the crisis. Aiding disadvantaged, impoverished, and vulnerable victims of violence and working with children, adolescents, and families often become a priority for humanitarian interventions.

Because of the relative stability of post-war settings, many successful MH interventions focus on long-term goals such as social transformation, development of community-based interventions, or family based health promotions for vulnerable and disadvantaged groups.

Often, the needs of the population are so extensive that MH interventions are most beneficial when they go beyond focusing only on some MH conditions, such as trauma. Such comprehensive interventions can include enhancing emotional regulation in youth, daily functioning, and employment programs, as Betancourt et al. (2014) demonstrated when working with war-affected youth in Sierra Leone.

Armed Conflict and War

Impact Factors

Armed conflicts and wars destroy communities and divide nations. In addition to many people losing their lives or becoming disabled, wars leave a trail of broken administrative, economic, and social infrastructure and shattered health services that cannot cope with increased needs.

Although each conflict is unique, they all have much in common.

- Although wars often begin for political reasons, once started, they do not discriminate; anyone can become a victim at any moment.
- Wars create massive collateral damage: many who do not directly participate in the conflict are affected physically and mentally.
- Conflicts produce massive numbers of refugees.
- War trauma can become a part of the collective identity, which carries an intergenerational impact.
- Wars have the propensity to recur unless massive violence prevention and peacebuilding efforts are implemented.

MH Impact

Whether an armed conflict is caused by tribal or sectarian violence or it is a freedom war to defend the country from external aggression, its impact is complex and systemic and extends far beyond the individual survivors. Much work needs to be done to rebuild dispersed communities, reestablish infrastructure, and restore the fabric of life.

Armed conflicts take a heavy MH toll on both civilians and combatants. In addition to trauma and destroyed infrastructure, war severs family and community ties and interrupts the transmission of cultural legacy. Common war-related traumatic experiences include witnessing violence, death and destruction, loss of loved ones and friends, destruction of homes and livelihoods, forced relocation, lingering unpredictability and fears about the future, and the realization that there may not be any safe place for anyone.

When assisting with war trauma, providers must be prepared to address acute stress reactions, severe trauma, and multiple losses. For every person, there is something different that becomes the core of their traumatic memory. For some, it is seeing injured or dead people; for others, losing all their belongings and memorabilia or having to make the difficult decision to flee while leaving behind those who are unable to move, abandoning pets, or hearing the sounds of sirens and waiting for the bombs to fall.

For children, exposure to war can be very traumatizing and dramatically increases their MH vulnerabilities in the future.

The psychological impact of wars greatly depends on the nature of the conflict.

Freedom wars or wars to defend their land often strengthen national identity and cohesions, give meaning to suffering, and serve as inspiration. They remind people of historic experiences of perseverance: every culture has heroic epic poems that portray the nations' heroes and emphasize their strength.

Unfortunately, it is not uncommon for the other side of the conflict to draw their strength from the same source: propaganda often portrays offense and aggression as self-defense (Cherepanov, 2023b).

Civil wars, on the other hand, are always a national tragedy. Such wars destroy personal and historical ties, alter collective identity, and their impacts reverberate through generations.

A civil war is a form of armed conflict that occurs when different groups of citizens within the same country are fighting each other. Such wars cut across the community and families and turn people against each other.

Interventions

Post-conflict GMH assistance involves supporting recovery for traumatized individuals and families, teaching communities about coping and mutual support, and identifying those who need a higher level of MH care. The priorities are often assisting those with PTSD and grief, providing connections to resources, helping to improve sleep and other trauma-related symptoms, and managing anger.

Aiding people affected by armed conflicts underscores respect for the different perspectives in a divided nation. Although GMH providers must refrain from taking sides according to the humanitarian principle of neutrality, this can be particularly hard when assisting victims of war.

PFA, MHPSS, and grief support have been identified as best practices. Expressive arts therapy, CBT (cognitive-behavioral therapy), and EMDR (eye movement desensitization and reprocessing) to deal with trauma reactions, stress, and anxiety management have demonstrated effectiveness in war zones as well (Hassan et al., 2016, pp. 36–37).

When responding to a conflict, it is essential to rely on local resources. As it happens with other CEs, local providers in armed conflicts may also be affected—demoralized, dispersed, traumatized, having other priorities, and in need of support and empowerment to step back into this role.

Sources of Resilience

Family ties and community support remain the main sources of resilience during an armed conflict and are important for both adults and children. Betancourt and Khan (2008) suggested approaching protective factors for children affected by war not from a trauma perspective alone but by also including social-ecological and developmental components such as coping, meaning-making, and social connections.

Special Considerations

The situation in conflict zones can change rapidly and without warning, and the personal safety of providers becomes the most serious concern. MH providers can travel to these sites only with established organizations that can monitor security, advise on developments on the ground, and assist with evacuation if needed.

> Any solo traveling to war zones is considered unprofessional and is categorically advised against.

The gender, race, ethnic, and cultural identities of providers do matter in terms of their safety and ability to establish trust with service recipients. For example, if the ethnicity of an MH provider is one the opposite side identifies with (even in remote generations), it may be triggering for survivors, become a matter of safety for aid workers, and create additional barriers to establishing trust.

The role of international MH providers during armed conflict becomes particularly sensitive. They can be deliberately targeted or taken as hostages with the intent to exchange them for ransom or imprisoned militants. If this occurs, relief operations can be compromised.

The issue of war neutrality becomes especially contentious during armed conflict or genocide. Those who assist victims and hear their sides of the story may have a hard time remaining neutral. Self-awareness of personal biases can help people navigate such complex situations.

Wars carry the propensity to set up cycles of retaliatory violence, which presents significant challenges for reconciliation and peacebuilding efforts. This is why retaliatory violence prevention must be incorporated into all MH relief activities. At the same time, jumping to reconciliation or peacebuilding efforts too quickly can be perceived by victims as insensitive and wrong.

From multiple personal conversations, I can conclude that international recognition of injustice and violence remains very important to victims. It acknowledges their suffering and makes them feel validated even when little can be done.

Special Groups in Armed Conflicts

In armed conflicts, where everyone can become a victim, MH providers face special challenges when meeting the needs of the survivors of war rape, child soldiers, and former.

Rape as Warfare

Although the MH impact of war rape carries some similarities with sexual gender-based violence, using rape as a tool of warfare adds a political aspect to this targeted victimization. Often, MH providers are the first to learn about such incidents from their clients, and they must alert international human rights organizations, such as Human Rights Watch at https://www.hrw.org.

War rape is the use of sexual violence as a tactic of war to humiliate, dominate, instill fear in, disperse, and/or forcibly relocate civilian members of a community or ethnic group (OHCHR, 2008). Political "justification" distinguishes war rape from other forms of sexual gender-based violence and legally makes it a crime against humanity.

History has many examples of when raping the enemy in the context of war is used to intimidate, demoralize, inflict humiliation and shame, and break the resistance of the opposing side (Doja, 2019; García-Moreno & van Ommeren, 2012). War rape can also be used as a form of torture or an act of genocide to dilute genetics, or to spread diseases like HIV, which amounts to ethnic cleansing (Poloni-Staudinger & Ortbals, 2012; Sharlach, 2000; Tol et al., 2013).

Although war rape has been a common occurrence throughout human history, it was first recognized as a war crime and persecuted by an international tribunal only following the 1992–1995 Bosnian war (Leaning et al., 2009; Crowe, 2013) when an estimated between 10,000 and 50,000 of women and 3,000 men were raped. (Henigsberg, 2010)

The true prevalence of rape in a war context is difficult to estimate because of underreporting. What is known suggests that it is widespread and continues to be widely used.

There also have not been too many studies on the aftermath of war rape in the victims. Those that are available have demonstrated extremely high rates of PTSD, depression, and suicidal ideation a year later (Lončar et al., 2006). Survivors and the children born from war rape can face serious, often lifelong medical and MH issues, identity problems, and social isolation in their own families and communities, which often end up blaming the victims (Weitsman, 2007; Russell, 2014; Cherepanov, 2020a).

Because the survivors of war rape cannot always count on family and community support, the humanitarian community sets its hopes on supporting grassroots initiatives where survivors are able to support and empower each other. Such initiatives, run by survivors, bring survivors together and create a sort of auxiliary community where they may draw strength from and support each other (Poloni-Staudinger & Ortbals, 2012).

In addition to psychoeducation, the survivors in such programs learn various vocational skills to support themselves and improve access to economic opportunities.

These initiatives empower survivors to champion advocating for themselves and their peers, and to fight stigma. Most of these programs are for women. Men can be victims of war rape as well, but they have fewer supporting resources, and the programs that do target males receive far less funding because most donors choose to donate to women. This gender inequality has led to accusations by social justice advocates of gender discrimination and biases against men (Cherepanov, 2020b).

City of Joy is a grassroots program aimed at creating a safe space and promoting leadership opportunities for female survivors of sexual violence in the Democratic Republic of Congo (DRC), a region affected by ongoing conflict (See: CityOfJoyCongo.org).

Living Peace was a 2012 program in Burundi and the DRC for men affected by war rape. It provided psychosocial and trauma support and focused on developing coping skills, mutual support, and nonviolent conflict-resolution skills (See: Promundo. *Living peace*. https://promundoglobal.org/programs/living-peace/).

Women for Women International (WfWI) has established a site in Bosnia and Herzegovina to focus on social and economic empowerment for women survivors of war rape (See: https://www.womenforwomen.org).

Such grassroots initiatives have been found effective in supporting and empowering survivors. Their limitations relate to difficulties in securing long-term funding, especially for services for men.

Child Soldiers

When working in post-conflict regions, GMH providers must be aware of the possibility that if their clients are of a specific age, they may have been either child soldiers or their victims. It should become an important consideration in treatment planning and accessing resources and support.

A child soldier is any person under 18 years of age who is part of any regular or irregular armed force in any capacity. The recruitment and use of children is a grave violation of international humanitarian law and child rights (UNICEF, 1997). The UN (2016) has warned of the devastating impact on children and has called to respect childhood.

The recruitment of child soldiers has been widespread in many countries: Uganda, Mozambique, Sri Lanka, Congo, Liberia, Sierra Leone, Somalia, Sudan, and Yemen. Militant organizations such as ISIS and Boko Haram have used children extensively (UN, 2016).

Singh and Singh (2010) have estimated that there are currently 300,000 child soldiers recruited in different countries. The actual number is expected to be much higher, and recruitment continues.

Recruited child soldiers are subjected to terrible violence and brainwashing. They are often forced to commit violence against militants and civilians (sometimes against their own villages), and acts of physical and sexual violence against each other, including their own community or even families, as an act of initiation or proof of loyalty. Many, especially girls but also boys have been subjected to sexual exploitation. Child soldiers are often given drugs to decrease their hunger and fear and increase their bravery and stamina (Pearn, 2003).

Former child soldiers present in treatment with high rates of PTSD, anxiety, and depression, and community acceptance has been shown to reduce the severity of MH issues (Betancourt et al., 2010; Singh & Singh, 2010; Kohrt et al., 2008; Wessells, 2017).

After the conflict is over, the former child soldiers are often stigmatized because of the roles they may have played in atrocities, which affects their transition to civilian life. Many experience difficulties reuniting with their families or being accepted back into the community. In addition to addressing the MH and trauma issues directly, GMH providers can participate in the reintegration efforts, which require a delicate act of negotiating between the children and the community.

Former Combatants

The post-war influx of traumatized veterans can change the psychological, social, and political landscape of society.

Many war veterans have been wounded, traumatized, and morally injured, and they experience difficulties with readjustment after decommission. Some of them were prisoners of war or tortured. The significant increase in rates of interpersonal and community violence, substance use, homelessness, crimes, and suicides among veterans in post-conflict regions is well documented (Asare-Doku et al., 2021).

Despite the tremendous need, international humanitarians are rarely directly involved in providing humanitarian MH relief to active-duty service members or recent veterans. One reason is that any foreign involvement can inadvertently be perceived as foreign influence in military action or an attempt to collect sensitive information.

After the war is over, assisting war veterans with readjustment issues, treating PTSD, and preventing substance use, violence, and suicide quickly become a priority in the affected and recovering regions.

Training local MH providers in supporting off-duty veterans and their families may be a better option for GMH professionals.

Genocide

Genocide is a legal term that pertains to the "acts committed with intent to destroy, in whole or in part, a national, ethnical, racial or religious group." (UN, 2019)

The declaration of a genocide carries strong international moral condemnation and has heavy political and economic consequences. Sometimes, a genocide is declared long after it occurs: the 1915 Armenian genocide was recognized by the European People's Party (2015) only 100 years later.

The international reaction to genocides has often been delayed or inconsistent, which has raised the issue of morality in humanitarian response (Slim, 1997). Even when the act of genocide has not been declared, there can be actions qualified as having genocidal intent, such as dehumanization of the opposing side, war rape, killing based on ethnic identity, kidnapping of women and children, and others.

Genocide is a crime against humanity, and suspected acts of genocide must be reported to international human rights watch organizations such as Human Rights Watch at https://www.hrw.org.

Mental Health Impact

Genocides inflict severe trauma through deliberate victimization based on ethnic, cultural, or religious identity. Genocides leave behind a long-lasting, often inter- and transgenerational legacy of pain and social fears and distrust, powerless, and belief that the genocide will happen again. The memories of victimhood and survivorship become a fundamental part of a collective and cultural identity.

Studies have demonstrated that Holocaust survivors and their descendants display high rates of anxiety and depression, or "survivor syndrome" (Niederland, 1968). The survivors reported higher rates of recurring nightmares, anhedonia, lack of energy, withdrawal from social interactions, psychosomatic complaints, difficulty concentrating, irritability, and a mistrustful attitude toward the world. Such experience alters parental styles and affects their children (Danieli, 2007). The descendants of the survivors often express worries that genocide will recur in the future. When I asked in different regions with recent history of genocidal action about the scariest part—the response often was as such:

> The scariest part is seeing your neighbors, family friends, coworkers with whom you celebrated cultural holidays and shared food and work, children played together and went to the same school, some even got married. So, you open the door, and here they are, standing at your doorstep, wanting to kill you and your family. The world, as we knew it, is gone forever. It is tough after that to restore trust. (Cherepanov, personal communication with a survivor)

Reconciliation often seems impossible. However, this may be the only solutions.

> They have no choice but to continue living together—migration is okay only temporarily, but everyone cannot migrate. The globe is not big enough for everyone to escape. They must learn to live together. (Cherepanov, personal communication with a senior migration officer)

Interventions

In the wake of acts that perceived as genocidal, MH specialists use PFA, grief support, trauma-specific cognitive-behavioral interventions, cognitive restructuring, and expressive art therapy to support survivors of violence, to bring immediate relief to the sufferers, and to assist with overcoming losses and severe trauma. Keeping perpetrators accountable is an integral part of restoring a sense of justice.

The horrific social, political, and humanitarian fallout from genocides demonstrates that the world must do everything it can not only to help people recover but also to prevent it from happening in the future.

My experience working with the descendants of the survivors of the Armenian genocide, Holodomor, Bosnians, Crimean Tatars deported under Stalin, Greeks, Chechens, and Rwandans has demonstrated that taking pride in collective survivorship, perseverance, and preserving ethnic identity can become a powerful tool in restoring a sense of belonging and overcoming.

Special Considerations

It is believed that historical conflicts cause genocides. In fact, history can be manipulated to justify genocides. Still, they are more often inspired, triggered, and encouraged by modern politics in which the government is at least responsible for their actions or inactions.

In ethnic conflicts, persons belonging to mixed marriages offer a glimpse of hope that 1 day, the divided country will be able to come together the same way how people found the way to reconcile their cultural differences. However, they and their children can become targets from both sides and need support in the divided nation.

> Children born from mixed marriages where both ethnicities are at war can be susceptible to identity crises: "I have a civil war replayed inside of my head," as one person born from a mixed family once told me.

Genocides carry a high potential for recurrences in a form of repeated or retaliatory violence, which is why violence prevention becomes an important step for interrupting cycles of re-victimization. The cultural memories of genocide can easily be triggered and cause an overreaction to current real or perceived threats.

Creating places of memory, preserving narratives, and setting up memorials allow us to preserve the memories of genocide and ensure the victims are not forgotten. However, these memorials must include components that illustrate the strength and hope for the future.

The descendants of the perpetrators may need MH support to restore their positive identity; working with them can be a part of future violence prevention efforts.

Complex Political Contexts (CPCs): Authoritarian States and Dictatorships

Political violence increases risks for both the aid workers and the aid recipients. Authoritarian Complex Political Contexts (CPCs) have been recognized in both low- and high-resource settings and wherever belonging to a particular political, religious, tribal, ethnic, or gender identity group or expressing political convictions make a person a target of violence, institutional discrimination, and systematic persecution. (Cherepanov, 2020a, 2023a)

Examples of CPCs are countries with an ongoing or a recent history of tyranny, dictatorship, authoritarian and nationalistic regimes, or other forms of political oppression and injustice that target people based on their collective identity.

Dictators use indoctrination and create an echo chamber to promote conspiracy theories. They deliberately foster informational and economic isolation from external and independent sources of information. Xenophobia and anti-LGBTQ sentiments are used to divert attention from the government's failures. Science, healthcare, education, art, and sports, all became politicized.

Political violence and violations of human rights set CPCs apart from other settings with high rates of criminal violence. In CPCs, the government abuses power and control for no other reason than for power and control. Such regimes place blame on minorities to oppress and justify attacks against them and employ informants or secret police. For example, the SARS pandemic was used in Russia to prevent the opposition from gathering. At the same time, the pro-government forces had no problems staging mass propaganda events (Cherepanov, personal communication).

Political violence is used to achieve political goals or force the opposition into obedience. The administration can deny or limit access to resources for marginalized groups. (Conteh-Morgan, 2003)

Such regimes are comparatively well organized and can be economically stable for some time, but they are built on isolation from the rest of the world and always end with a humanitarian calamity of unimaginable proportions. Extermination of their own citizens, violations of human rights, and disregard for the rule of law result in a catastrophic implosion of the state, igniting wars, disasters, and triggering famines and starvation. At the same time, the administration often attempts to hide the true extent of humanitarian needs and thwarts the delivery of life-saving foreign aid to avoid international exposure. For instance, this happened during Holodomor in Ukraine from 1932 to 1933 and later in North Korea from 1994 to 1998. There are many more such examples.

In the states with CPCs, dictators attempt to enlist MH providers as informants to report on alleged disloyalty and to employ punitive psychiatry as a means of punishing dissidents. This practice was widespread in the USSR (Bloch & Reddaway, 1977) and has remained prevalent in the Russian Federation. A similar tactic was reported in Somalia during the 1970s, where psychologists were tasked with reporting disloyal individuals, and recent reports of the same are coming from Uganda and other countries (Cherepanov, personal communication).

Most recently, in the Russian Federation, there was a proposed amendment to the professional code of ethics for psychologists and psychiatrists demanding that they inform law enforcement agencies if their clients disclose that they don't support military operations (Cherepanov, personal communication). They are also encouraged to report draft dodgers and disloyalty, and to use their psychological expertise to encourage young people to join the army. (Professor Kupratov, president of the Professional Medical Psychotherapeutic Association, October 22, 2022, https://www.youtube.com/watch?v=JdUuPZ2DCzo)

Psychological and MH Impact

Living in a dictatorship can result in complex trauma, deep distrust, and suspicion of strangers and authorities—including health and MH service providers. Distrust translates into difficulties in disclosing weaknesses and vulnerabilities and seeking assistance. Studies have indicated that these social cognitions have the potential to persist in shaping worldview and influencing social behaviors across generations (Cherepanov, 2020a). The component of deliberate and targeted political victimization and abuse by the government invokes a multitude of emotional, behavioral, and cognitive reactions in people, which effect in some ways parallels the effects of interpersonal abuse (Cherepanov, 2023b).

Sustained trauma is often complex and chronic. It stems from accumulated hardships and traumatic losses, such as missing, tortured, or imprisoned friends or family members. Many either become victims or witnesses of violence; some endure torture or are familiar with those who have. The transgenerational toxicity of social trauma is apparent, creating societal and cultural trauma that impacts cultural identity across generations.

Emotional impact can be severe. Prolonged and chronic exposure to fear, anxiety, and unpredictability contributes to emotional overreactions or emotional withdrawal.

Behavior reflects social fears and helplessness. Individuals may adopt a low-profile lifestyle and escapism, exhibiting hypervigilance and attempting to evade unwanted attention or exposure from authorities. Some resort to self-harming behaviors, such as excessive drinking or even suicide.

Social cognitions are marked by profound distrust of the administration, which translates into social fatalism, apathy, and learned helplessness. The distrust of official figures is passed on to healthcare providers.

The distrust, fear, and shame associated with CPCs prevent *the aggregation* of traumatic experiences, meaning that people don't feel comfortable disclosing or sharing their personal experiences. It prevents them from empathizing and supporting each other. The lack of aggregation compromises the community's capacity to come together and develop mutual support systems (Cherepanov, 2023a).

MH Interventions

In CPCs, GMH interventions prioritize mitigating societal stressors, strengthening resilience and self-determination, and preventing cycles of violence and revictimization in the future. These objectives can be realized by

- Providing MH support to victims or witnesses of violence and torture, as well as those who have endured traumatic losses due to murder, suicide, or the disappearance of family members.
- Assisting oppressed, marginalized, and vulnerable groups by validating and normalizing their experiences and connecting them to individual internal strength and external support.
- Identifying community strengths and resources and facilitating mutual support.
- Correcting misinformation.

Operating in a complex environment means navigating political challenges while balancing the safety and the needs of vulnerable populations that may be afraid to speak out. The contextual specifics of CPCs determine the principles of interventions (Cherepanov, 2021) that MH providers need to keep in mind.

Safety and vigilance. In CPCs, prioritizing the safety of both beneficiaries and providers is a paramount task. Merely the act of reaching out for help can attract unwanted attention, elevating personal risk. To manage these risks, providers routinely engage in safety discussions and planning with clients and remain vigilant about their security, including the possibility of being followed. The risks and political challenges to international humanitarian assistance can be so significant that it brings up the question of whether this aid is feasible or if the risk may outweigh the benefits for the providers and recipients.

The international humanitarian community is well aware of the extent of humanitarian needs in CPCs, and the cost-benefit ratio has been a part of humanitarian debates.

Confidentiality. Confidentiality is a basic requirement in any MH intervention, but there can be only limited expectation thereof in CPCs. Authorities can go a long way to access sensitive health information by searching records, using listening devices, or even recruiting staff or interpreters as informants. Records and electronic devices can be searched, misused, or confiscated, underscoring the inherent limitations of confidentiality. Any GMH programming in CPCs must have formal protocols for preserving the confidentiality of the participants, establishing emergency communication and security protocols, and developing safety plans for urgent program termination.

Trauma-, culture-, and politically informed approach. MH programming should work toward enhancing trauma, cultural, and political competencies in any interventions.

Importance of provider affiliation. Working with an established international agency can provide additional security, support, and advocacy if something doesn't go right. But if this organization becomes blacklisted by the government, it can create additional challenges for the providers and the people they assist.

Preferring small interventions over ambitious agendas. In CPCs, predicting all the consequences of large intervention is challenging. In CPCs, there is a high degree of uncertainty, which makes it difficult to calculate the long-term impact of any intervention. The cautious approach implies that strategically selected small-scale interventions that can generate a systemic impact, such as psychoeducation or training local providers, are more favorable than ambitious and sweeping projects that aim to fundamentally transform community life.

Exploring available choices. It is important to explore with clients the available choices, even if these choices are limited; focusing on the present and the immediate future helps to restore feelings of being in control.

Special Considerations

Customizing mental health interventions to the CPC is imperative for delivering safe and competent services. The complexity of such situations necessitates specialized competencies for GMH providers, including an understanding of politically informed interventions (Cherepanov, 2023a).

Authoritarian administration often promotes a siege mentality by depicting an external enemy as conspiring against the nation's progress. The people served may internalize this indoctrination, which will have a direct impact on their relationship with GMH providers if they are affiliated with that designated enemy (often the West). Trust (or the lack thereof) and fear of punitive psychiatry pose significant barriers to reaching out and accepting MH assistance and support.

In CPCs, the distinction between perpetrators and victims can be blurred, with former victims sometimes becoming perpetrators and vice versa. Fostering trusting and supportive family relationships boosts resilience, strengthens coping mechanisms, and helps individuals resist indoctrination and brainwashing (Cherepanov, 2020a, 2023a). Engaging in conversations with clients about whom they can trust can be advantageous.

Torture

In CPCs, torture is used for various reasons—to crush the spirit of those who disobey or disagree with the government administration and to scare those who may attempt to overthrow the regime.

> Physicians for Human Rights (PHR) define *torture* as the intentional infliction of severe mental or physical pain or suffering by or with the approval of state agents See: https://phr.org/issues/torture). Torture is prohibited under international law, and PHR expressed commitment to documenting it, supporting the survivors, connecting them with legal services, and raising awareness of these practices.

In addition to the trauma of deliberate victimization, anxiety, and depression, torture survivors often have multiple medical needs that must be addressed concurrently with MH interventions (Steel et al., 2009). Medical providers must be mindful of the possible history of torture in their patients and explore interventions that are trauma-sensitive because some practices can be triggering. For example, even a minor surgical treatment of torture survivors can become a highly retraumatizing experience (Schippert et al., 2023).

Torture survivors often sustain physical injuries and need medical attention. They may have been beaten, raped, sustained traumatic brain injury, and have other medical conditions. Increasingly often perpetrators use electric shock delivered through cables attached to genitalia, as reported by refugees from Iraq, Uganda, and other countries (Cherepanov, personal communication). Survivors can be severely traumatized and suffer from moral injury, especially when, under torture, they may have revealed information or falsely accused friends or family members. They continue blaming themselves even though moral judgment is hardly applicable to such situations.

Punitive psychiatry can also be considered a form of torture when persons who question the administration's policies can be imprisoned in psychiatric facilities where they are needlessly and forcibly administered high doses of antipsychotic medications (van Voren, 2010). The mental and physical impact of such psychiatric punishment can be long-lasting, as has been reported by political prisoners from the former Soviet Union. The fear of being locked up in a psychiatric institution strongly contributed to the reluctance to seek MH services.

Interventions

Psychoeducation can be used to normalize trauma reactions, challenge internalized stigma, and provide information on coping. It suggests sources of strength and resilience and encourages mutual support.

Authoritarian administrations can impose limitations on the choice of interventions. For instance, the administration can view holistic practices like yoga as contradicting the governing ideology (Cherepanov, personal communication). In an environment characterized by distrust, the efficacy of talk-based methods like trauma processing, cognitive-behavioral therapy, or group therapy may be limited. Employing expressive arts, play therapies, and body-oriented approaches reduces the need for personal disclosure, allowing individuals to symbolically convey thoughts and emotions that might be difficult or unsafe to articulate literally.

Refugees from countries affected by complex political contexts (CPCs) carry social assumptions about themselves and others, shaped by societal trauma and a fundamental distrust of the administration, health authorities, and other community members. This distrust has the potential to complicate the process of integration with the host community.

To maintain the appearance of neutrality, MH providers should refrain from engaging in civic activities or demonstrations, as it can heighten risks for them and the people they serve.

What to Avoid

When working in the countries affected by CPCs, MH providers must be very sensitive to personal boundaries of their clients.

Avoid:

Excessive questioning. Instead, focus on treatment-relevant information to prevent the feeling of an interrogation.

Asking for trust. Trust may or may not naturally develop in building rapport. Many MH interventions do not require any trust.

Attempting to "uncover the truth." Honesty is not a prerequisite for receiving mental health support.

Insisting on disclosures. Allow clients to volunteer important information rather than pushing for it.

Taking sides in protests and discussing politics. Instead, help clients explore their decisions' pros and cons and the associated risks.

Creating electronic records or clients' lists. Minimize the use of electronic medical record-keeping and protect against potential hacking and monitoring.

Ethics in Political Emergencies: Mr. Jones Dilemma. Exercises

Working in complex political contexts (CPCs) can come with significant ethical challenges, underscoring the awareness of the limits and priorities of one's role. These challenges can be so complex that sometimes providers decide against setting the MH program in the region with CPC.

One dilemma that is characteristic to CPCs is the advocacy versus "do no harm" dilemma. Advocacy is integral to GMH work but balancing it with the "do no harm" principle can be daunting. I call it the Mr. Jones dilemma based on the film with the same title.

The film *Mr. Jones* (Holland, 2019) provides an example of this dilemma through the story of journalist Gareth Jones, who faces the moral choice of revealing evidence of the Holodomor, the famine created by the Soviet Union administration that resulted in mass starvation in Ukraine. Jones, who witnessed mass mortality, chose to go public about it, putting the lives of the hostages held by Stalin's regime at risk.

Similarly, providers may feel compelled to publicly uphold their beliefs against human rights violations and bear witness in order to mobilize international support. It is crucial to recognize that in CPCs, any involvement in public activities can pose a threat to the safety of beneficiaries, potentially hindering future assistance. Seeking supervision can help balance the beneficiaries' needs with the GMH mission and identify reasonable measures to minimize such risks.

Exercises. Ethical Dilemmas in CPCs

Instructions

Pick a scenario and place it in the context of any country with an authoritarian regime to add more concrete details.

Examine different decisions and their intended and unintended potential consequences.

Discuss different options for how such situations should be handled by a GMH provider to minimize harm.

1. Watch Mr. Jones film and explore different solutions from the role of Mr. Jones. Imagine that you must make a decision about publically disclosing the witnessed atrocities. There is a risk that hostages who are fellow British engineers will be killed.

   What will you do?
2. A non-disclosure agreement

   A licensed MH professional Peter who works for a local NGO is contacted by a nearby prison and asked to assess the mental status of a political detainee, John Doe, who has been exhibiting signs of severe depression and anxiety and may be suicidal. Peter agrees to conduct the assessment.

   Upon arrival, Peter is presented with a nondisclosure agreement by the facility's administration. The agreement states that any information obtained during the assessment, including John Doe's mental status and any discussions held during the evaluation, must remain confidential and cannot be disclosed to anyone outside of the facility.

   Although Peter wants to help for humanitarian reasons, signing the agreement may limit the MH provider's ability to share important findings and advocate for the release of a political prisoner. However, if he doesn't sign the agreement, he may be denied access entirely and will not be able to help.

3. Offering a sensitive information
   Samantha, a passionate political activist from a country where human rights violations are rampant, has gathered substantial evidence of atrocities committed by the government against its citizens. Determined to bring international attention to these violations, Samantha reached out to Dr. E., a MH expert with extensive experience in working with trauma survivors and human rights advocacy. Dr. E. is currently in the country where they assist people with serious mental illnesses.

   In her initial correspondence, Samantha explains the gravity of the situation in her country and expresses the urgent need to share crucial information with someone who can help amplify the voices of the oppressed. She requests a confidential meeting with Dr. E. to disclose the details of the human rights violations, emphasizing the importance of discretion due to the potential risks for herself and others involved in exposing the truth.

   Upon receiving Samantha's message, Dr. E. acknowledges the sensitivity and seriousness of the matter. Understanding the potential implications for Samantha and the delicate nature of the information she wishes to disclose, Dr. M. must decide whether to meet with her.
4. Facing imminent persecution
   Ahmed, a vocal LGBT advocate in a country known for its oppressive regime and anti-LGBT sentiments, finds himself increasingly targeted and at risk of persecution due to his gender identity and outspoken criticism of the government's persecution of other gay people. Fearing for his safety and well-being, Ahmed decides to seek asylum in a neighboring country where he hopes to find refuge and protection from the authorities.

   Recognizing the daily risks and psychological toll of living under constant threat and the trauma of potential persecution, Ahmed reaches out to Mr. M, a MH provider known for their expertise in working with individuals facing persecution and forced migration. In his initial communication, Ahmed explains his situation and expresses his urgent need for assistance in fleeing the country and accessing MH support to cope with the challenges ahead. Mr. M. acknowledges the unique challenges Ahmed is facing.
5. Participation in a political rally
   Ms. V. who is a GMH who provides psychosocial support to victims of gender-based violence and is committed to advocating for human rights, receives an invitation to participate in a political rally organized by a local grassroots movement protesting widespread human rights violations in their community. Ms. V. recognizes the rally as an opportunity to raise awareness, show solidarity, and demand justice for those affected, but has reservations about joining this event because she is a foreigner.

You may find suggested protocols for navigating such dilemmas further on in Chap. 10.

Takeaways

- Complex political emergencies are humanitarian crises caused by government dysfunction and associated with political violence and human rights violations.
- Examples are failed or fragile states, armed conflicts, genocides, and complex political contexts (CPCs) or tyranny.
- Ineffective governance makes regions prone to poverty, crimes, and surging gang violence, which leads to disasters and famines.
- Most political emergencies are precipitated by the administration's inability or unwillingness to protect their citizens; they may involve political violence and other forms of deliberate victimization.
- In instances of political violence, people are targeted based on their collective identity, which distinguishes such situations from regions with high rates of random violent crimes.
- The experience of political violence has inter- and transgenerational toxicity and alters social cognitions, beliefs, and attitudes.
- People in political emergencies are exposed to severe trauma and victimization but may be afraid to seek assistance.
- Political emergencies increase risks for MH services providers and beneficiaries and produce unique ethical dilemmas.

References

Asare-Doku, W., Donnir, G. M., Ayuurebobi Ae-Ngibise, K., Peprah, J., Awuviry-Newton, K., & Acquah, F. (2021). Psychiatric disorders among the military in West Africa: A systematic narrative review. *Behavioral Sciences (Basel, Switzerland), 11*(10), 138. https://doi.org/10.3390/bs11100138

Betancourt, T. S., & Khan, K. T. (2008). The mental health of children affected by armed conflict: Protective processes and pathways to resilience. *International Review of Psychiatry, 20*, 317–328.

Betancourt, T. S., Borisova, I. I., Williams, T. P., Brennan, R. T., Whitfield, T. H., de la Soudiere, M., Williamson, J., & Gilman, S. E. (2010). Sierra Leone's former child soldiers: A follow-up study of psychosocial adjustment and community reintegration. *Child Development, 81*(4), 1077–1095. https://doi.org/10.1111%2Fj.1467-8624.2010.01455.x.

Betancourt, T. S., McBain, R., Newnham, E. A., & Brennan, R. T. (2014). Context matters: Community characteristics and mental health among war-affected youth in Sierra Leone. *Journal of Child Psychology and Psychiatry, and Allied Disciplines, 55*(3), 217–226. https://doi.org/10.1111/jcpp.12131

Bloch, S., & Reddaway, P. (1977). *Russia's political hospitals: The abuse of psychiatry in the Soviet Union*. Victor Gollancz Ltd..

Cherepanov, E. (2020a). *Understanding the transgenerational legacy of totalitarian regimes: Paradoxes of cultural learning*. Routledge. https://doi.org/10.4324/9780429030338

Cherepanov, E. (2020b). Sexual and gender-based violence as warfare. In R. Geffner, V. Vieth, V. Vaughan, A. Rosenbaum, L. Hamberger, & J. White (Eds.), *Handbook of interpersonal violence across the lifespan*. Springer. https://doi.org/10.1007/978-3-319-62122-7_106-1

Cherepanov, E. (2021). Mental health interventions in complex political contexts. *Intervention, 19*(2), 149–154. https://doi.org/10.4103/intv.intv_14_21

Cherepanov, E. (2023a). Refugees from countries with complex political contexts: Politically informed approach to health and mental health services. *Frontiers in Public Health, 11*, 1323259. https://doi.org/10.3389/fpubh.2023.1323259

Cherepanov, E. (2023b, January 27). *Abuse of political power is the abuse of people. When are we going to re-elect dictators? Transforming society*. Bristol University Press and Policy Press. https://www.transformingsociety.co.uk/2023/01/27/abuse-of-political-power-is-the-abuse-of-people-when-are-we-going-to-stop-re-electing-dictators/

Conteh-Morgan, E. (2003). *Collective political violence: An introduction to the theories and cases of violent conflicts*. Routledge.

Crowe, D. M. (2013). *War crimes, genocide, and justice: A global history*. Palgrave Macmillan. ISBN 978-0-230-62224-1.

Danieli, Y. (2007). Multicultural, multigenerational perspectives in the understanding and assessment of trauma. In J. P. Wilson & C. Tang (Eds.), *The cross-cultural assessment of psychological trauma and PTSD* (pp. 65–89). Springer.

Doja, A. (2019). Politics of mass rapes in ethnic conflict: A morphodynamics of raw madness and cooked evil. *Crime, Law and Social Change*. SpringerLink, *71*(5), 541–580. https://doi.org/10.1007/s10611-018-9800-0. ISSN 1573-0751. S2CID 149928004.

Duffield, M. (1994). *Complex political emergencies: An exploratory report for UNICEF with reference to Angola and Bosnia*. School of Public Policy, University of Birmingham.

European People's Party. (2015). *Resolution adopted by the EPP Political Assembly (3rd March 2015) on "The Armenian Genocide and European Values."* European People's Party (EPP). https://web.archive.org/web/20150402104820/http://www.epp.eu/sites/default/files/content/documents/Final_Res_Armenian%20Genocide.pdf

Fiedler, C., Mroß, K., & Grävingholt, J. (2016). *Building peace after war: The knowns and unknowns of external support to post-conflict societies* [Briefing Paper 11/2016]. German Development Institute/Deutsches Institut für Entwicklungspolitik. https://www.idos-research.de/en/briefing-paper/article/building-peace-after-war-the-knowns-and-unknowns-of-external-support-to-post-conflict-societies/

García-Moreno, C., & van Ommeren, M. (2012). *Mental health and psychosocial support for conflict-related sexual violence: Principles and interventions*. World Health Organization. https://www.unicef.org/protection/files/Summary_EN_.pdf

Hassan, G., Ventevogel, P., Jefee-Bahloul, H., Barkil-Oteo, A., & Kirmayer, L. J. (2016). Mental health and psychosocial wellbeing of Syrians affected by armed conflict. *Epidemiology and Psychiatric Sciences, 25*(2), 129–141. https://doi.org/10.1017/s2045796016000044

Henigsberg, N. (2010). Mental health consequences in men exposed to sexual abuse during the war in Croatia and Bosnia. *Journal of Interpersonal Violence, 25*(2), 191–203. https://doi.org/10.1177/0886260509334288

Holland, A. (Director). (2019). *Mr. Jones*. Performance by James Norton, Vanessa Kirby, and Peter Sarsgaard. Production Kinorob, Film Produkcja, and Jones Boy Film.

Kohrt, B. A., Jordans, M. J. D., Tol, W. A., Speckman, R. A., Maharjan, S. M., Worhtman, C. M., & Komproe, I. H. (2008). Comparison of mental health between former child soldiers and children never conscripted by armed groups in Nepal. *JAMA, 300*(6), 691–702. https://doi.org/10.1001/jama.300.6.691

Leaning, J., Bartels, S., & Mowafi, H. (2009). Sexual violence during war and forced migration. In S. F. Martin & J. Tirman (Eds.), *Women, migration, and conflict: Breaking a deadly cycle* (pp. 173–199). Springer.

Lončar, M., Medved, V., Jovanović, N., & Hotujac, L. (2006). Psychological consequences of rape on women in 1991–1995 war in Croatia and Bosnia and Herzegovina. *Croatian Medical Journal, 47*(1), 67–75.

Niederland, W. G. (1968). Clinical observations on the "survivor syndrome". *International Journal of Psycho-Analysis, 49*(2), 313–315.

OHCHR. (2008). *Rape: Weapon of war*. United Nations Human Rights, Office of the High Commissioner. http://www.ohchr.org/en/newsevents/pages/rapeweaponwar.aspx

Pearn, J. (2003). Children and war. *Journal of Paediatrics and Child Health, 39*, 166–172.

Poloni-Staudinger, L., & Ortbals, C. D. (2012). Rape as a weapon of war and genocide. In *Terrorism and violent conflict: Women's agency, leadership, and responses*. Springer.

Russell, D. (2014). *Children of rape*. SURF Survivors Fund. https://survivors-fund.org.uk/awareness-raising/children-of-rape/

Schippert, A. C., Dahl-Michelsen, T., Grov, E. K., Sparboe-Nilsen, B., Silvola, J., & Bjørnnes, A. K. (2023). Torture survivors' experiences of receiving surgical treatment indicating re-traumatization. *PLoS One, 18*(10), e0287994. https://doi.org/10.1371/2Fjournal.pone.0287994

Sharlach, L. (2000). Rape as genocide: Bangladesh, the former Yugoslavia, and Rwanda. *New Political Science, 22*(1), 89–102. https://doi.org/10.1080/713687893

Singh, A. R., & Singh, A. N. (2010). The mental health consequences of being a child soldier—An international perspective. *International Psychiatry, 7*(3), 55–57. https://www.ncbi.nlm.nih.gov/pmc/articles/PMC6734971/

Slim, H. (1997). Doing the right thing: Relief agencies, moral dilemmas and moral responsibility in political emergencies and war. *Disasters, 21*, 244–257.

Sondorp, E., & Zwi, A. B. (2002). Complex political emergencies. *BMJ, 324*(7333), 310–311. https://doi.org/10.1136/2Fbmj.324.7333.310

Steel, Z., Chey, T., Silove, D., Marnane, C., Bryant, R. A., & van Ommeren, M. (2009). Association of torture and other potentially traumatic events with mental health outcomes among populations exposed to mass conflict and displacement: A systematic review and meta-analysis. *JAMA, 302*(5), 537–549. https://doi.org/10.1001/jama.2009.1132

Tol, W. A., Stavrou, V., Greene, M. C., Mergenthaler, C., van Ommeren, M., & García-Moreno, C. (2013). Sexual and gender-based violence in areas of armed conflict: A systematic review of mental health and psychosocial support interventions. *Conflict and Health, 7*, 16. https://doi.org/10.1186/1752-1505-7-16

Tyagi, J. (2012). Weak states. In G. Ritzer (Ed.), *Wiley-Blackwell encyclopedia of globalization*. https://doi.org/10.1002/9780470670590.wbeog809

UN. (2016). Together for the protection of children affected by armed conflict. *Office of the special representative of the secretary-general for children and armed conflict*. https://childrenandarmedconflict.un.org/

UN. (2019). Genocide background. *Office on genocide prevention and the responsibility to protect*. http://www.un.org/en/genocideprevention/genocide.shtml

UNICEF. (1997). *Cape Town Principles and best practice on the prevention of recruitment of children into the armed forces and demobilization and social reintegration of child soldiers in Africa*. https://openasia.org/en/wp-content/uploads/2013/06/Cape-Town-Principles.pdf

van Voren, R. (2010). Political abuse of psychiatry—An historical overview. *Schizophrenia Bulletin, 36*(1), 33–35. https://doi.org/10.1093/schbul/sbp119

Weitsman, P. (2007). Children born of war and the politics of identity. In C. Carpenter (Ed.), Born of war: Protecting children of sexual violence survivors in conflict zones (pp. 110–127). Kumarian Press.

Wessells, M. G. (2017). Children and armed conflict: Interventions for supporting war affected children. *Peace and Conflict Journal of Peace Psychology, 23*(1), 4–13.

Chapter 9
Acquiring Professional and Humanitarian Competencies

Professionalization of Global Mental Health

This chapter zooms in on the knowledge and skills that MH professionals require to adequately respond in their professional capacity to humanitarian crises. It is in addition to their core professional expertise.

GMH is a growing and versatile field that has only recently solidified as a professional specialization. This move coincided with the call for professionalization of humanitarian action and came with the need to increase professional competencies of all humanitarian actors. In GMH, professionalization means humanitarian responsibility, incorporating best practices and quality assurance so the work is conducted effectively, ethically, and accountably.

GMH providers who come from different professional and cultural backgrounds and perspectives, training, experience, and expertise, first and foremost must be skilled in their primary professions. To ensure consistency in interventions, they also need to have a working knowledge and understanding of humanitarian relief systems and must be on the same page with other humanitarian actors when implementing interdisciplinary and intersectional collaborations.

Many large humanitarian organizations have already responded to the call for professionalization of aid by spelling out the expected specialized professional competencies as a part of hiring eligibility or including them in pre-deployment orientation and training. However, a standardized training module is yet to be developed.

Wessells (2009) has recognized that training MH professionals in a specific approach is not enough. He acknowledges that a universal approach may not be effective in all circumstances and calls for ensuring contextually and cultural appropriateness of interventions. According to Wessells, such skills can be achieved by

E. Cherepanov, *Humanitarian Competencies for Global Mental Health Professionals*, Contemporary Humanitarian Action and Emergency Management,
https://doi.org/10.1007/978-3-031-74268-2_9

using critical self-reflection, greater specificity in ethical guidance, a stronger evidence base for intervention, and improved methods of preparing GMH professionals.

Here we focus on outlining the core competencies and the path to acquiring them which is an important step toward developing professional standards and standardized training with possible credentialing. Although the degree of relevance of every professional and humanitarian skill may vary based on the settings, the development of professional standards and competencies is envisioned as a blueprint for the further professionalization of GMH.

Professionalization in GMH Work

GMH work exposes providers to situations with a high degree of uncertainty, intractable ethical dilemmas, and moral ambiguities that will make providers question much of what they have learned before in their professional training. Navigating such situations requires specialized expertise in addition to professional training.

> *Professionalization* in the multidisciplinary GMH action refers to obtaining professional knowledge and skills for providing MH and psychosocial care in a humanitarian context.

The challenges associated with GMH work clearly demonstrate that being a qualified MH professional is essential but not sufficient—this work must also incorporate specialized knowledge and skills that allow for an effective, contextually appropriate, and ethical response to humanitarian emergencies.

There are several reasons that elevate the importance of professionalism in GMH. The extreme vulnerability of service recipients sets high expectations for professional self-determination integrity. The lack of ready-to-go solutions makes GMH providers responsible for every decision they make because the price for a mistake in the humanitarian space can be exceptionally high. Professional competencies prepare GMH providers to make informed and ethical decisions in challenging circumstances when there may be little access to peer support, professional supervision, or consultations.

Navigating humanitarian situations without clear directions or established protocols places a greater emphasis on professional self-determination backed by competencies and training. Such situations call for flexibility and contextuality in the approaches, which involves understanding not only the letter but the spirit of interventions and making an informed determination about the best way to reach the goal.

A GMH Professional

Working in a humanitarian setting requires specialized expertise and skills. A GMH professional is a specialist who:

- Has professional integrity and is committed to humanitarian values, ethics, and the code of conduct.
- Has both core and specialized professional knowledge and skills.
- Is aware of the limitations of their expertise and makes efforts to receive additional training when needed.
- Has knowledge of the MH reactions to extreme stress and trauma and the dynamics of natural healing.
- Has trauma, cultural, and geopolitical awareness and understands the MH impact of political impact and the effects of climate change.
- Understands the multidisciplinary systems of humanitarian relief.
- Is able to make ethically sound and responsible decisions under duress.
- Is able to be a team player and also to work independently.
- Acts in a respectful, non-discriminative, and non-prejudiced manner to service recipients, other providers, and peers.
- Maintains professional boundaries and protects the dignity and privacy of the people served and the image of the profession.
- Is open-minded and culturally and globally curious, able to think critically and outside of the box.
- Has excellent interpersonal skills and good self-awareness and understands the importance of self-care.

Building Blocks of Professionalization: Developing a Training Curriculum

Four Groups of Professional Competencies

First and foremost are the *core professional competencies* that include generic professional knowledge and skills. These are the only competencies that are specific to the MH profession. It basically means that a GMH professional must be a good specialist in their primary profession, whether it is MH, psychiatry, social work, or others.

The second group comprises specialized *context-specific competencies* shared with other multidisciplinary MH and psychosocial support professionals and paraprofessionals. They all need to have the knowledge, understanding, and skills to work in a humanitarian environment when responding to a crisis.

The third group refers to *humanitarian competencies*. These are awareness of geopolitical situations and influences, global mindedness, understanding of humanitarian systems and professional cultures, and making responsible decisions in morally ambiguous situations.

There are also *personal competencies*, including empathy, compassion, self-awareness of one's biases, managing fantasies, and self-care. These are further examined in Chap. 13.

The core competencies are acquired during the standardized professional training; others are developed during elective training and supervised practice, and some are derived from the experience.

A professional license in good standing is often required in GMH professionals who provide direct mental health services internationally. A license issued by a professional regulatory body serves several important purposes. Having a license ensures standards of practice and protects people from malpractice. It indicates that the MH professional has demonstrated the knowledge, skill, and abilities to perform the services.

But this licensure requirement comes with a catch. According to MH regulations, a license is valid only within the area of its issuance, whether it is a country, state, or province. This limitation does not pertain to crisis response. Defining the primary scope of GMH service as a response to international humanitarian emergencies allows us to overcome such limitations imposed by the licensing requirements (American Red Cross, 2015).

In an emergency or disaster situation professional services can be conducted outside of the licensing area, nationally or internationally. In such situations, the deploying agency assumes responsibility for the integrity and quality of this work.

There is a difference between a professional license, which attests to the core professional competencies, and certification, which designates additional expertise or specialization. Currently, I am not aware of any certification options for GMH specialization and this is something to consider in the future.

There have been previous attempts to build a standardized curriculum for GMH specialization. For example, the American Psychiatric Association recommended covering topics for GMH expertise for psychiatrists (https://www.psychiatry.org/psychiatrists/international/global-mental-health). These areas of knowledge are:

- Cultural competency
- Service delivery in limited resource settings
- Epidemiology in cultural and geographic contexts
- Health systems and policies
- Access to treatment and care
- Ethics and human rights
- Structural determinants of mental health
- Education and supervision of nonspecialists

In another example, the Task Force on International Trauma Training has developed guidelines and a core curriculum for training on trauma in an international setting (Weine et al., 2002). The task force describes the challenges encountered in post-conflict environments. It has proposed the principles and essential components of training curricula that cluster around four dimensions: values, core curricular elements, monitoring, and evaluation.

Training Objectives for GMH Specialization

As a result of education and training, GMH providers should be able to

- Successfully apply their knowledge and skills in a multitude of global settings.
- Provide trauma-informed and culturally competent MH support, crisis interventions, and MH counseling in a humanitarian context.
- Conduct clinical assessments, evaluate risks, and know when to request a higher level of care.
- Have a toolbox of quick and easy-to-use interventions and recommendations for managing trauma symptoms and relieving stress or improving sleep.
- Understand the systemic impact of trauma.
- Understand the array of roles GMH providers can play in humanitarian emergencies.
- Conduct humanitarian research and needs assessments, understand the importance of data and outcome measures and
- Comply with ethical, professional, and regulatory guidelines.

Professional Competencies for GMH Professionals

The core courses can vary across countries and clinical MH specialties (psychologists, psychiatrists, psychiatric nurses, counselors, and clinical social workers). Still, there is the required coursework that makes providers eligible for a professional license or a diploma in countries where there is no established license to practice.

In the suggested systematic training curriculum below the titles of the courses are approximate and refer to the topics covered.

Core Courses in MH Counseling
The required core courses are the cornerstone of training for any MH professional, regardless of specialization.

Although training standards, course requirements, and even the exact names for the graduate programs in MH counseling or proxy disciplines can slightly vary, a typical curriculum consists of core courses, elective courses, and supervised practice in the form of practicum and internship.

Graduate programs in MH counseling typically offer the following required courses with some variation (sorted alphabetically):

Abnormal psychology
Accessing community resources and navigating the healthcare system
Basic counseling skills
Community mental health
Ethics and professional issues for MH practitioners
Human development across the lifespan
Mental health assessments
Personality and counseling theory
Perspectives in cross-cultural counseling
Theory and practice of individual and group mental health counseling

Elective Courses: Concentration

In addition to the required core courses, every program offers electives that allow trainees to diversify and advance knowledge and skills in specific areas of concentration.

Examples of such electives are courses suitable for GMH practice on posttraumatic stress reactions and interventions, public health and community MH, holistic approaches, and treating substance use disorders. Other subjects of study that can be helpful in fieldwork are research design and integrated approaches.

Field Experience: Practice

The third training block (or a mandatory supervised internship) offers opportunities to apply the learned theory and skills to real-life situations.

MH professionals interested in GMH specialization can choose placements where they will gain experience in working in low-resource settings, assisting people from low-income backgrounds, multicultural populations, people whose lives have been affected by severe trauma, or those affected by substance misuse. Should trainees decide to further their career in GMH, serving refugees allows them to gain a global perspective and master essential skills such as working with interpreters.

Interdisciplinary and Context-Specific Competencies

This cluster of competencies refers to the knowledge and skills essential for working in the multicultural and multidisciplinary context of a humanitarian emergency or contributing to system development in low- to middle-income countries (LMICs).

The competencies that GMH shares with other specializations can be acquired through postgraduate or continuing education or specialized professional training. These competencies aim at

- Increasing understanding of the systemic impact of complex emergencies and systems of trauma.
- Mastering multicultural skills and the ability to work in multidisciplinary and multicultural teams.
- Preparing for providing crisis intervention and disaster MH response and using approaches such as Psychological First Aid (PFA).
- Preparing GMH providers for training local providers, including healthcare providers, teachers, and humanitarians, in emergency response and PFA.

Psychological First Aid (PFA) and Trauma Training

Training in PFA and trauma-specific interventions can be a part of trauma concentration, or it can be taken as a standalone course or certification program. Many MH organizations have been offering certificates in trauma training, but only a few of them focus on global work.

GMH professionals are expected to be able to train in PFA and trauma-informed care health, and human services providers and community workers. Trauma and PFA training have demonstrated their relevance in the humanitarian space across sectors and include skills for emotional support, coping, and recovery that are important for anyone who aids in humanitarian emergencies, regardless of the discipline or training level. The training consists of basic trauma-informed skills that can be used in various situations. They are:

Empathy involves expressing a sincere desire to understand the person's experience, engaging in discussions about what matters most to them, and accurately acknowledging their emotions, even those not explicitly stated.

Genuineness entails being approachable and unguarded, favoring spontaneity over strict formality.

Respect calls for showing genuine regard for survivors, emphasizing respect in all interactions.

Active listening skills include asking clarifying questions, accurately rephrasing survivors' statements, verbally reflecting their emotions precisely, and using open-ended questions to help them clarify any mixed or inconsistent messages they may convey.

Problem-solving skills revolve around focusing on priorities, breaking down large tasks into smaller steps, and other approaches that allow a person to feel less overwhelmed and more in control.

Learning about *stress response and strategies for managing stress* helps to understand stress reactions, identify coping skills, and promote alternative perspectives and new behaviors (Young et al., 1998).

This training educates about *burnout, its prevention,* and the *importance of self-care.*

Context-Specific Competencies

The humanitarian context of work places certain expectations on GMH service providers. Multidisciplinary relief providers must be aware of how potentially volatile and not always predictable or safe environments impact services and learn to manage the imposed limitations.

The first group of contextual competencies includes basic knowledge about the theory and practice of disaster MH interventions.

The second group refers to the ability to adjust interventions to the specifics of the humanitarian crisis, being resourceful and flexible, thinking outside the box, and seeking alternative solutions when problem-solving and reaching goals.

In addition to trauma-informed and multicultural competencies, multidisciplinary relief, providers need to know the region's or group's history and current geopolitical processes and understand how the global and political contexts affect social cognitions, beliefs, and attitudes toward service providers (Cherepanov, 2021).

Finally, regardless of the profession, anyone in an emergency setting must have the basic skills to provide abbreviated risk assessment and increase safety for everyone involved—themselves, the aid recipients, and other service providers—and take reasonable steps to defuse and deescalate dangerous situations. These skills can include working with strong emotions, crisis intervention, and crowd control basics.

Humanitarian Competencies

Humanitarian competencies are shared between multidisciplinary and multisectoral humanitarian actors and are important for ensuring consistency and coordination of relief efforts with relief workers. Understanding the humanitarian systems helps professionals to find their place in humanitarian action, be effective, and strengthen collaborative efforts. The humanitarian competencies are as follows:

- Understanding humanitarian systems and professional cultures.
- Understanding the structure of the humanitarian sector and its operations.

- Understanding the mandates of the key humanitarian organizations and their specializations and priorities.
- Having a working knowledge of humanitarian principles, humanitarian accountability, international and humanitarian law, and the international legislation related to refugee law.
- Compliance with humanitarian ethics and the Humanitarian Code of Conduct.
- Understanding the safety imperative and following security protocols.
- At all times being respectful to fellow humanitarians, local providers, and consumers.

Takeaways

- Like other humanitarian actors, GMH providers responded to the call for professionalizing humanitarian action and have been working on defining their professional competencies.
- The importance of specialized expertise in GMH stems from the unique challenges that providers encounter in humanitarian emergencies and the extreme vulnerability of the service recipients.
- There are four building blocks of competencies that ensure the high standards of GMH practice. The personal competencies are discussed in Chap. 13. The rest are professional, interdisciplinary, and humanitarian competencies.
- The core professional competencies are part of the standardized professional training of MH professionals.
- GMH professionals share interdisciplinary competencies with other health and human services providers and relief workers. Interdisciplinary competencies include understanding the humanitarian context, the basics of disaster response and management, trauma-informed care, and skills for psychological first aid.
- The humanitarian competencies for all humanitarian actors include knowledge of the humanitarian relief systems and their culture, as well as humanitarian ethics.

References

American Red Cross. (2015). *Eligibility criteria for disaster mental health credentials*. Disaster Mental Health Introduction Handout. Retrieved from the Red Cross Disaster Mental Health Standards and Procedures https://www.counseling.org/docs/default-source/default-document-library/2015-disastermentalhealth_eligibility-05_2015.pdf?sfvrsn=0

Cherepanov, E. (2021). Mental health interventions in complex political contexts. *Intervention, 19*(2), 149–154. https://doi.org/10.4103/intv.intv_14_21

Weine, S., Danieli, Y., Silove, D., Van Ommeren, M., Fairbank, J. A., Saul, J., & Task Force on International Trauma Training of the International Society for Traumatic Stress Studies. (2002). Guidelines for international training in mental health and psychosocial interventions for trauma exposed populations in clinical and community settings. *Psychiatry, 65*(2), 156–164. https://doi.org/10.1521/psyc.65.2.156.19936

Wessells, M. G. (2009). Do no harm: Toward contextually appropriate psychosocial support in international emergencies. *American Psychologist, 64*(8), 842. https://doi.org/10.1037/0003-066X.64.8.842

Young, B. H., Ford, J. D., Ruzek, J. I., Friedman, M., & Gusman, F. D. (1998). *Disaster mental health services: A guidebook for clinicians and administrators*. National Center for Post-Traumatic Stress Disorder. http://www.ncptsd.va.gov/publications/disaster/index.html

Chapter 10
Ethics and Morale in Global Mental Health Work

Ethics for Global Mental Health

This chapter explains the importance of specialized ethics for GMH professionals and focuses on gray areas in ethical reasoning. Humanitarian situations routinely expose providers to psychologically difficult and sometimes traumatizing decision-making process in morally ambiguous and complex situations where there may not be any good solutions. Making informed, context-appropriate, and ethical decisions in such situations requires special competencies.

Obviously, unethical practices such as having sex with the clients or exploiting them in any other way are strictly prohibited under the professional code of ethics and discussing them falls outside of this chapter's agenda. These actions can undermine the profession's image, the spirit of humanitarianism and compromise the safety and well-being of both providers and the people they serve.

Ethics is an integral part of any professional decision-making process. The role of ethics increases exponentially in morally ambiguous situations, which are common in humanitarian emergencies. The profound vulnerability of people affected by humanitarian emergencies emphasizes the need for adherence to the most rigorous ethical standards.

Ethics for GMH is the system of professional and multidisciplinary values, competencies, and standards that provide ethical guidance and a frame of reference for reasoning the complex professional and moral dilemmas that arise within humanitarian contexts. (Cherepanov, 2018)

The GMH ethics establish the precedence of humanitarian principles and the directionality for the decision-making. Ethical guidelines offer grounding in

E. Cherepanov, *Humanitarian Competencies for Global Mental Health Professionals*, Contemporary Humanitarian Action and Emergency Management,
https://doi.org/10.1007/978-3-031-74268-2_10

situations marked by moral ambiguity. They flag unethical practices and emphasize the importance of self-awareness and self-care.

Sometimes, there is confusion about the difference between professional and GMH ethics, the code of conduct, and morals. While there is some overlap, they each reflect different facets of GMH work. Traditionally, humanitarian ethics refer to humanistic values and the decision-making process; the humanitarian code of conduct governs behavior; and morality is a prerogative of the norms imposed by society and personal convictions. They may coincide or, in some instances, conflict. The code of conduct guides the ethical side of humanitarian behavior. As previously described in Chap. 6, it was developed in response to highly publicized and consequential grossly unethical incidents such as sexual misconduct by aid workers.

The GMH ethics are reflective of the multidisciplinary and multicultural environment where all service providers must base their work. McGowan et al. (2020) have noted that although some ethical guidance is available to frontline humanitarians, much work must be done to assist them with day-to-day decisions. The GMH professionals committed to their professional ethics needed additional guidance in navigating the unique and intractable dilemmas that the humanitarian context provides in abundance.

Establishing the Need for GMH Ethics

In a humanitarian context, ethics take the central stage because an ethical indiscretion can have an extremely high price. Any problematic conduct or poorly made decisions can compromise not only the work in progress but also the image of the humanitarian organization and, as a result, jeopardize the aid delivery and safety of other aid workers.

Negotiating humanitarian dilemmas involves reconciling values coming from multicultural and multidisciplinary environments. This reconciliation must be done in a way that does not lower professional ethical standards.

Professional code of ethics articulates fundamental values; sets ideals, standards, and moral principles established by the profession; and is adopted by members as guidance for professional conduct and decision-making. They are so deeply engrained into the professional identity of MH specialists that it is almost impossible to imagine that the universal applicability of these key components may be questioned. However, in GMH work it can be the case. There are numerous justifications for the need for specialized ethics in GMH work, rooted in the unique mission and its dual identity as an MH and humanitarian specialty.

The professional code of ethics always remains at the core of any decision-making for any healthcare professional. Yet ethicists agree that disaster relief, trauma, and refugee work expose the limitations of normative and prescriptive professional standards and ethical protocols (Jenson, 1997).

Another difference is that professional ethics often address only health-related matters in a professional setting. In contrast, GMH works with people who have experienced humanitarian catastrophes that engulf their entire lives (De Torrenté & Stobbaerts, 2008).

Professional codes do not always offer clear solutions when different professional or humanitarian values collide or the ethical imperatives contradict the individual's benefits. An example can be navigating a situation where collective, individual, or social interests conflict. Such instances can occur when attempting to place the suspected individuals in quarantine against their will to prevent the spread of a deadly communicable disease such as Ebola. Another example can be the conflict between the Do No Harm principle and Advocacy when any exposure can be harmful to an individual. Still, the same exposure can benefit the whole group by bringing the world's attention to their desperate situation.

Values Over Protocols?

There are different ways to think about ethical guidance. The guidance can be linked to norms, outcomes, or values (i.e., virtues).

Virtue ethics prioritizes values over rigid norms or protocols to inform decisions (Behnke, 2005). The virtue-based approach to ethics has been finding growing support among both GMH and humanitarian professions because prioritizing humanitarian values helps to stay true to the professional mission.

Health and MH professional codes of ethics and humanitarian ethics are all built upon universal humanistic values and norms. The ethics for GMH establishes the contextual relevance of these norms: what is considered ethical in one context may not be so in a totally different situation (see Ethically Questionable Practices). GMH ethics provide a broader point of reference and directionality for negotiating intractable ethical dilemmas or conflicting professional or moral values (Cherepanov, 2018, 2019). We cannot decide which professional value is more professional or which moral value is more moral and must reference the humanitarian context of GMH work where these conflicts of values start making sense.

For example, the decision about whose benefits, an individual or a population, are more important can be decided only within the context of an epidemic. Another moral dilemma can occur when the provider must choose who to service and, consequently, who to reject, which may be morally difficult in an emergency. The case studies at the end of the chapter will give more similar dilemmas and suggest protocols for their negotiations.

Ethics in Humanitarian Research

The significance of data for planning humanitarian interventions and the dependence and vulnerability of the research subjects exponentially elevate the role of ethical standards in humanitarian research.

> *Humanitarian research* is the systematic collection and analysis of data that applies to qualitative or ethnographic information or quantitative data. It can include needs assessments, determination of the prevalence of certain MH conditions, program monitoring and outcomes evaluation, and data collected for advocacy purposes. (IASC, 2007)

Humanitarian research plays an increasingly important role in humanitarian theory and practice and is used for assessing needs, evaluating the impact of humanitarian assistance, planning, coordinating relief efforts, and allocating aid. GMH research can be a powerful tool for social justice and advancing the scientific body of knowledge. It contributes to a deeper understanding of human resilience and reactions to severe stress and trauma, facilitating progress in psychosocial interventions, pioneering solutions, and advocacy (Lambert, 2015).

The Inter-Agency Standing Committee (IASC) has issued ethical guidelines for conducting mental health and psychosocial research in emergency settings, identifying the main ethical challenges. The guidelines recommended strategies for addressing validity, confidentiality, potential for inflicting emotional distress, informed consent, and the researcher's responsibility. It has been suggested that the participatory research model can mitigate some of these challenges (IASC, 2007; Lambert, 2015).

In the past, questionable research practices have been exposed. Ponterotto and Casas (1991) and Pittaway et al. (2010) have revealed widespread issues such as practices based on coercion and exploitation of participants, negative impacts on the community, and unreliable findings. This is in addition to disrespect to the local culture, disregard for the safety of participants and the future of the community, and failure to address the limitations in data validity—all of this undermines the professional community's trust in the integrity of humanitarian research, and the quality of collected data. In humanitarian emergencies, the use of children as research subjects calls for an additional layer of protection due to children's vulnerability, their dependence on adults, and the possible lack of child protective services (Collins et al., 2011).

The humanitarian situation creates a significant power differential between the researchers and the research subjects. Marshall and Batten (2004) linked the power dynamic between the researcher and the respondents to the inherent privileges of researchers holding power in the form of money, education, and knowledge over the research subjects, which easily can lead to actual or perceived coercive components in the relationship.

The areas that are always most challenging for humanitarian researchers are risks to validity, informed consent, data ownership, and culturally appropriate research protocols.

Cultural Validity: The PAR Approach

Difficulties with translating research instructions and questions to local languages are not limited to the language only. Some concepts may not have a corresponding meaning or existence in other cultures. Failure to account for these incongruences can lead to miscommunications, misunderstandings, and erroneous conclusions. While there have been attempts to establish a "thesaurus" of cultural idioms of distress, the translation may still not be enough to achieve the true equivalence of meaning. The questions or item formulations may carry different connotations for participants from different subcultures or age groups even when responders come from the same country (Bolton, 2001a, b; Lambert, 2015; Wessells, 2009).

To mitigate the risks to cultural validity, Allden et al. (2009) proposed employing the method of participatory action research (PAR).

> Researchers and participants in PAR model work together to define a problem, identify its causes, and negotiate solutions. (Reason & Bradbury, 2008) The most significant advantage of PAR is that it involves the community in developing research questions, assuring culturally appropriate language, instructions, tools, and accountability in how the results can be used for initiating transformative changes. (McTaggart et al., 2017, p. 28)

Informed Consent

Voluntary and informed consent to participate is the cornerstone of any ethical research. Leaning (2001) cautioned against overlooking the power differential between researchers and participants when asking for informed consent for participation. The consent to participate as a research subject must not be linked to potentially coercive practices such as receiving a substantive award like food or currency. If a reward for participation is offered, the participant must be able to withdraw from participation without returning the award.

Any perception of coercion may affect the voluntary components of consent (why a person agrees to participate), the sampling (who will agree to participate), and the integrity of data. In such situations, the participants may feel that they must participate "to please the researchers" or because their or their family's or community's well-being depends on their answers.

Educating adults, children, and parents on the research goals and protocols and letting them know that they can decline participation at any time without any repercussions or having to return any offered reward or incentives needs to be a routine conversation in humanitarian settings.

Informing the participating community leaders about the research goals and how the data will be collected and used can help reduce possible tension and decrease risks for participants.

Data Ownership

The issue of data ownership has become a point of increasing contention in humanitarian research.

It is reasonable to expect GMH researchers to share their findings with the participants or community. Sharing results helps to avoid the perception of exploitation (Darou et al., 1993). The community that understands the potential benefits of research is less likely to feel exploited or taken advantage of and is more likely to engage in future research and cooperation (Cherepanov, 2018).

Confidentiality

Ensuring confidentiality can be challenging when community members closely monitor each other. In politically unstable regions, merely participating in research could jeopardize the safety of individuals. Breaches in confidentiality concerning sensitive matters like histories of sexual assault, political affiliations, religious beliefs, and sexual orientations could place participants and their families at high risk (Beyrer & Kass, 2002; Mackenzie et al., 2007; Pittaway et al., 2010).

In addition, some people who are in abusive relationships may be coerced to disclose their answers, which can by itself be a problem if research deals with a sensitive reality such as surveying the prevalence of intimate partner violence.

Furthermore, even when individual identities are concealed in published data, participants can be blamed for disclosing negative information about their community. Sometimes, gathering indirect or collateral data instead of direct interviews may be a better, less risky option. In case of domestic violence, it can be the number of women seeking medical services for particular injuries.

Either way, serious planning must be done to protect the records and health-related information in case researchers must quickly evacuate.

Potential for Emotional Distress

Some widely used tools for evaluating trauma include questions about adverse experiences (Labott et al., 2013). Recognizing the potential for research participants to experience emotional distress, fear, or anxiety because of participation in research activities, the World Health Organization (WHO, 2012) has provided specific guidance on minimizing psychological risks for research participants. Their advice is that the researchers should proactively anticipate any distress that can occur and be ready to provide remedies, such as training interviewers to provide Psychological First Aid if needed.

Duty to Intervene

Sometimes research subjects, either children or adults, disclose that they are subjected to ongoing abuse, neglect, maltreatment, or trafficking. What is the responsibility of a GMH researcher in such instances?

As mandated reporters, health and MH researchers have an ethical obligation to report suspected abuse, neglect, or maltreatment to the authorities or law enforcement personnel. However, in a humanitarian crisis, following this guideline can become a complicated task. There may be no functioning child protection agencies in the area, the authorities may not prioritize the child's safety, and there is no assurance that family members or the community will not become aware of the accusations and retaliate.

Frequently, children's statements are closely monitored by their parents, or they demand disclosure afterward. This situation also presents a moral dilemma for the GMH workers: How can we advocate for the prevention of child abuse if a child risks punishment for reporting it? And what are the limits of our duty to intervene without causing further harm?

Identifying and addressing concerns about respondent safety must be integral to thorough preplanning. To reduce some of these risks, the World Health Organization (2017) has proposed a guideline emphasizing that researchers, designated authorities, and healthcare providers should advise the child or adolescent and their caregivers about the limits of confidentiality before conducting interviews.

Managing Ethical Challenges

Ethical Review Boards (ERBs) have become a powerful tool for managing ethical challenges in humanitarian research. ERBs ensure the ethicality of the research and provide oversight against unethical practices. In humanitarian research, ERBs aim to protect the dignity, rights, well-being, and welfare of research participants and communities (Schopper et al., 2009). They also serve to raise awareness of specific challenges in humanitarian research.

Humanitarian ERBs have been advocating for accountability and promoting ethically sound research models in humanitarian emergencies. It is important that an ERB's advisors have the humanitarian experience and GMH expertise.

Ethically Questionable Practices: Trauma Tourism, "Playing God," the Savior Complex, and the "Magic Pill of Happiness"

In addition to clearly unethical practices such as exploiting or taking advantage of beneficiaries, a whole host of situations can be considered ethically questionable.

> *Ethically questionable practices* are those regarded as ethical in some circumstances but deemed unethical in others. (Cherepanov, 2018)

Some of the examples below have been previously described in the literature, others came from the providers' and beneficiaries' reports, or were drawn from the author's experience.

Iatrogenic Practices

Even the best of intentions can inflict harm when well-minded GMH providers do not fully recognize the potentially damaging social and cultural impacts of their interventions.

> *Iatrogenic harm* is damage created as a byproduct of an intervention by a service provider or caretaker of any type or from a procedure or technique. (Caplan & Caplan, 2001, p. 22)

Using clinical language and diagnoses to label normal psychological reactions, trying to treat conditions that are not pathological, or persuading people in distress that they are ill and need treatment can undermine traditional or individual ways of healing and coping. Already Illich (1974) expressed concerns that the pathologizing approach in GMH is not only not helpful but can harm community members who used to rely on traditional and cultural practices. This way, external interventions can negate the need in self-regulation and self-determination. Illich believed that medicalizing routine life can have grave consequences for people's resilience and their capacity to withstand and cope with future adversities.

"Playing God": Going Outside of the Professional Role

Exposure to strong emotions induces a powerful countertransference, making it difficult for GMH professionals to maintain impartiality and professional boundaries. Going outside of the professional role can violate boundaries and cause confusion in the people served. Examples can be establishing personal relationships with beneficiaries, such as friendship or romantic relationships, inviting them to travel to the provider's homeland, offering to send invitation to visit or financial support, or giving them gifts or money. Such practices are considered unethical even when done out of the best intentions because of their potential to violate professional boundaries or create negative dynamics in the community.

In the field, expatriate GMH providers must be aware that just by virtue of their citizenship or the color of their skin, they can be holders of tremendous privilege and power in making important decisions about the people they serve, and humanitarian agencies take their opinions and recommendations very seriously. Such actions that are socially accepted and even encouraged in high-resource settings can become exponentially problematic in humanitarian space.

It is not uncommon for MH providers in Western countries to advocate for their clients so they may have faster access to resources or receive services sometimes ahead of others. Such advocacy in low-resource regions can become a source of tensions and be perceived by other people as unfair leading to accusations of special relationships, bribery, or suspicion of ulterior motives.

"White Savior Complex"

Due to the power differential, a person in a role of power and privilege (e.g., service provider) must consider not only what is said or done but also how those with less power can perceive it.

The "white savior" trope refers to a Westerner portrayed as a messiah-like figure who rescues non-white people from disastrous circumstances. Humanitarians have long been raising awareness of this pervasive stereotype in charitable advertisements. According to Ogard (in Gharib, 2017), selfies taken with African children, for instance, can perpetuate the notion that only Western aid and charity have the power to "save the world." Ogard contends that these children are depicted as helpless and pitiful, while the volunteer is portrayed as the superhero coming to rescue them from their misery. To spotlight these stereotypes, a "Barbie Savior" Instagram parody account has been established where the public contributes staged photos depicting a Barbie doll traveling to a low-income country doing photo-ops at disaster sites and in hospitals.

More recently, the public media revived this "white savior" trope concerning the activities of MrBeast, an American YouTube personality, after he provided shoes for children in Africa (https://twitter.com/velvetsuite/status/1633955270551388162).

"Trauma Tourism"

Disaster or trauma tourism doesn't have a formal definition, yet the connotation refers to unqualified and unorganized volunteers who travel to a disaster zone driven by voyeuristic curiosity and rationalized by the intent to help. Although appearing innocent, at a humanitarian disaster site, this form of unsolicited prosocial behavior may have multiple negative implications, including hindering the relief work and increasing risks for everyone involved.

Trauma tourism, which involves visiting destinations where human tragedy is the main attraction, has been known to the tourist industry for a long time (Clark, 2009). It has been recognized in setting stops for tourists to take pictures with backgrounds of Nagasaki, the Phnom Penh "killing fields" (the Choeung Ek monument), and the different concentration camps in Poland.

Human and professional curiosity is an understandable motivation to travel. However, those visiting impoverished or disaster-stricken regions must be aware of the potentially destructive nature of such unorganized travel and whether they are acting like "white saviors " instead of truly trying to help.

Trauma tourism is fueled by some MH professionals' belief that their professional training makes them qualified to respond to any humanitarian emergencies without additional training. They seize the opportunity to "learn on the go" and gain more experience without much understanding of what such work entails.

Using humanitarian emergencies to satisfy professional curiosity or as a training opportunity without having humanitarian competencies is irresponsible and unethical.

Some genuinely believe that a crisis provides an occasion to test and promote their newly developed interventions or gather data for their research. These practices are highly concerning from an ethical standpoint.

In humanitarian emergencies, only organized relief activities are acceptable. When contemplating a trip, one should ask themselves what will benefit people more: this trip or donating the funds allocated for travel to basic needs instead.

Humanitarian aid workers on the ground are often ambivalent about the influx of "fly in and fly out" "foreign experts." These MH providers are often ill-equipped to provide relief work, lacking specialized professional skills and humanitarian competencies. They have a limited grasp of local culture and don't have direct connections with local agencies or the affected population.

Probably the most revealing and well-documented incident of trauma tourism occurred in the wake of the Haiti earthquake (Redfield, 2013), which Van Hoving et al. (2010) called a medical shame. Haiti's crisis created a virtual form of trauma tourism.

In post-earthquake Haiti, Kaussen (2015) noticed the emergence of a new form of trauma tourism: *virtual disaster tourism*, when providers reach out to survivors via Zoom.

Virtual disaster tourism has reached enormous proportions during the response to the war in Ukraine, when a great number of foreign MH professionals have been reaching out to offer direct care, and provide training and supervision to local MH providers. Despite good intentions, this work has mainly remained unorganized, and providers did not coordinate with each other, the relief agencies on the ground, or with Ukrainian MH providers. These interventions have created a lot of fragmentation, confusion, inconsistency, redundancy, and conflicting recommendations—and even competition for access to clients between national and international MH providers.

A more subtle forms of trauma tourism include MH professionals who travel "to show their compassion and help sufferers" by "bringing self-help books on psychology," teaching them "how to dance or do crafts to get in touch with higher power" or teach "evidence-based practices" that may or may not be relevant to the situation, or just "making people happy" by giving them opportunity to share their stories with the MH professional who later publishes it without consent.

"A Magic Pill of Happiness"

In a humanitarian crisis, where desperate people can be susceptible to seeking quick fixes, psychotropic drugs are often perceived as an ideal solution.

In addition to the hypothesis that our knowledge about the use of medications may be socially constructed (Cohen, 2009; Safer, 2002; Schulman et al., 2002), any use of drugs during a humanitarian crisis comes with a long list of cautionary considerations.

Psychotropic medications in complex emergencies may be indicated in a limited number of situations when a person is unable to cope and function, presents a risk to self or others, or is psychiatrically fragile.

However, there have been mounting concerns about the use of psychotropic medications in humanitarian emergencies without proper oversight, managing side effects, and education of the patients. An artificially improved mood can quickly turn problematic when it takes away the focus and energy needed for survival. Reliance on the "magic pill of happiness" can potentially interrupt the natural healing process and create psychological dependence.

This example below illustrates the pervasive and possible irreversible shift in attitudes in the community once mood-altering medicine was introduced.

When working in an African remote village, I was approached by a man who asked for a pill "to be happier." He went on to explain that previous doctors were very kind and used to give him "feel good" medication all the time. That medication made him not think as much about his life. Reportedly, everyone could get these pills if they felt sad. I examined this person, assessed the risks, and offered several tools he can use to manage his mood and anxiety. He seemed disappointed: "Why cannot you be like others and just give me the pill. It is so much faster and easier."

In addition, the lack of education can lead to the situation in which people who can share the medications with the family members: "It helped me, and I want my family to feel better!".

Other ethical questions revolve around the discontinuation of psychotropic medications. Unstable and highly unpredictable environments make it difficult to ensure a consistent supply.

As far as using psychiatric medications for people with serious MH conditions and psychotic symptoms is concerned, prescribers face a difficult cost-benefit dilemma.

Unless the treatment occurs in established facilities with human resources and steady supply of medications, there may not be guarantees that the patients will be able to continue with treatment regimen raising concerns about medication discontinuation. There may be difficulties in monitoring adherence to treatment along with managing the side effects.

Understandably, there are different opinions about prescribing medications in such situations. Some believe that even if a person gets to feel better for a short time, it is worth the try. Others feel that the risks outweigh the benefits.

Ultimately, one thing is clear—medicine cannot replace people's own work on the recovery and overcoming but they can interrupt the natural self-healing process.

Moral Convictions

Moral values remain an essential component of directing humanitarian activities because they connect practice to humanistic ideals.

Where ethics mainly refer to professional activities; morals reflect deeply seeded personal convictions, most of which are shared across humankind and imprinted in cultural and religious tenets.

In humanitarian work, GMH providers encounter various ethical and moral dilemmas, some of which can shake their personal beliefs to the core. Relying on only moral values for guidance can interfere with professional ethics and complicate navigating professional dilemmas. Furthermore, engaging morality in professional decision-making when each solution comes at a moral cost can have a paralyzing effect.

When humanitarian situations create intractable dilemmas, professionalism and not morale becomes a primary source for decision-making.

Morals and beliefs are at the core of human identity and make us who we are. However, when these moral principles become overly rigid, a person can start valuing their beliefs over the well-being of other people. The awareness of moral relativity helps avoid moralistic stances and self-righteousness. This said, it remains important that a person retains unaverred convictions that cannot be compromised to serve as a moral compass. There should not be too many of such moral beliefs because most of them are relative and can apply differently in different circumstances.

In many situations with serious and unsolvable moral dilemmas, professional thinking precedes moral convictions. Let's examine such humanitarian thinking using an example of the "*tale of a pill.*"

This hypothetical situation is used in humanitarian training to demonstrate humanitarian reasoning and illustrate the contextual relativity of moral beliefs when they interplay with professional priorities.

Imagine: During an epidemic in a war-ravaged country, there is only one pill available that can save one person, a child or a parent from a deadly tropical disease. Due to security risks, the delivery of more medicine anytime soon is improbable. A provider should decide who will get it.

Although our moral inclination would be to save the child, it will be a waste of valuable resources that can help someone else because the child is entirely dependent on the parent and will not survive without them.

Another way to look at morals is through the lens of social consciousness, and the perception of morality of the humanitarian organization's choices has high visibility (Slim, 2015). Great importance is given to not only what humanitarian organizations do but also to the moral image they project (Otegui, 2022).

This image is very important and determines the public attitude toward humanitarian agency. Often, these organizations are so large and powerful that their decisions about aid provision carry significant social and political implications that affect the lives of hundreds of thousands of people. For the benefit of beneficiaries, it is always important that the image of humanitarian agencies project kindness, concern for alleviating injustice, and compassion for the plight of people. They also must be inclusive and promote the active role of beneficiaries in their recovery.

Two Protocols for Negotiating Ethical and Moral Dilemmas

Intractable Dilemmas

Many ethical dilemmas in GMH work are driven by the conflict of underlying paradigms.

- This can be *a conflict between professional values* when one is forced to choose to attend to the immediate versus long-term needs of survivors.
- It can be *a conflict between professional ethics and humanitarian guidelines* when a provider must abandon the people served because of security protocols.
- Or it can be *a conflict between ethics and moral convictions* when providers must make decisions that go against their moral beliefs like it happens when having to choose who is prioritized to receive life-saving services.

When looking closer, such dilemmas present a false opposition. They cannot be resolved by deciding which professional or moral value is more important. The precedence of humanitarian priorities, accountability, and situational relevance provides a strategic path for negotiating competing agendas (Cherepanov, 2019).

A conflict between individual or collective benefits will be navigated differently if the provider functions in a public health or a clinical capacity. The conflicting priorities about the importance of healthcare or educational program will also be different based on whether it is a humanitarian emergency or a development situation.

Two suggested protocols can be helpful when navigating intractable dilemmas. They are "Weighing and Negotiating" and "Multidimensional Reasoning." The following exercise provides an opportunity to practice applying these protocols in dilemmas loosely based on real-life situations.

Protocols for Navigating Intractable Dilemmas

1. Weighing and Negotiating
   The values-based ethical approach in GMH allows us to move from excessively focusing on unpredictable outcomes to the decision-making process. When any

solution carries the potential to bring harm, weighing and negotiating the following four aspects of a specific situation can help to determine the least harmful option. This template can be used in various situations, narrowing down the available choices and guiding the decision-making.

- *Accountability* is the determination of whom a GMH provider is primarily accountable to in their current role: the people served, society, or their moral convictions. It guides humanitarians to use their resources wisely and assume responsibility for their immediate and long-term actions.
- *Contextual awareness* is choosing the most beneficial and least harmful actions in the specific context.
- *Professional self-awareness* recognizes one's professional expertise and its limits, roles, cognitive biases, and fantasies, which can influence decision-making.
- *Personal self-awareness* recognizes one's moral convictions, where some are firm and may not be negotiable under any circumstances. In contrast, others can depend on the context.

2. Multidimensional Reasoning
   The second protocol is rooted in the idea that there can be different dimensions or levels of reasoning through which the issue is approached. They are associated with different perspectives that can be approached on an emotional, moral, rational, or professional level. The awareness of choices or perspectives comes with the realization that there may be other levels of reasoning.

   For example, one can realize that they have considered a decision on an emotional level. At the same time, they can be aware that professional-level reasoning would yield different results: It is their choice and, consequently, their responsibility to choose a perspective for judgment. In a professional role, they may prioritize a professional decision-making level and be aware of other factors influencing their reasoning, such as countertransference or fantasies (see Chap. 13). This approach emphasizes the importance of self-awareness (understanding the reasons for the decisions), contextuality in navigating dilemmas, and deciding on the most appropriate choice based on the situation and the role of the decision-maker (Cherepanov, 2019).

Let us use a hypothetical situation to illustrate how this multidimensional reasoning works.

> A GMH provider has been aiding victims of violence or traumatized children. After the security situation worsens, the provider is ordered to evacuate.

Here is an array of possible decisions:

1. Refusal to evacuate: "I cannot abandon the people I was helping and who have come to trust me. I must share their hardship. It is the moral thing to do."
2. Following the instructions, evacuate with the deploying organization, can mean abandoning the people served and leaving them in danger.

Discussion

This is a difficult decision to make. A provider who decides *emotionally* may be compelled to stay behind and share the hardship and risks with people they serviced because our moral convictions tell us to do so. As professionals, we are taught not to abandon the people we serve.

However, *rational* decision-making brings up a tricky question: Will staying behind meaningfully help the victims? Or will it just put the provider at greater risk? In the meantime, in the bad-case scenario of food, medication, or shelter shortages, having an extra person could mean fewer resources and less survivors' protection.

The *professional lens* introduces yet another perspective where the decision is made based on the biggest benefits for the professional role, which includes weighing the consequences. If a provider who decides to stay behind for moral reasons becomes captured or abducted and a ransom is demanded, the money and rescue resources spent to release them could have been put to better use, like aiding more people. Such a situation will likely create a media frenzy and take attention away from the victims. The volunteer's decision not to follow the agency's recommendation undermines the discipline in the field, which is crucial for everyone's well-being and safety. As a result, it can reduce the agency's capacity to respond to an emergency effectively.

Regardless of the decision, self-awareness will help decide which level of decision-making is most appropriate to the situation and the role of the GMH provider. Either way, any of these decisions can be emotionally draining, and seeking psychological support after the fact may be a good idea.

Practice and Exercises

Practice 1

Objective

To practice using the Multidimensional Reasoning protocol to negotiate ethical and moral dilemmas.

Instructions

1. Read the dilemmas and identify the underlying conflict of values.
2. Explore the decisions that can be made on the emotional, moral, cognitive, and professional levels.
3. Compare outcomes and brainstorm each decision's possible professional and personal implications.

REMEMBER: There may not be any clear answers or good solution

Case scenarios for discussion

1. A dying child

   A terminally ill 3-year-old boy has several days to live if he receives oxygen. The medical team informs the child's family that he has only a few days left to live. Boy's parents, who arrived from far away to the clinic, are understandably devastated by the prognosis and expressed their desire to take him home so he can spend his remaining time surrounded by the whole family's love and familiar environment. There boys can receive last rites by local minister. The family believes it's crucial for boy's peace and comfort in his final moments.

   However, the treating medical provider expresses concerns about transporting boy home. They fear that the stress and logistics involved in moving him could potentially worsen his condition or even lead to his death during transport. They argue that keeping child in the hospital ensures access to immediate medical care and support, which may be crucial given his fragile state.

   This situation presents a challenging ethical and moral dilemma. On one hand, there's the emotional and psychological well-being of the boy and his family, who desire to be together in a familiar environment during his final days. On the other hand, there's the medical team's duty to prioritize a child's physical health and safety, which they believe may be compromised by transporting him home.

   Additional question:

   What can be the role of MH provider in this situation?
   How can MH providers moderate decision-making?
   What if this child is suspected to have an infectious disease?

2. An angry mob

   In a refugee camp where a medical compound provides care for severely ill individuals, a chaotic scene unfolds as a crowd of enraged people pursues a man, accusing him of war crimes committed during a conflict in the region. The man, realizing the danger he's in, flees toward the medical compound in a desperate attempt to seek refuge.

   As he reaches the gates of the medical compound, he pleads with the medical staff for shelter and protection. He explains that he's being wrongly accused and fears for his life if caught by the angry mob outside.

   The medical staff, torn between their duty to provide care for their patients and their lack of authority in matters of justice, find themselves facing a moral dilemma. They understand the gravity of the accusations against the man and the potential repercussions of harboring someone accused of such serious crimes. However, they also recognize their obligation to provide medical assistance and uphold the principles of humanitarian aid, which include providing refuge to those in need regardless of their background or circumstances.

Additional questions:

What can be the role of MH provider during and after the incident?
What if it was a female victim of domestic violence who is pursued by the angry husband and asks to hide on the compound?

3. Food distribution
   In a remote area where resources are scarce, a children-focused organization arrives to deliver a limited supply of food intended to feed the children. However, upon their arrival, they are met by community leaders who insist that the food should be distributed to older adults first, arguing that they are the most valuable members of the community due to their wisdom and value for the community.
   The organization is faced with a challenging dilemma: while their primary mission is to address the nutritional needs of children, they also understand the cultural significance placed on respecting and prioritizing older members of the community. Moreover, they realize that challenging the authority of community leaders could potentially strain their relationship with the community and hinder future efforts to provide aid.
   Recognizing the delicate nature of the situation, the organization seeks guidance from a MH provider who is well-regarded within the community. This MH worker holds trust among community members, making them a potential mediator in this conflict.
4. Security concerns
   A GMH provider assists survivors of an armed conflict. Violence breaks out and threatens the aid workers. The site director orders an evacuation.

   A. The survivors fear the worsening security situation and beg you not to leave them in danger.
   B. A car is sent to evacuate the expatriates. The car is full. At the last moment, a local pastor's family with little children asks you to let them in.

Practice 2

Below is an actual case that received much attention in the media.

- Renee Bach is an American missionary with no medical training who founded the charity Serving His Children in Uganda.
- She opened a malnourishment center and treated 940 malnourished children; 105 children died, and some of their families sued her.
- The controversy and ongoing legal battles have been the subject of multiple journalistic investigations in various mediums.
- An independent investigation by the Uganda Medical and Dental Practitioners Council in response to a 2019 suit against Bach found no evidence that Bach represented herself as a doctor or had provided medical care.

- Bach is now the subject of a controversial HBO documentary, *Savior Complex*, directed by investigative journalist and documentarian Jackie Jesko.
- Bach's time in Uganda has made her the face of white saviorism in Africa.

Read the description of the case below and answer the following questions:

What was the intent of founding this charity in Uganda?
Were there any ethical violations?
What could be unintended consequences?
What should have been done differently?

For more information, see the full story in Haasch's (2023) report entitled Renee Bach believes God called her to save Ugandan children. Their families say she killed them (https://www.insider.com/where-is-renee-bach-savior-complex-uganda-hbo-2023-9).

Takeaways

- Humanitarian work produces unique ethical dilemmas and moral conflicts.
- Most of them are not true dilemmas but reflect the conflict of underlying paradigms.
- In GMH work and humanitarian research, ethical guidance comes from both the professional code of ethics and humanitarian ethics.
- The obvious and blatant disregard for professional ethics, such as taking advantage of people served, clearly violates a professional code of ethics and the humanitarian code of conduct and will not be tolerated in the humanitarian space.
- The gray areas in ethical guidance are called ethically questionable practices. They are practices that can be deemed ethical in some situations but appear unethical in a humanitarian emergency, e.g., trauma tourism.
- When negotiating moral conundrums with no good solutions, professional guidance can take precedence over moral convictions.
- "Weighing and Negotiating" and "Multidimensional Reasoning" are two protocols that can be used to navigate complex dilemmas in GMH.

References

Allden, K., Jones, L., Weissbecker, I., Wessells, M., Bolton, P., Betancourt, T. S., & Sumathipala, A. (2009). Mental health and psychosocial support in crisis and conflict: Report of the Mental Health Working Group. *Prehospital and Disaster Medicine, 24*(S2), s217–s227. https://doi.org/10.1017/S1049023X00021622

Behnke, S. (2005). On being an ethical psychologist. *Monitor on Psychology, 36*(7), 114.

Beyrer, C., & Kass, N. E. (2002). Human rights, politics, and reviews of research ethics. *Lancet, 360*(9328), 246–251. https://doi.org/10.1016/S0140-6736(02)09465-5

Bolton, P. (2001a). Cross-cultural validity and reliability testing of a standard psychiatric assessment instrument without a gold standard. *Journal of Nervous and Mental Disease, 189*(4), 238–242.

Bolton, P. (2001b). Local perceptions of the mental health effects of the Rwandan genocide. *Journal of Nervous and Mental Disease, 189*(4), 243–248.

Caplan, G., & Caplan, R. (2001). *Helping the helpers not to harm: Latrogenic damage and community mental health.* Routledge.

Cherepanov, E. (2018). *Ethics for global mental health: From good intentions to humanitarian accountability.* Routledge. https://doi.org/10.4324/9781351175746

Cherepanov, E. (2019). Ethical dilemmas in global mental health. *BJPsych International, 16*(4), 81–83. https://doi.org/10.1192/bji.2019.10

Clark, L. B. (2009). Coming to terms with trauma tourism. *Performance Paradigm, 5*, 162–184.

Cohen, D. (2009). Needed: Critical thinking about psychiatric medications. In M. St-Onge & S. Dumont (Eds.), *Social work and global mental health.* Routledge.

Collins, P. Y., Patel, V., Joestl, S. S., March, D., Insel, T. R., Daar, A. S., Bordin, I. A., Costello, E. J., Durkin, M., Fairburn, C., Glass, R. I., Hall, W., Huang, Y., Hyman, S. E., Jamison, K., Kaaya, S., Kapur, S., Kleinman, A., Ogunniyi, A., et al. (2011). Grand challenges in global mental health. *Nature, 475*, 27–30. https://doi.org/10.1038/475027a

Darou, W., Kurtness, J., & Hum, A. (1993). An investigation of the impact of psychological research on a native population. *Professional Psychology: Research and Practice, 24*, 325–329.

De Torrenté, N., & Stobbaerts, E. (2008). *MSF and accountability: From global buzzwords to specific solutions.* Humanitarian Practice Network. http://odihpn.org/magazine/msf-and-accountability-from-global-buzzwords-to-specificsolutions/

Gharib, M. (2017, November 26). Volunteering abroad? Read this before you post that selfie. *Goats and Soda, NPR.* https://www.npr.org/sections/goatsandsoda/2017/11/26/565694874/volunteering-abroad-read-this-before-you-post-that-selfie

Haasch, P. (2023, September 29) *Renee Bach believes God called her to save Ugandan children.* Their families say she killed them. Business Insider. Retrieved from https://www.businessinsider.com/where-is-renee-bach-savior-complex-uganda-hbo-2023-9

IASC. (2007). *Guidelines on mental health and psychosocial support in emergency settings.* Interagency Standing Committee.

Illich, I. (1974). *Medical nemesis: The expropriation of health.* Calder & Boyars.

Jenson, E. (Ed.). (1997). *Disaster management ethics, disaster management training programme* (1st ed.). Department of Humanitarian Affairs of the General Secretariat of the United Nations for the Disaster Management Training Programme (DMTP). http://reliefweb.int/sites/reliefweb.int/files/resources/2561747D821E0256C1256DB70053E6D4-undp-ethics-1997.pdf

Kaussen, V. (2015). Zooming in: Virtual disaster tourism in post-earthquake Haiti. *Sir Arthur Lewis Institute of Social and Economic Studies, 64*(3/4), 33–77.

Labott, S. M., Johnson, T. P., Fendrich, M., & Feeny, N. C. (2013). Emotional risks to respondents in survey research: Some empirical evidence. *Journal of Empirical Research on Human Research Ethics, 8*(4), 53–66. https://doi.org/10.1525/jer.2013.8.4.53

Lambert, J. (2015, January 27). *Ethical considerations for research with victims of political violence and human rights violations.* StressPoints. https://www.istss.org/education-research/traumatic-stresspoints/2015-january/ethical-considerations-for-research-with-victims-o.aspx

Leaning, J. (2001). Ethics of research in refugee populations. *Lancet, 357*(9266), 1432–1433. https://doi.org/10.1016/S0140-6736(00)04572-4

Mackenzie, C., McDowell, C., & Pittaway, E. (2007). Beyond 'do no harm': The challenge of constructing ethical relationships in refugee research. *Journal of Refugee Studies, 20*(2), 299–319. https://doi.org/10.1093/jrs/fem008

Marshall, A. & Batten, S. (2004). Researching across cultures: Issues of ethics and power. *Forum: Qualitative Social Research, 5*(3), article 39. https://doi.org/10.17169/fqs-5.3.572

McGowan, C. R., Baxter, L., DuBois, M., Sheather, J., Khondaker, R., Cummings, R., & Watkins, K. (2020). Preparing humanitarians to address ethical problems. *Conflict and Health, 14*, 72. https://doi.org/10.1186/s13031-020-00319-4

McTaggart, R., Nixon, R., & Kemmis, S. (2017). Critical participatory action research. In L. L. Rowell (Ed.), *Palgrave international handbook of action research* (pp. 21–35). Springer.

Otegui, D. F. (2022). *Symbolic approach to humanitarian action: It takes one to know one*. Springer International Publishing.

Pittaway, E., Bartolomei, L., & Hugman, R. (2010). "Stop stealing our stories": The ethics of research with vulnerable groups. *Journal of Human Rights Practice, 2*(2), 229–251. https://doi.org/10.1093/jhuman/huq004

Ponterotto, J. G., & Casas, J. M. (1991). *Handbook of ethnic/racial minority counseling research.* Charles C. Thomas.

Reason, P., & Bradbury, H. (Eds.). (2008). *The Sage handbook of action research: Participative inquiry and practice*. Sage.

Redfield, P. (2013). *Life in crisis: The ethical journey of doctors without borders*. University of California Press.

Safer, D. J. (2002). Design and reporting modifications in industry-sponsored comparative psychopharmacology trials. *Journal of Nervous and Mental Diseases, 190*, 583–592.

Schopper, D., Upshur, R., Matthys, F., Singh, J. A., Bandewar, S. S., Ahmad, A., & van Dongen, E. (2009). Research ethics review in humanitarian contexts: The experience of the independent ethics review board of Médecins Sans Frontières. *PLoS Medicine, 6*(7), e1000115. https://doi.org/10.1371/journal.pmed.1000115

Schulman, K. A., Seils, D. M., Tirnbie, J. W., Sugarman, J., Dame, L. A., Weinfurt, K. P., Mark, D. B., & Califf, R. M. (2002). A national survey of provisions in clinical-trial agreements between medical schools and industry sponsors. *New England Journal of Medicine, 347*(17), 1335–1341. https://doi.org/10.1056/nejmsa020349

Slim, H. (2015). *Humanitarian ethics: A guide to the morality of aid in war and disaster*. Oxford University Press.

Van Hoving, D. J., Wallis, L. A., Docrat, F., & De Vries, S. (2010). Haiti disaster tourism—A medical shame. *Prehospital and Disaster Medicine, 25*(3), 201–202. https://doi.org/10.1017/s1049023x00008001.

Wessells, M. G. (2009). Do no harm: Toward contextually appropriate psychosocial support in international emergencies. *American Psychologist, 64*(8), 842. https://doi.org/10.1037/0003-066X.64.8.842

World Health Organization (WHO). (2012). *Assessing mental health and psychosocial needs and resources: Toolkit for humanitarian settings*. World Health Organization. SBN: 9789241548533.

World Health Organization (WHO). (2017). *Responding to children and adolescents who have been sexually abused.* https://www.who.int/publications/i/item/9789241550147

Chapter 11
Joining Humanitarian Sector. Finding Deployment Opportunities

Becoming a Humanitarian Volunteer

Humanitarian action frequently relies on volunteers to provide direct care and assist people in need in other ways. Making informed choices about the path forward involves understanding the humanitarian employment opportunities, knowing the advantages and disadvantages of working locally or internationally, choosing an agency, and finding one's role in the multidisciplinary and cross-sectorial relief response.

> *A volunteer* is one who voluntarily offers their services in any capacity (Oxford English Dictionary). Volunteers participate in many aspects of humanitarian work. Some volunteers respond to humanitarian emergencies work for free, others receive a stipend or are paid by foundations or grants, and some choose to invest their funds in exchange for the opportunity to help others.

When one begins to ponder putting their humanistic ideals into practice and joining humanitarian action, many practical questions arise: Can I do it? Do I have what it takes? What is the process? How can I prepare? Where do I start?

There are multiple avenues for MH professionals to get involved in a professional capacity with aiding people affected by humanitarian crises. Numerous employment and volunteering opportunities are available for those interested in fieldwork, assisting refugees at their places of resettlement, joining an established NGO, or launching their own projects.

E. Cherepanov, *Humanitarian Competencies for Global Mental Health Professionals*, Contemporary Humanitarian Action and Emergency Management, https://doi.org/10.1007/978-3-031-74268-2_11

Why Work in the Humanitarian Sector?

Working in a humanitarian context offers invaluable professional and personal experience. The global perspective enriches our understanding of human reactions to extreme stress and our appreciation of the miracle of human survivorship, diversity, and resilience in coping with the most dire circumstances. It allows MH professionals to learn about different ways of life and people's cultures worldwide. But, most of all, it can lead to professional and personal discoveries about the importance of their role in bettering the world.

Humanitarian work is not easy, but it can be incredibly rewarding. It expands our knowledge about the world and our role in shaping the global future and can become a life-changing experience. GMH providers who respond to humanitarian emergencies often feel that they can make a real difference in the lives of others.

> Humanitarian work experience provides an empowering sense of purpose, reminds them of their personal and professional mission, and offers a better understanding of the value of humanity. Later, many report nostalgia for "this sense of clarity about my personal and professional purpose". (Cherepanov, personal communications)

This humanitarian experience is in stark contrast with routine professional life, where health providers sometimes are left feeling that they are just a small part of a heavily regulated healthcare apparatus in which most decisions are made for them.

In a Humanitarian Setting, GMH Volunteers Can Pursue a Variety of Activities

While many MH providers imagine the GMH field as an opportunity to provide direct care to populations affected by wars or famines, GMH practice is much broader and involves many other activities.

In a humanitarian space, most aid providers are called volunteers unless they are professional humanitarians, administrators, or managers.

As volunteers or employees, GMH providers engage in various projects:

- Delivering individual and group MH services and support in a humanitarian emergency.
- Responding to disasters and providing psychological first aid.
- Engaging in advocacy and policymaking.
- Building community resilience and improving the capacity to cope with adversity.
- Conducting needs assessment and humanitarian research.

- Developing community supports and referral systems.
- Facilitating community recovery.
- Promoting child and adolescent mental health and welfare, supporting caregivers, and strengthening child protection.
- Providing MH support to aid workers and preventing burnout.
- Offering supervision, training, and peer support.
- Advising and administering projects.
- Devising substance misuse, suicide, and violence prevention initiatives, and peacebuilding.
- Providing targeted support for vulnerable groups, such as victims of gender-based violence or children affected by war.

For example, in their research, GMH volunteers can work on identifying the pervasive MH patterns in response to a disaster in order to assess pressing needs. They may evaluate how the community copes, the availability of resources, sources of strength and resilience, and the need for external assistance. Such research opens the opportunity to enhance our understanding of the efficacy of prevention and interventions and to focus on developing innovative responses.

GMH professionals can participate in policy development, identifying priorities, and advocacy. They actively initiate collaborations and engage with other entities to identify, develop, and advance interventions.

Providers engage in prevention and building community resilience. Such an approach encourages community leaders and members to take a broader responsibility for their health, well-being, and the future. The transition from illness-focused interventions to health and recovery-focused preventions is a basis for promoting and managing health and recovery (Cherepanov, 2015).

Who Can Do This Work?

Forming an informed decision about engaging in GMH work is important to making this experience successful and rewarding. This process begins with reviewing one's motivations, professional knowledge and skills, and physical and mental fitness.

Sometimes, MH providers ask themselves: can any person with good intentions and professional expertise engage in GMH work in a humanitarian context?

In addition to professional competencies, certain personal qualities and interpersonal skills shape the GMH experience. Some of these qualities are

- The ability to wait and act fast in a narrow window of opportunity.
- The awareness of one's own professional and personal limitations and needs.
- Global-mindedness and cultural humility.
- Empathy and compassion.
- Good decision-making and problem-solving skills.
- Healthy personal and professional boundaries.

- A high tolerance for unpredictability, ambiguity, and the expression of strong emotions.
- Human and professional curiosity.

Reflecting Upon Motivation

People decide to join humanitarian work for various professional and personal reasons. Some do it out of compassion; others out of personal and professional curiosity, pushing professional boundaries, or learning about human resilience while traveling the world. And sometimes, "It almost feels like we have no choice" (Cherepanov, personal communication).

Ultimately, it seems like the source of motivation doesn't matter as much as one's awareness of their reasons for volunteering. Without this self-awareness, unrecognized motivations can interfere with the decision-making process in ambiguous situations, contribute to the emergence of toxic fantasies (further discussed in Chap. 13), and lead to problematic boundaries and burnout.

> For example, a person who recently lost a child signs for the humanitarian mission "to save other children." In the fieldwork, they kept "recognizing" their child in every other child they tried to help and were grieving those losses as a personal loss. Countertransference complicated this person's bereavement and quickly led to burnout, a subsequent emotional breakdown, and serious health problems. Eventually, this person could not continue the work and left for home. (Cherepanov, personal communication)

National or International Work

The first choice a future humanitarian must make is whether they are more interested in providing GMH assistance locally, nationally, or seeking to travel internationally.

While international work often appears more adventurous and carries a romantic appeal, much can be done locally or nationally by those who may be unable to take a long time away from work or family or have limitations imposed by their health or family obligations.

As a rule, international fieldwork comes with a significant time investment. This work sometimes takes place in remote, hard-to-reach locations, where travel, organizing, and logistics require a lot of time. It is not unusual for agencies to ask volunteers for several months of commitment. However, this time can be much shorter in an emergency or disaster situation, or when providers possess sought-after skills such as unique language capacity.

Even when international travel seems out of reach, there are disaster response agencies like the American Red Cross that deploy MH volunteers locally and nationally to respond to flooding, forest fires, and other natural and manmade disasters that have resulted in massive displacement. Although technically this is not GMH work, it can provide valuable experience and teach skills.

Another way to get involved is to assist underserved and marginalized populations locally, such as servicing undocumented migrants, who face significant barriers to accessing health and MH services as well as other resources.

Employment

Initially, relief interventions were primarily undertaken by only a few organizations. As the scale and complexity of crises have increased, so have the number and variety of humanitarian organizations, creating more employment opportunities (Schweer, 2011). Significant efforts have been made to organize the humanitarian space, consolidate the human resources, and standardize the hiring process to ensure the quality and accountability of the actors.

Currently, the humanitarian landscape consists of numerous large and small humanitarian agencies as well as local and international nongovernmental organizations (NGOs). Some NGOs are funded by the United Nations (UN), the largest intergovernmental organization. Other NGOs secure funding from international donors, faith-based organizations, or through public appeals to aid victims of armed conflict, famines, and natural disasters.

The Berkeley Library (2024) has compiled a list of prominent humanitarian organizations. Most now employ the MH modules and routinely engage MH providers in operations. Many more large and small NGOs involve MH services as part of their social, educational, or resettlement services, health promotion, and work in connecting vulnerable individuals to resources (Global Review, 2013). Here is the list:

Doctors Without Borders mainly comprises doctors and health workers assisting populations in distress and victims of disaster and armed conflict.

International Medical Corps assists those in urgent need, providing first response, healthcare, and health-related emergency services.

Islamic Relief Worldwide is an independent humanitarian and development organization with a presence in over 40 countries across the globe.

The *International Rescue Committee (IRC)* is a humanitarian organization that offers emergency assistance to persons displaced by war, persecution, or natural disaster.

The *International Committee of the Red Cross* helps people affected by conflict and armed violence and promotes laws that protect victims of war.

The *International Federation of the Red Cross and Red Crescent Societies* carries out relief operations to assist victims of disasters, combined with development work.

Oxfam International works to create solutions for poverty using sustainable development programs, public education, campaigns, advocacy, and humanitarian assistance.

Refugees International advocates for lifesaving assistance and protection for displaced people and promotes solutions to displacement crises.

World Vision is a global Christian relief, development, and advocacy organization that works with children, families, and communities to overcome poverty and injustice.

UNICEF, the United Nations International Children's Emergency Fund, is a humanitarian aid organization developed as part of the UN mandate. It primarily provides assistance to children, focusing on their education and protection.

Choosing Deploying Agency

As GMH providers explore employment opportunities in the humanitarian sector (volunteering is considered a form of employment), they first outline for themselves what population or issues they are interested in, what kind of work best fits their expertise, and whether they want to seek deployment opportunities with the agency or launch their own project (which will be discussed in next Chap. 12).

Deploying Organizations

Humanitarian aid agencies organize and manage operational and logistical support to humanitarian aid operations. Although only some of these operations directly relate to MH work, its footprint has grown exponentially.

Deploying organizations are responsible for operations, programming, hiring and supporting volunteers, and organizing travel, accommodations, and the workplace. Often, they prefer hiring people who can contribute to already established projects or those that are planned for the near future. Of course, GMH providers with unique skills and vision can propose a project.

Choosing a humanitarian agency that can fulfill the applicant's interests is an important step that will define their overall GMH experience.

During the hiring process, GMH volunteers must first decide whether they prefer to work with large transnational organizations or smaller international or local NGOs. Large and small agencies operate differently, and working with each has its own advantages and disadvantages.

Larger agencies often operate more like corporations. They have a greater amount of funds at their disposal and can offer better financial and other benefits for the volunteers, like stipends, health insurance, or paid time off. They are also better positioned to manage security and provide psychological debriefings and professional and peer support. On the other hand, they sometimes struggle with less flexibility and inertia in emergency response due to excess bureaucracy and control in operations management. Smaller NGOs, for their part, can offer much more flexibility and independence in the providers' decision-making, but they lack many of the advantages that more prominent NGOs enjoy.

Humanitarian agencies often develop their own organizational culture: They have their way of doing things, and talking to other volunteers will provide a sense of what to expect and how their agency operates.

Other important aspects to examine are whether the agency has had previous experience with humanitarian projects, the overall scope of services they provide, and the populations they serve, the expertise and experience of the leadership, who is on the advisory board, the sources of funding, are how these funds are allocated.

Questions to ask are how much of the donations are spent on administrative overhead, what specialists they usually employ, and whether they have established peer support and collaboratives on the ground.

For example, Doctors without Borders (MSF) report that they spend 83% of funds on programs, 16% on fundraising, and only 1% on management and general administration. (retrieved from https://www.doctorswithoutborders.org/careers/work-field/find-role/clinical-psychologists)

Finally, it is important to inquire about the organization's priorities: their mission, agenda, and the ground values governing their work. How do they support their volunteers? Do they offer health insurance in case of an emergency? How do they monitor security? Do they have a whistleblower policy or structure allowing for confidential feedback and complaints?

When Institutional and Professional Values Collide

To summarize, it is expected that a deploying humanitarian agency

- Has spelled out a mission, their values, and a mandate (the scope of work).
- Has structures responsible for quality assurance, supervision, and peer support.
- Offers health insurance, MH healthcare, and post-deployment peer support.
- Takes security seriously.
- Has anti-discrimination, anti-harassment, and whistleblower policies in place, and has a channel to raise concerns about unethical practices safely and without repercussions.

- Treats national and international staff equally with respect and dignity and does not discriminate.
- Provides transparency about where the funding comes from and how it is spent.

On some occasions, the professionals' understanding of their mission can conflict with the organizational values. For example, organizational and professional beliefs can diverge drastically regarding attitudes toward birth control when supporting rape victims, stances on advocacy, or disagreements about interventions.

These examples illustrate the importance of due diligence in clarifying institutional values and expectations before deployment. MH providers can still work with NGOs whose ground values or religious affiliations they do not fully share. But they should make an informed decision about how much of their convictions they can compromise in exchange for the opportunity to help others.

Eligibility Determination and the Hiring Process

Applicants can start by researching professional employment opportunities directly on the agency's websites and assembling their resume. The hiring process varies greatly from agency to agency; the description here reflects general tendencies and what to expect.

The applicant must be prepared for the rapid deployment or a possible waiting period even after a successful interview because deployment decisions are prioritized based on the best fit for the project depending on the applicant's expertise, language capacity, skills, and availability. To improve suitability for the position, an applicant must refer to the list of expected professional qualifications (see Chap. 9) and can obtain additional training if needed. In addition, there are other criteria to consider.

Holding a professional license in good standing. When hiring to provide direct services, the humanitarian organization can ask for a valid professional license. There is an expectation that being licensed will provide basic assurance of the necessary training and the quality of work.

Mental fitness refers to high-stress tolerance and the ability to put personal problems on hold during the deployment so they don't interfere with the work. Of course, this doesn't include family emergencies.

Physical fitness is the ability to adjust to physically demanding situations with uncomfortable accommodations and the inability to get privacy or enough sleep. In fieldwork, access to healthcare or medications may be limited.

Time commitment. A deployment can be as short as 2 weeks to assist with disaster relief or as long as several months. The latter is more common for MH providers unless someone possesses unique skills. The short-term assignments tend to put more pressure on the receiving agency, which requires more resources to manage the short visit.

Ability to travel. Having a valid travel passport and being eligible for an entry visa would allow a provider to enter the region.

Language capacity is always a great asset that allows providers to establish direct contact with the people they serve. If this is not feasible, working with interpreters can substantially compensate for not speaking local languages.

Hiring eligibility. When applying for a volunteer position, applicants must be prepared to go through a background and credentials check. This is done to ensure quality and for liability purposes.

The Job Interview

The hiring process typically involves checking qualifications, credentials, and references and screening for criminal background.

Contrary to common perception, employment and volunteer opportunities in the humanitarian sector are very competitive. The hiring process can be grueling in large agencies because they value their reputations and hold their applicants to the highest standards. Any poor judgment from the employee's side can cast doubt on the whole agency and its mission, and affect relief operations.

The applicant's resume must accurately describe their qualifications, expertise, and experience. Private practice or office work is important but may not add many points in a competitive environment. Ideally, the applicant will underscore their experience of working in low-income and low-resource environments, assisting marginalized people in the community, and working with interpreters.

The applicants must be prepared to be asked about their availability: how quickly they could deploy should the opportunity arise, how much advance notice they need, and for how long they can work in the field.

Usually, casual professional attire is the best choice for a job interview.

Preparing for Deployment

Preparation for travel must be taken seriously. Many deploying organizations offer pre-deployment briefings and resources for getting ready. This includes a list of necessary vaccinations, a proposed list of personal items, and other things that international humanitarian travelers must be aware of.

Prior to traveling, it is helpful to research the destination country's history, culture, geopolitical, and economic situation, and the most current developments. More information can be found at ReliefWeb (https://reliefweb.int/countries) or other available sources. It is always a good idea to learn about the etiquette of the local culture, dress appropriately, and know a few phrases in the local language.

An excellent resource for international humanitarian travelers is the most recent edition of the Centers for Disease Control's *Yellow Book* (Kivlehan & Kayden,

2023), which provides information about how to prepare for travel, including the most current health travel advisories, vaccine recommendations, and recommendations on what to pack and how to remain safe during the trip. Additional resources on engaging in humanitarian work are

> "Humanitarian Aid Worker: How to Craft a Career Assisting with Global Issues," Maryville University, August 5, 202, shares basic tips for the humanitarian aid career, https://online.maryville.edu/blog/humanitarian-aid-worker-career-guide/.
>
> The International Medical Relief site offers detailed information on how to pack for the mission and how to find volunteer opportunities, https://internationalmedicalrelief.org/resources/mission-preparations/mission-packing-list/.
>
> The CDC (https://wwwnc.cdc.gov/travel/page/humanitarian-aid-workers) proposes a list of suggested items to pack for humanitarian health providers:
>
> - Book for leisure reading or notepad for possible journaling
> - Cash (new or crisp bills can often be exchanged at better rates)
> - Contact lenses, prescription glasses (extra pairs, if applicable)
> - Energy and memory bank for electronic devices
> - Disposable gloves
> - First aid kit
> - Hand sanitizer
> - Headlamp and spare batteries
> - Insect repellent
> - Mosquito net (if traveling to areas where insect-borne diseases are endemic)
> - Laundry detergent
> - Long pants, shirts that cover the shoulders
> - Photocopies of important documents, such as your passport, driving and professional license (and leave copies of these documents at home with a loved one)
> - Personal hygiene supplies
> - Mobile telephone, equipped to work internationally (or preferably unlocked)
> - Money belt
> - Sewing kit
> - Sturdy work boots (particularly in disaster or rudimentary settings)
> - Sunglasses
> - Sunscreen
> - Laptop or tablet
> - Toilet paper

There may be a need to bring medications for personal use for acute and chronic medical conditions, such as upset stomach, pain, diabetes, or asthma. Travelers must be aware that some prescribed medications that are considered legal in the West can be prohibited in other countries and bringing them may result in fines or even arrest.

Professionals often benefit from bringing a reference (e)book with information about treatment recommendations or medication management protocols.

Talking to other volunteers who recently traveled to the same place will provide more first-hand information.

Exercise: Exploring Motivation

The awareness of personal motivation for choosing humanitarian work can help with understanding how it can be used for choosing the area of the involvement and also with managing the emotional over-involvement that can make operations unsafe or lead to violation of professional boundaries.

Goal

To identify the personal and professional sources of motivation for engaging in humanitarian relief.

Instructions

Compile, write down, and discuss in groups three personal and one professional drivers for your interest in the humanitarian cause and joining the movement.

Discussion

How does this motivation affect your choices in work and life?
How will this motivation help you to achieve your goals?
How can this motivation interfere with your goals?
How can this impact be mitigated?

Takeaways

- There are many avenues for MH providers to join the humanitarian action in a professional capacity. The easiest way is to work with humanitarian agencies, which offer a wide variety of opportunities and supports.
- The first step in getting involved in GMH work is creating an inventory of personal and professional interests and skills and obtaining the relevant training, if needed.
- Following steps include exploring choices: opening positions, choosing between national or international work and between large or small agencies, all of which have advantages and disadvantages.
- Researching the deploying agency's mission, values, priorities, expertise, and experience will help one make the right employment decision and reduce misunderstandings and miscommunications during fieldwork.
- Volunteers must prepare for a competitive hiring environment, which often includes checking competencies, verifying professional licenses, and a background check. Language capacity is always an asset.
- The fieldwork can be psychologically and physically demanding, and there are checklists that help to prepare for the deployment.

References

Berkeley Library. (2024). *Non-governmental organizations (NGOs)*. University of California. https://guides.lib.berkeley.edu/c.php?g=496970&p=3626027

Cherepanov, E. (2015). It takes a village: Psychological recovery in complex emergencies. *International Journal of Psychology and Behavioral Sciences, 5*(1), 16–25.

Global Review. (2013). *UNHCR's mental health and psychosocial support for persons of concern*. United Nations High Commissioner for Refugees.

Kivlehan, S., & Kayden, S. (2023). Humanitarian aid workers. In *CDC yellow book 2024*. Centers for Disease Control and Prevention. https://wwwnc.cdc.gov/travel/yellowbook/2024/work-and-other-reasons/humanitarian-aid-workers

Schweer, C. (2011, June 30). *The changing landscape of humanitarian aid*. Center for Security Studies. https://css.ethz.ch/en/services/digital-library/articles/article.html/130108

Chapter 12
Humanitarian Initiatives: Launching a Project

From Acts of Altruism to Humanitarian Work

Launching a humanitarian project requires thorough planning and organization, even when we think we just want to help people in need. However, not every act of volunteering and pro bono work can be qualified as humanitarian work.

> To increase the social impact of an individual's volunteer work and make it a humanitarian Acts of altruism become humanitarian work when they extends beyond aiding one or even several people and into addressing underserved groups' similar needs in a systemic and organized way.

Initiatively, there are typically several steps to follow.

The first is to define a target group of people who struggle with similar issues, assess their needs, and begin raising awareness and advocating for them. Other considerations include securing funding, engaging other like-minded peers, possibly diversifying assistance, identifying other available resources, monitoring the quality of work, and assessing the social and health imprint.

Even when MH professionals are open to providing pro bono services, securing funding is important to sustain their humanitarian efforts. Funds are needed for technology, recordkeeping, renting office space, and reimbursing volunteers' expenses. Funds can come from various sources, such as grants, crowdfunding, or soliciting personal donations.

Other steps involve determining what services will be offered and who is eligible to receive them because it is impossible to help everyone. There must be clear eligibility criteria and criteria for who should be prioritized for free care. Such

E. Cherepanov, *Humanitarian Competencies for Global Mental Health Professionals*, Contemporary Humanitarian Action and Emergency Management,
https://doi.org/10.1007/978-3-031-74268-2_12

determination can be based on people's age, refugee status, health or mental health cognitions, and more.

If other volunteers are joining the project, there should be selection criteria and eligibility determinations to verify their backgrounds and professional competencies.

Let's use an example to illustrate the difference between altruism and humanitarian work.

> An MH professional in private practice has been offering pro bono services to undocumented migrants who have no health insurance and cannot pay. Can this be considered a humanitarian project?

Discussion
Yes and no. Although helping behavior is inspired by humanistic values, it can be qualified as a humanitarian work only when it meets specific criteria: It must be regular, organized, and coordinated. In addition, humanitarian work is population oriented and aims at assisting a group of people with similar needs as opposed to helping an individual.

In our example, an MH provider who realizes that there may be more people with similar needs identifies a group of newly arrived refugees with no access to healthcare because they lack insurance. To address this need, the MH provider can then gather data on how many people may need such services, advocate for their needs, and survey the interest of peers to participate in this project. Inviting other specialists, social and community outreach workers and possibly registering an NGO can help with applying for grants.

Voluntourism, MONGOs, and GINGOs

With a clear understanding that solo, unorganized travel to a disaster zone is never a good idea (to say the least), MH professionals can still initiate a humanitarian project and assist in humanitarian emergencies in an organized manner.

Working with established humanitarian agencies is just one facet of GMH work. Another option is to launch a project that reflects the values and mission of the founders and allows them to use professional resources effectively.

Lately, there has been a growing variety of privately initiated or faith-based humanitarian initiatives and projects where individuals or several like-minded providers seek the best application for their humanitarian interests and passion. In humanitarian lingo, they are called voluntourism, GINGOs, and MONGOs, and they are the emerging trends that Schnabel (2016) has called "do-it-yourself aid." These initiatives present with various ratios of benefits versus concerns, and an awareness of the problematic sides can help to avoid these pitfalls in humanitarian programming.

Voluntourism

The Oxford Languages Dictionary defines *voluntourism* (a portmanteau of the words "volunteerism" and "tourism") as a form of tourism in which travelers participate in voluntary work, typically for charity.

The term describes the emerging trend where volunteering and tourism combine to form a popular international work and travel mode. In this type of travel, participants dedicate their time and energy to assisting others while immersing themselves in a new country and culture.

Voluntourism usually involves short-term initiatives that prioritize the participants' experience over their tangible impact on the communities in need. Voluntourism has faced criticism from humanitarian actors, mainly directed at volunteers who travel abroad primarily to enrich their resumes, bolster their college applications, or fulfill a sense of obligation to "give back" to disadvantaged areas without considering how much (or little!) their work contributes to making a sustained difference (Denny, 2021).

GINGOs

Another option is to join an existing GINGO, which stands for Grassroots International Nongovernmental Organization. They often operate on small budgets, less than USD 250,000 (Davis, 2020).

These groups often are personal initiatives started by Westerners with a college degree but lacking formal training or professional experience in international development (Schnable, 2016). Schnable further highlights that grassroots aid initiatives sometimes originate in a personal and relational context and may not consistently align with or contribute to a humanitarian relief plan.

Examples of GINGO initiatives include adoptive parents who want to start a charity, MH, or training program in their child's native country; MH providers who are first or second generation immigrants who want to give back to their country of origin; and a professor seeking to set up a research or graduate training program. It can be an expert in a particular area who is interested in establishing a program servicing special needs groups or groups of interest, such as supporting children of war, victims of gender-based violence, or persons affected by HIV.

MONGOs

The abbreviation MONGO stands for "My Own NGO" (Polman, 2013). Some professionals choose to visit areas affected by disasters as independent professionals without any organizational affiliations. Acting solely on personal motivation, they are not entirely assimilated into a more structured system. Instead, this self-driven approach leads to the creation of smaller individualized projects (Paul, 2019).

Polman (2013) identified two critical problems with these groups: They often lack specific skills and do not understand how humanitarian systems work. The latter makes it hard to coordinate and integrate their activities into humanitarian responses, which can cause confusion and interfere with ongoing relief operations. Consequently, these practices have been generally considered problematic.

That said, professional initiatives can be beneficial when coordinated and in communication with other humanitarian actors to fill existing service gaps and avoid duplication or interference with existing services.

Planning a Humanitarian Project

When MH professionals choose to develop their own GMH project, they usually have generic professional skills. They may have experience working with refugees or responding to local or national disasters with disaster management agencies such as the American Red Cross. However, they often lack an understanding of the humanitarian relief systems, humanitarian ethics, codes of conduct, and operational guidelines. Without proper planning and execution, such initiatives can create more problems than solutions.

Problematic outcomes include risks for service fragmentation, establishing competing MH modules, and employing ethically questionable practices. The thorough planning of a GMH project can mitigate some of these concerns.

When an MH provider contemplates putting humanitarian ideals into practice, there are several steps to consider before programming begins. Perhaps, after exploring everything the project entails, a provider may want to consider other forms of engagement in humanitarian work: There are many humanitarian needs around the world. One suggestion is to begin by helping refugees locally or nationally, which can become a sort of bridge between national and international work.

Next, I offer the steps to determine the feasibility of their prospective program can help to organize the decision-making and be used as a practical guide for launching a GMH or integrative project.

Exploring Professional and Personal Interests and Readiness

"What population am I interested in and prepared to service?"

When a GMH professional begins thinking about providing humanitarian assistance, they are encouraged to explore their interests and competencies and to narrow down their choices.

Will it be a specific population, age, culture, or region? There are various reasons why a MH professional may want to zoom in on a particular region or population. Sometimes, the interest comes from personal investment (e.g., ancestors came from the same region), professional interests, or expertise. Another part is reviewing personal and professional readiness, competencies, and skills, and getting additional training if needed.

Target Population and Scope of Service

"Who are the people who will be served, what are their needs and what services will be provided?"

The region where the work will take place and the group of potential service recipients must be defined as clearly as possible in terms of the population and their needs. Other factors are an approximate estimate of the serving capacity, available resources, and the criteria for service (in)eligibility.

Providers identify the target populations to determine the focus and scope of services they plan to provide. The project must not be planned to serve "everyone who needs help" or "whoever comes."

The target group and the eligibility must be clearly defined in terms of age, life experiences, MH issues, or needs. Consequently, the scope of the service can be as narrow as assisting persons with a particular condition or experience, or it can be as broadly defined as mental health support to disaster survivors. Not having a clearly defined target group can result in a situation where the program becomes overwhelmed by people seeking assistance, and it will be more morally difficult to send them away. Precise criteria will allow practitioners to inform people about their eligibility ahead of time.

Access

"How will I find the people I want to service?"

This planning step involves researching how to locate the target group and gain access to them—how these people will be found, reached out to, and engaged.

Physical access requires a lot of planning for travel to a conflict zone or disaster-stricken region, addressing security concerns, shelter, and other accommodations. A big part of programming is informing, advertising, and explaining services to beneficiaries and other humanitarian agencies on the ground who will be making referrals.

Researching access always involves knowledge of travel advisories and real-time updates about security and epidemiological situations.

Needs Assessment

"How do I know who needs assistance and what kind of help people will most benefit from?"

A needs assessment allows us to identify the priority needs of the target population and the challenges that prevent addressing them. Typically, a needs assessment pursues the following objectives:

- Establishing a comprehensive picture of interrelated humanitarian, health, and MH needs.
- Examining the existing barriers to meeting them.
- Identifying the gaps in services and evaluating available resources.

The needs assessment can include an approximate estimate of how many people have particular MH needs and how many people can be serviced given the available service capacity and resources. A part of an MH needs assessment is learning about local resources, traditional local and cultural ways of coping and healing, or how people in the past used to cope with similar challenges.

A needs assessment takes many different forms. The most common formats include surveys, interviews, focus groups, and key informant interviews. Each has its advantages and disadvantages.

The World Health Organization (2012) has published an excellent toolkit for assessing MH and psychosocial needs and resources in humanitarian settings, which can be used as further guidance in determining the need for a new program.

Creating an Inventory of Resources

"Are my resources sufficient for meeting the needs and, if not, how can I expand the service capacity of my organization?"

The next step in designing a project is to review and map the resources needed for its successful execution. There are four groups of resources.

First are the locally available resources, locally positioned NGOs, or official systems of care. It is beneficial to reach out to these established programs on the ground and coordinate plans with them.

The second group is human resources, which means the availability of providers, community workers, and their associates, such as interpreters, who can commit to doing this work.

The third group involves assessment and intervention tools with available translations.

And the fourth group refers to organizing logistics—lodging, food, and transportation to the place where the work will take place.

Funds

"How will I fund the project?"

Before launching a project, a provider must ensure the availability of financial means to sustain the project and evacuation in the case of an emergency.

Although many who are involved in this line of work are ready to volunteer their services and even cover expenses, funding remains essential to support the work without putting more burden on the host organization and community. The support staff, interpreters, cooks, and drivers must be paid, and there are many other associated expenses. Funds can be used to bring art supplies and technology to local schools or for any other token of appreciation that a good guest would offer to express their appreciation for being welcomed.

Whenever financial matters are involved, accountability to the donors becomes a focal point. Even when personal money is used, strict accounting practices still must be incorporated in any planning, partially to prove that funds are used responsibly and to avoid accusations of mishandling or misappropriation. Registering the organization as a nonprofit, opening a designated bank account, and hiring an accountant are often good practices.

The chaos that ensued during conflicts or emergencies makes monitoring discretionary spending difficult. Furthermore, there is a delicate balance between efforts to increase control over spending and those to avoid excessive bureaucratic barriers. Establishing a financial monitoring and control system beforehand assures stakeholders that funds are accounted for, spent responsibly, and are not getting into the wrong hands or used for corruption.

Programming

"How do I plan the program and provision of service?"

Programming involves goal setting, defining outcomes, and other components that determine a project's integrity and success. Measures for quality control and establishing ongoing access to supervision or peer support must be built into any project planning.

In a humanitarian space, inadequate planning can border on unethical and inflict even more harm than professional malpractice. Examples of problematic planning include inadequate needs assessment, failure to plan for sustainability and termination, and fostering dependence on external aid. The plan of interventions must be based on and consistent with identified goals and strategic objectives. They should aim at addressing unmet needs and be accompanied by monitoring the quality and integrity of interventions and the outcomes to measure their impact.

Each project proposal must include concerns for sustainability and capacity building. For example, it can include plans for training the local providers to continue providing services to the community and maintaining the gains achieved after the GMH providers leave.

Planning for termination is an essential part of any programming in GMH. Such a provision must be considered from the very beginning and is supposed to answer the questions about what will happen to the people served after the program ends or loses funding and how to mitigate this impact. How and where will they be able to receive support in the future? Are there any coping skills they can learn to use on their own? These and other plans must be discussed so people do not feel abandoned or exploited.

Another essential component of programming is provisions related to the safety of the beneficiaries, such as securing the confidentiality of records after the program's termination.

Potential Ethical Concerns and Political Implications

The proposed project must be carefully examined for potential ethical concerns that may emerge during its execution, and a plan must be developed to address them. Social and political implications, both intended and unintended, need to be examined, and efforts must be included to mitigate them. For example, if a women empowerment project conflicts with local cultural traditions, the participation can leave beneficiaries at greater risk than before. Recognizing and mitigating these risks must be a part of any program planning. For example, there can be plans to engage community leaders in developing the project and facilitating the discussion about its potential benefits for the community.

Group Exercise: "Do-It-Yourself" Aid

Objective
This practice exercise asks readers to practice thinking about factors that constitute a successful GMH project, and practice developing such project. This activity will also increase the understanding of existing humanitarian programs.

Instructions

In a small group, propose a GMH project and then follow the steps to do programming, examine its potential implementation and potentially problematic practices, and investigate alternative problem-solving strategies.

The programming steps:

- Exploring professional and personal interests and readiness
- Target population and the scope of service
- Access
- Needs assessment
- Creating an inventory of resources
- Funding
- Programming
- Potential ethical concerns and political implications

Defend the proposed humanitarian project in the large group.

Takeaways

- Humanitarian work is an activity that is regular, organized, and coordinated. It aims at meeting the group's needs.
- There are various ways GMH providers can develop a humanitarian project that best fits their interests and skills.
- Understanding the humanitarian context and ethical practices in humanitarian emergencies is key to successful humanitarian projects.
- To make the project viable, responsible, and ethically sound, the provider must identify the target population and the scope of service, conduct the needs assessment, secure funding, research best practices, establish collaborations, and address any potential ethical concerns.
- The project must be carefully planned and include provisions for program termination, capacity building, and sustainability.

References

Davis, J. M. (2020). Canada's GINGOs: Who are they, what are they doing, and what role for the future? *Development in Practice, 30*(6), 738–750. https://doi.org/10.1080/09614524.2020.1801584

Denny, L. (2021, October 28). What's the difference between volunteering abroad and voluntourism? *Go Overseas*. https://www.gooverseas.com/blog/what-is-the-difference-between-voluntourism-and-volunteering

Paul, B. K. (2019). Channeling disaster aid: Process and problems. In B. K. Paul (Ed.), *Disaster relief aid* (pp. 43–99). Palgrave Macmillan.

Polman, L. (2013). *The crisis caravan: What's wrong with humanitarian aid?* Henry Holt and Company. http://rbdigital.oneclickdigital.com

Schnable, A. (2016). The era of do-it-yourself aid: Possibilities and perils. *Bridge/Work, 2*(1), article 2. http://scholar.valpo.edu/ilasbw/vol2/iss1/2

World Health Organization (WHO). (2012) *Assessing mental health and psychosocial needs and resources*. Toolkit for humanitarian settings. Geneva: 2002.SBN: 9789241548533

Chapter 13
Managing Mental Health Impact of Humanitarian Work

Mental Health Impact of Humanitarian Work

Increased Security Concerns

This chapter serves a dual purpose. It offers recommendations for GMH providers on delivering MH support to national and international aid workers and also prepares workers to recognize the toll this work takes on them. Some recommendations have been drawn from personal experiences providing MH support to humanitarians; others are informed by supporting frontline responders during the COVID-19 pandemic (Cherepanov, 2020).

The escalating scale of armed conflicts, displacement, and humanitarian crises have heightened levels of insecurity and increased the threat of violence against humanitarians. Guterres, the secretary-general of the United Nations, has recognized these risks and drawn attention to the MH needs of aid workers and the emotional wellbeing of the humanitarian workforce. He has praised them for their commitment to humanitarian causes and expressed concerns over the MH impact of increasingly challenging working conditions (See: https://www.un.org/en/healthy-workforce-home).

A substantial body of evidence has emphasized the importance of acknowledging and proactively addressing MH issues within humanitarian work environments (Cardozo et al., 2012; Ager et al., 2012). Prominent humanitarian organizations have recognized the impact of work-related stressors on the health and wellbeing of their personnel and now place a greater emphasis on supporting the MH needs of field workers. They have instituted various forms of psychological support, including predeparture psychoeducation and MH assistance in the field (e.g., debriefing in the aftermath of a traumatizing incident). They have implemented peer support networks to help volunteers cope with trauma, stress, and MH challenges after the

E. Cherepanov, *Humanitarian Competencies for Global Mental Health Professionals*, Contemporary Humanitarian Action and Emergency Management,
https://doi.org/10.1007/978-3-031-74268-2_13

mission. Furthermore, many large NGOs have contracted external referral systems, such as EAPs (employee assistance programs), to cater to those with more extensive mental health needs.

Cultivating self-awareness is vital for recognizing and managing potentially harmful cognitive biases and burnout. This self-awareness allows individuals to promptly identify the need for self-care and seek support, whether in the field or during readjustment.

Burnout Management

Risks of the Burnout

Humanitarian work is associated with a high risk of burnout which presents a major challenge for humanitarian work. Aid workers often work in physically and morally demanding environments affected by violence, political instability, and poverty. They encounter extensive suffering, severe trauma, and moral dilemmas and face tough professional and personal choices.

According to one UNHCR staff wellbeing survey, up to 38% of respondents directly working with people in humanitarian settings reported symptoms of secondary traumatic stress, with a risk of various dimensions of burnout ranging from 9% to 43%. (See: https://www.unjiu.org/sites/www.unjiu.org/files/jiu_rep_2023_4_english.pdf)

Empathizing with suffering, identification with victims, and being away from families and friends, coupled with limited professional and personal support, can give way to feelings of isolation and difficulties adjusting (Foo et al., 2023). The internalized anger common in a humanitarian emergency, emotional over-engagement due to countertransference, secondary trauma, compassion fatigue, and professional fantasies exponentially increase the susceptibility for burnout.

When burnout is not addressed, chronic workplace stress can lead to increased accident and illness rates, recklessness, decreased performance, and reduced work commitment and engagement, which can result in premature termination of the project (Elwafaii, 2020; Cheney, 2020).

Burnout negatively affects work and personal wellbeing and physical health. The signs of burnout typically include feelings of exhaustion, a sense of detachment, loss of meaning in the work, indifference, negative attitudes, diminished professional effectiveness, and the emergence of medical problems and problematic substance use habits.

To summarize, in a humanitarian emergency, the factors that significantly elevate the risk of burnout are
Exposure to overwhelming needs, mass suffering, and severe trauma.
Mission failure when a provider cannot complete the project or agenda.
Intractable moral and ethical dilemmas and having to make difficult decisions in high-stress situations.
Limited resources when some have to do more than it was planned.
Long hours of work.
Being unable to help everyone who needs it, which leads to the feeling that the work is meaningless in the face of a complex emergency.
Professional and personal isolation due to being far away from professional and personal support.
Unresolved pre-deployment social or psychological problems such as conflicts with friends or family.

Additional factors contributing to occupational burnout in fieldwork may be a lack of privacy, the provider's previous traumatization, or problems at home (Cherepanov, 2018).

Misdirected Anger

Humanitarian workers frequently encounter a lot of anger; indeed, anger is often the most prevalent and pervasive emotional reaction in an emergency. Anger can be expressed by those receiving aid and internalized by aid workers who become angry with their peers and deploying organizations.

> In emergencies, humanitarian organizations often become a lightning rod for a lot of anger and blame from beneficiaries and aid workers alike. At times, it may even create an appearance that the humanitarian agency is the main enemy. Although these organizations are far from perfect, yet the irony of the situation is that they are part of the solution. There are possible psychological explanations for this phenomenon: It is not the first time in history when a person in a helping role has faced hostility from the people they are trying to help.

This misplaced anger places additional pressure on the MH providers and managers as they grapple with the frustration coming from the very people they are trying to assist. This can be emotionally draining, especially when providers believe they have been doing everything within their means to help.

This anger often substitutes deeper and more complex emotions such as fear, desperation, helplessness, or sadness that are hard to recognize and even harder to accept or express. Understanding and addressing these underlying emotions, and being aware of the incongruency to the situation, help to avoid taking this anger personally or internalizing it.

Here are helpful tips on dealing with anger for GMH workers that were previously described by Cherepanov (2020) during the response to the COVID-19 pandemic:

- Respond to emotions and not to words.
- Look beyond anger: Assist individuals in identifying and expressing underlying feelings appropriately.
- Recognize that anger directed at you is not necessarily about you, and don't have to take it personally.
- Venting anger is not always helpful. Redirect if emotions become counterproductive: Shift the conversation toward other important topics.
- Choose words that offer comfort, stability, and predictability. For example, "I assure you we will do everything to help your loved one."
- Try to establish a dialog.
- Prioritize personal safety and the safety of others.

Burnout Resilience

Peer support, self-awareness, and self-care are the main resources for building burnout resilience (Everall & Paulson, 2004).

The offered recommendations on preventing and reversing burnout are derived from experience when providing psychological wellbeing of field workers as a part of pre-deployment training (Cherepanov, 2020).

The skills suggested below help with increasing the understanding of the nature of burnout and gaining mastery of its management.

Tools for improving burnout management are:

Understand the signs of burnout, its impact on mental health and the importance of self-care.
Learn to recognize signs of the burnout.
Create inventory of your vulnerabilities, strengths, supports, and sources of resilience.
Identify, mobilize support, and review coping skills that helped in the past, such as journaling, reading, arts, and spirituality.
Bring a non-professional book for personal reading.
Use any opportunity to get privacy and physical exercises.
Learn to accept moral ambiguity.
Compartmentalize: as much as possible try to establish clear boundaries between personal and professional life.
Listen to peers when they express concerns about your psychological wellbeing.
Do not make any life-changing decision when in the field.

Reach out and talk to peers even if you want to talk only about the weather.
Discuss concerns about the quality of work life with the supervisor or manager.
Plan for re-entry and re-adjustment.
Take breaks between assignments.
Reach out to professional help if symptoms persist or worsen.

Peer Support: When to Seek Professional Help

Peer support is a form of mutual support for first responders and relief workers who deal with severe occupational stress every day in their professional lives. It aims to improve the quality of professional life, but it is not a substitute for professional MH interventions.

The peer support format has been steadily gaining recognition as a first line of MH support for emergency workers, and more humanitarian agencies have been instituting peer support modules as part of routine practice. Many humanitarian agencies now offer training for peer support volunteers where they learn active listening skills, the most effective coping strategies, and indicators that suggest the need for referral to professional services.

Peer support helps field workers feel understood, validated, and supported. The peer support format fits into the culture of peer camaraderie and fellowship of emergency responders. The frontline workers often come to trust only their peers, who, they believe, are the only ones who can truly understand them.

Peer support is not treatment and Do and Don't tips for peer supporters can help anyone who wants to be emotionally available to their peers (Cherepanov, 2020).

Tips for Peer Support

Dos

Check-in on each other and be aware of those who are in distress.

Random acts of kindness, small compliments, and favors, e.g., offering a bottle of water or a box of tissues, can go a long way.

Be available when someone wants to talk. Be also clear with setting time limits. Avoid sending mixed signals.

Accept that one may remain distressed even after talking to peers, and it is okay.

Respect the individual's way of dealing with difficulties.

Give feedback if stress affects the job performance or makes the provider unsafe.

Don'ts

Never, ever assume the role of psychotherapist for your peers.
Avoid emotional incongruency, like being too cheerful or "Pollyannaish."
Don't try to fix others or solve their life problems for them.
Don't suggest they relax or calm down.
Don't assume that talking about feelings always is going to make people feel better.
Don't tell a peer not to think about work at home or home at work. They wish they could avoid doing it!
Don't neglect practical assistance or offer help with small tasks when possible.
Avoid labeling peers' behavior or feelings as pathological or diagnose them.
Don't forget that you also need support.

Aid workers must be referred to professional services as soon as possible if they are unable to function or sleep, their relationships and jobs suffer, conflicts at work or home escalate, they are at risk of losing their job, or if they report increased substance use, worsening depression, or suicidal ideations.

Self-Care and Self-Awareness

Self-Care

Self-care in MH professionals is a matter of professional competence and ethics. Self-care helps with stress management, increases energy, improves job satisfaction, and prevents burnout. Self-care involves paying attention to one's needs, practicing self-compassion, and setting aside time for activities that enhance physical and mental health and overall wellbeing.

Practices like meditation, mindfulness, grounding exercises, and daily small self-care-centered actions can have a big impact (Cardozo et al., 2012).

Although much literature exists on self-care, many available recommendations are hardly realistic in fieldwork, where having privacy is sometimes a luxury. For example, some common self-care suggestions are spending more time doing pleasurable things, improving diet, or spending more time with loved ones. However, many other things can be done to reduce the emotional burden of burnout (based on NIMH, 2024).

(Recommendations)
To prevent burnout, humanitarians, when possible, should do the following:

- Use any opportunity to engage in physical activity, even for a short period of time. This can mean walking, pushups, practicing yoga, or participating in sports activities.

- Maintain a healthy, regular eating pattern and stay adequately hydrated. Additionally, limit the consumption of caffeinated, sugary, or alcoholic beverages.
- Prioritize sleep. Adhere to a consistent sleep schedule to ensure you get the required amount of rest.
- Schedule regular times for enjoyable, relaxing, and healthy activities like journaling. Incorporate mindfulness, meditation, progressive muscle relaxation, or breathing exercises in daily activities: Doing them doesn't take a long time, sometimes just minutes at a time.
- Establish priorities. Determine what tasks are urgent and what can be postponed. Learn to decline new responsibilities if you feel overwhelmed. Focus on acknowledging what you have accomplished at the end of the day rather than dwelling on unfinished tasks.
- Foster connectedness. Stay in touch with peers, friends, or family members who can offer emotional support and practical assistance.
- Practice self-compassion. Treat yourself with kindness, understanding, forgiveness, and empathy.

The active promotion of self-care in helping professions has demonstrated its indisputable benefits and made it a vital element in contemporary healthcare. However, when it comes to practice, especially in emergencies, the philosophy of self-prioritizing sometimes meets resistance. Focus on self can be perceived as a distraction from prioritizing patients' needs, which may disadvantage peers and create a sense among responders that their judgment about their ability to carry on their work cannot be trusted.

Self-Awareness Offers Choices

Self-care is vital for MH work, and the self-awareness framework underscores the significance of being mindful of and attending to one's physical and MH needs. It allows professionals to trust their judgment when deciding about the best time and means to meet these needs. This approach opposes externally imposed and almost mandatory self-care, which can sometimes invoke resistance in the heat of an emergency. Understanding one's limitations and needs enables professionals to make the best decisions regarding safety and self-care to suit the circumstances and their professional role.

In an emergency, self-awareness becomes a powerful tool in balancing the health and wellness of the responders, preventing burnout, and ensuring that self-care doesn't compromise the integrity of care. Self-awareness is a necessary condition for realizing risks and available choices. Recognizing countertransference, fantasies, cognitive distortions, and biases must become a part of GMH professional training (Cherepanov, 2020).

Countertransference and Fantasies

The emergency setting and trauma work can increase the first responders' susceptibility to developing cognitive distortions, illusions, and fantasies, especially for those who are exposed to strong emotions, trauma, and suffering.

Countertransference is a cognitive aberration that can occur when a client's experience triggers a provider's traumatic memories and elicits personal emotional reactions that can compromise the provider's ability to respond to the client's needs. Williams (2012) has identified countertransference as the biggest threat to professional and personal boundaries in those who work with severe trauma because other people's trauma may trigger providers' personal experiences and cause them to act in ways that they would not otherwise.

Countertransference presents a serious challenge to the integrity of care and, if not recognized, quickly leads to burnout. Self-awareness plays a vital role in managing countertransference and other cognitive biases.

The cognitive distortions known as *fantasies* predictably alter the perception of the professional role in relation to others. Acting on these fantasies increases the risk of professional boundaries violation, contributes to burnout, affects the quality of care, and increases reckless behavior.

Fantasies are associated with an altered perception of professional roles, blurred boundaries, and a sense of omnipotence and irreplaceability. Fantasies also alter the perception of the people served, who become viewed as helpless and incapable of making their own decisions. Cherepanov (2020) identifies three common fantasies related to relief workers in emergency settings: the Rescuer, the Superman, and the Helper.

The *rescuer fantasy* is "a subconscious belief that one must rescue or save another person from something bad, posited as a motive for certain actions or choices" (Oxford Dictionary, s.v. "rescuer fantasy"). A MH provider who acts upon this fantasy feels they must do everything to rescue others, even when it goes against presumed victims' will.

The *Superman fantasy* is the belief that the primary role of the MH provider is locating and fixing the problem. Such a fly-in-and-out intervention is never well-planned or collaborative. A GMH provider in the role of Superman often favors quick solutions that may conflict with the natural healing process. They tend to go for immediate fixes without seeking lasting and sustainable solutions. MH providers in the role of Superman tend to overestimate their role and undermine teamwork, which carries a negative impact on collaborative efforts.

The *helper fantasy* refers to a cognitive bias where MH providers primarily identify their role as someone who must do everything themselves with little regard for other people's own resources, strength, and resilience. The reliance on external recognition makes a helper depend on outside approval. MH providers who act out this fantasy tend to foster dependence in the people served. In contrast to a provider with the helper's fantasy, those who truly want to help assist the beneficiaries to regain self-efficacy and independence (Brueck, 2020).

In a helping profession, this fantasy is difficult to challenge because it resonates with the professional mission. The antithesis is the understanding that we do this work not for the people served but for ourself, for personal and professional fulfillment, because it feels morally right. This is why we do not need external approval to feel good about our work.

Risk (Mis)perception and the Safety Imperative

We cannot completely eliminate risks in humanitarian settings, but we can improve safety by accurately recognizing and managing these risks. This is called the human component in risk management.

The main factors that negatively affect risk perception and hinder compliance with the safety imperative, are existential despair, burnout, countertransference, fantasies (see above), the "dual loyalty" dilemma, the "humanitarian impunity bubble," and compromised personal support.

In humanitarian settings, there is an absolute and undisputed priority of personal safety for the aid workers—the safety imperative—which is a matter of professional and ethical competency. The heightened security risks and exposure to mass trauma and suffering that can lead to stress and burnout also affect the perception of risk. In some cases, humanitarians wrestle with uncertainties about the meaning of their work, questioning the significance of the impact and the value of their contributions: so-called *existential despair*. In turn, this may cause individuals to reevaluate the perceived value of their own lives, potentially leading to increased risk-taking behaviors (Cherepanov, 2018).

The *dual loyalty dilemma* refers to situations when loyalty to the organization and loyalty to the people served conflict. This can happen, for example, when providers must choose between following the deploying agency's order to evacuate or refusing to leave behind the people served, who will likely be left in danger.

Sometimes, the rush to help in emergencies or being in *a "humanitarian mode"* which is a rush to help also limits self-awareness; the fantasies may become overpowering and affect the provider's perception of risks and sense of self-preservation.

Emergency responders are aware of such danger and use several phrases to remember the safety imperative and provide grounding:

"There is no need to multiply the victims."

This sentiment, common among first responders, emphasizes that self-sacrifice won't contribute to resolving the situation but instead will result in helping fewer patients.

"Your life doesn't belong to you only."

Identification with victims can lead to questioning the value and purpose of work and life. This statement reminds responders of their responsibility to their families, who are concerned about their wellbeing and trust that their loved ones will do everything they can to avoid unnecessary risks. This is why compromised personal support can exponentially increase unsafe behavior and negligence toward one's own safety.

"Humanitarian workers must do everything possible to be safe. It is a job requirement."

Diligently following security rules and safety precautions during field operations helps regain sense of control in unpredictable situations (Bickley, 2010).

In humanitarian work, self-sacrifice is never a good idea. However, when confronted with existential despair and survivor's guilt, the providers may feel tempted to consider sharing fate with the victims as the only existing moral choice. For example, an MH provider may feel compelled to offer themselves in exchange for hostages. (Cherepanov, personal communication)

In such a dramatic development, this decision is unlikely to help the hostages. It will, however, put the provider in harm's way, which will complicate the provision of humanitarian aid and affect many more people.

A GMH provider who does not value their own life will be unable to help and empower others.

Another factor distorting risk perception is the so-called *humanitarian impunity bubble.*

The "*humanitarian impunity bubble*" refers to an illusion of invincibility. According to Allan (2015), humanitarians live in a sort of cognitive bubble where they rely on rules and norms that are abstract and detached from real-life challenges in the field, increasing their vulnerability.

This illusion can create a false sense of safety when the rules and norms create reassuring and sometimes empowering erroneous perceptions of seemingly coherent and predictable spaces.

Having to choose between assuring one's safety and the duty to help has always been an emotionally difficult dilemma for any helping professional. Clear instructions on prioritizing personal safety are part of the organizational codes of conduct. Positioning safety as an imperative assists decision-making in morally ambiguous situations (Bickley, 2010, p. 182).

> For example, the instruction that aid workers must prioritize their safety (Sphere, 2018) seems clear and easy to follow. However, in a security breach, international providers are expected to follow the organization's order to evacuate over safety concerns. This also means leaving behind the national personnel and clientele. For an expatriate provider, evacuation means abandoning clients and months of work, and leaving behind colleagues and friends. This decision is never morally easy as it goes against the most deeply seeded moral convictions.

Return from the Mission: Preparing for Readjustment

> It is common for humanitarian aid workers to express more hesitancy and worries about readjustment when returning home than when going to the mission. (Cherepanov, personal communication)

Return to normalcy is often associated with stresses of readjustment, which unfortunately have not received appropriate attention from MH professionals. The readjustment brings specific stresses that, if overlooked, can significantly affect wellbeing, health, professional functioning, and personal relationships. For these reasons, some agencies have extended peer support to generously cover reentry time, when trained peer support specialists reach out to the returning volunteers and assist them through the readjustment period.

Numerous studies of emergency responders have demonstrated that readjustment can be very stressful, leading to lingering depression, anhedonia, lack of energy and drive, increased conflicts at work and home, social isolation, and even job loss, which further depletes much-needed support. The stresses of reentry and the adjustment issues heighten risks for substance abuse and suicidal ideations (Hodgkinson & Stewart, 1998; Cherepanov, 1999).

Upon returning from a mission, providers may anticipate

- Difficulty being fully emotionally present with family and friends.
- Emotional detachment, inability to experience happiness, and other intense emotions.
- Relationship difficulties with a significant other. Potential escalation of conflicts at home and work.

- Anhedonia (lack of energy and motivation).
- Problems with sleep, heightened anxiety, hypervigilance, depression, irritability, or anger.
- Social isolation, lacking the desire or energy to engage in social activities.
- Traumatic symptoms like intrusions, flashbacks, nightmares, or survivor guilt.
- Increased alcohol and drug use.
- Being fixated on the past, always thinking and talking about the field experience.
- Exacerbation of preexisting somatic problems such as hypertension and diabetes.

Typically, these symptoms resolve quickly—within a month. However, if they persist or worsen, or if the person feels that life is not worth living or experiences suicidal thoughts, seeking professional support is necessary.

Preparing for Readjustment

Reentry may be easier if one begins preparing before the deployment, which involves preparing the family, the social network or community, and the self. Here are some suggestions.

Preparing Family
Discuss with family in advance that you might be emotionally distant for some time and reassure them that it does not diminish your love for them.

Preparing Social Networks and the Community
The responses to the Ebola and SARS epidemic demonstrated that aid workers in regions with complex epidemiological situations can encounter stigma upon their return to the community (Wester & Giesecke, 2019; Cherepanov, 2020). Educating the community about the nature of your work is beneficial to countering potential misinformation and making it clear that the provider is not contagious. As a precaution against stigma, it may make sense to refrain from visiting children's playgrounds and attending large public gatherings for some time after returning home.

Preparing Self
A provider can anticipate and prepare for a period of "sluggishness" marked by physical and mental fatigue. Making too many plans can be unattainable and lead to self-disappointment. Allowing yourself to feel tired, sad, and less productive and planning for self-care will make readjustment easier.

DO NOT plan on changing your job, making other important life decisions, or committing to another mission until the adjustment cycle is complete.

Adaptive Readjustment

As readjustment progresses in an adaptive way, the adjustment stresses are gradually reduced, and a person can notice that they are now capable of

- Attending to their own physical and mental needs: nutrition, exercises, meeting friends, taking time before starting work.
- Emotional responsiveness and interest in current events.
- Experiencing a range of emotions, which include pleasure and joy.
- Increased and enjoyable socialization.
- Thinking about the future.
- Using field experience for personal and professional growth (Cherepanov, 1999).

The factors that strengthen resilience during the reentry period are

- Good social support and the ability to discuss feelings and reach out for help.
- Stress management skills and a sense of humor.
- Maintaining good sleep and physical health.
- Adaptive coping strategies.
- Good problem-solving and conflict-resolution skills.
- Cognitive flexibility: ability to accept other's views and opinions.
- Secure relationships, employment, and housing.

Despite recognizing the importance of readjustment, studies of emergency personnel have demonstrated that the great majority of professionals never ask for professional help and are confident that they would never disclose to their agencies the need for assistance (Hodgkinson & Stewart, 1998; Orsillo et al., 1998; Koppel, 2002). This means that peer support outreach and self-awareness are crucial for promoting positive adjustment and enhancing access to behavioral health for those who need it. More attention must be given to this part of the humanitarian experience.

Takeaways

- GMH professionals are often asked to provide MH support to humanitarians, and they also must recognize and attend to their own psychological needs.
- The stresses associated with humanitarian relief work can take an emotional toll on aid workers and affect their mental and physical health.
- Increased threats against humanitarians, exposure to mass suffering, trauma, and death, and compassion fatigue increase the risk for burnout.
- Countertransference can lead to over-identification with victims, creating difficulties with maintaining their professional role, and possibly leading to boundaries violations.
- The common cognitive biases in disaster response are metaphorically labeled as Rescuer, Helper, and Superman fantasies. They increase the potential for burnout and alter risk perception.
- Self-awareness helps providers to recognize fantasies, manage burnout, and determine the need for self-care.
- It is sometimes easier to adapt to emergencies than to reentry. Preparing self, family, and community helps mitigate the readjustment stresses and maximize personal and professional gains from the humanitarian experience.

References

Ager, A., Pasha, E., Yu, G., Duke, T., Eriksson, C., & Cardozo, B. L. (2012). Stress, mental health, and burnout in national humanitarian aid workers in Gulu, northern Uganda. *Journal of Traumatic Stress, 25*(6), 713–720. https://doi.org/10.1002/jts.21764

Allan, T. (2015). Life beyond the bubbles: Cognitive dissonance and humanitarian impunity in northern Uganda. In S. Abramowitz, C. Panter-Brick, & P. Piot (Eds.), *Medical humanitarianism: Ethnographies of practice* (pp. 96–119). University of Pennsylvania Press.

Bickley, S. (2010). *Safety first revised: A safety and security handbook for aid workers*. International Save the Children Alliance. http://www.eisf.eu/resources/library/

Brueck, H. (2020, May 14). WHO: Healthcare workers are being attacked with rocks and bleach for treating coronavirus patients. Some have stopped wearing uniforms to stay safe. *Business Insider*. https://www.yahoo.com/news/healthcare-workers-being-attacked-rocks-174000091.html/

Cardozo, L. B., Gotway Crawford, C., Eriksson, C., Zhu, J., Sabin, M., Ager, A., Foy, D., Snider, L., Scholte, W., Kaiser, R., Olff, M., Rijnen, B., & Simon, W. (2012). Psychological distress, depression, anxiety, and burnout among international humanitarian aid workers: A longitudinal study. *PLoS One, 7*(9), e44948. https://doi.org/10.1371/journal.pone.0044948

Cheney, C. (2020, May 4). Researcher: Coronavirus pandemic increases risk of physician suicide. *HealthLeader Media*. https://www.healthleadersmedia.com/clinical-care/researcher-coronavirus-pandemic-increases-risk-physician-suicide/

Cherepanov, E. (2018). *Ethics for global mental health: From good intentions to humanitarian accountability*. Routledge. https://doi.org/10.4324/9781351175746

Cherepanov, E. (2020). Responding to the psychological needs of health workers during pandemic: Ten lessons from humanitarian work. *Disaster Medicine and Public Health Preparedness, 16*(2), 734–740. https://doi.org/10.1017/dmp.2020.356

Cherepanov, E. (1999). *Return from mission. Trauma News, 8*(4), 5–7.

Elwafaii, O. (2020, April 29). Why are COVID-19 doctors committing suicide? *CGTN*. https://newsus.cgtn.com/news/2020-04-29/Why-are-COVID-19-doctors-committing-suicide%2D%2DQ4yi8yhYB2/index.html

Everall, R. D., & Paulson, B. L. (2004). Burnout and secondary traumatic stress: Impact on ethical behaviour. *Canadian Journal of Counselling, 38*(1), 25–35.

Foo, C. Y. S., Tay, A. K., Yang, Y., & Verdeli, H. (2023). Psychosocial model of burnout among humanitarian aid workers in Bangladesh: Role of workplace stressors and emotion coping. *Conflict and Health, 17*, 17. https://doi.org/10.1186/s13031-023-00512-1

Hodgkinson, P., & Stewart, M. (1998). *Coping with catastrophe*. Routledge.

Koppel, T. (2002). *A good man in hell: General Roméo Dallaire and the Rwanda genocide.* Interview with General Dallaire. Speaker's series. United States Holocaust Memorial Museum. https://www.ushmm.org/confront-genocide/speakers-and-events/all-speakers-and-events/a-good-man-in-hell-general-romeo-dallaire-and-the-rwanda-genocide

National Institutes of Health (NIMH). (2024). *Caring for your mental health*. National Institute of Mental Health. https://www.nimh.nih.gov/health/topics/caring-for-your-mental-health

Orsillo, S., Roemer, L., Litz, B., Ehlich, P., & Friedman, M. (1998). Psychiatric symptomatology associated with contemporary peacekeeping. *Journal of Traumatic Stress, 11*, 609–611.

Sphere. (2018). *The Sphere handbook: Humanitarian charter and minimum standards in humanitarian response* (4th ed.) www.spherestandards.org/handbook

Wester, M., & Giesecke, J. (2019). Ebola and healthcare worker stigma. *Scandinavian Journal of Public Health, 47*(2), 99–104. https://doi.org/10.1177/1403494817753450

Williams, M. B. (2012). Ethics. In C. R. Figley (Ed.), *Encyclopedia of trauma: An interdisciplinary guide* (pp. 233–235). Sage.

Chapter 14
Conclusions and Recommendations

Conclusions

It is my hope is that this book will inspire MH professionals to join the humanitarian cause, prepare them to respond to crises in the increasingly dangerous world, equip them with an understanding of what this work entails, and offer the necessary skills.

There has been a growing understanding of the MH's central role in shaping the global health agenda, building resilience, and preventing violence. Mental health support for people affected by disasters, armed conflicts, famines, and epidemics alleviates suffering and saves lives. It is an essential factor of health and wellbeing and is a human right.

The introduction of global context to the MH profession has encouraged the MH field to reflect on its place and role in the changing world, its achievements, and the unacceptable price for staying disconnected from the bigger world.

The MH professionals' response to humanitarian emergencies has demonstrated a strong commitment to humanistic values, professional interest, and compassion. Introducing humanitarian competencies to MH work is envisioned as the next step toward the professionalization of GMH and establishing it as a specialization with its distinct scope of services and framework.

The GMH innovations have already altered the landscape of the mainstream MH field and humanitarian action. The GMH experience promoted contextuality in understanding the MH needs in humanitarian crises and offered new opportunities for learning from global experiences. As a result of professional advocacy and education, humanitarian agencies now routinely incorporate GMH modules into their operations and turn their attention to the MH needs of aid workers. The GMH providers who respond to humanitarian emergencies have equally realized the need for humanitarian competencies to understand the humanitarian context of their work and know about the humanitarian relief systems and the humanitarian culture.

E. Cherepanov, *Humanitarian Competencies for Global Mental Health Professionals*, Contemporary Humanitarian Action and Emergency Management,
https://doi.org/10.1007/978-3-031-74268-2_14

The GMH's perspective has accelerated moving away from the narrowly defined professional siloed approaches to establishing truly interdisciplinary collaborative and integrative practices such as psychosocial, integrated primary care practice, and community-based interventions. Global optics spearheaded rapid advances in MH studies and practice that, in some ways, have outpaced their theoretical substantiations, concept development, and the evidence for empirically designed practices.

The GMH experience has enabled several other paradigmatic shifts in the mainstream MH: from focusing on individuals to concentrating on populational needs, from the disease-oriented paradigm to strengthening coping and resilience, and from problem-solving for people to partnering with them to finding solutions and fostering self-reliance.

The contemporary developments in GMH underscore the importance of tailoring research and interventions to the context and the humanitarian settings characterized by the massive humanitarian and MH needs, compromised or destroyed infrastructure, power differential, profound service recipients' vulnerability, and elevated security risks.

As a specialization of MH, GMH is concerned with providing MH support and assistance to people affected by humanitarian emergencies. Thus, the GMH's scope of service primarily falls under the relief or crisis response modality. However, more than ever, humanitarian relief now incorporates thinking about long-term solutions, such as sustainability, resilience, and capacity building. These efforts can consist of training and supporting local service providers and building referral and child protection systems.

GMH providers build their work upon existing strengths and resources. These interventions prioritize strengthening resilience, enhancing coping, and improving access to community resources and professional services.

GMH work is not about "repairing broken people," solving their problems, or changing their lives or society they live in. It is supposed to support people affected by a catastrophic event cope, recognize, and mobilize their personal and cultural resources and enables them to seek their own solutions. GMH interventions enable people to do their best under the circumstances, support each other, and regain mastery over their lives. They assist survivors and the community realize available choices, even when limited, and recognize and take pride in their endurance and strength.

The GMH work is collaborative by nature and, in addition to the core professional expertise, this professionally, psychologically, and morally demanding work requires specialized interdisciplinary, humanitarian, and personal competencies. Aiding people with interconnected needs can take many shapes and forms: conducting direct services, advocacy, research, and policymaking.

When GMH professionals respond to humanitarian crises, they become a part of humanitarian space, which is the interplay of massive and pressing humanitarian needs and multidisciplinary humanitarian relief efforts. To an amateur, the humanitarian emergency site may appear chaotic. However, when disaster strikes, the zone of the impact quickly becomes an arena of concerted humanitarian relief, a system of multidisciplinary relief organizations, aid workers, donors, and health and MH providers interacting with each other and the aid recipients.

Humanitarian competencies strive to ensure that all interventions are conducted systematically, collaboratively, and in a coordinated manner and that they are consistent with humanitarian regulations and ethics.

Here are the main conclusions:

Humanitarian emergencies carry a systemic impact and affect the entire lives of the people and not just some aspects of their lives. Understanding the systemic nature of a humanitarian situation helps maximize the benefits of MH interventions and increase the sustainability of the recovery. Complex and interconnected needs call for interdisciplinary approaches. Systemic thinking about needs involves the understanding that most people will cope and recover independently if they have good support or that small interventions can lead to significant changes. There may not be a need to treat everyone or focus on symptoms only. Often, engaging family and community support becomes the strategically chosen priority.

The impact of humanitarian emergencies exceeds the ability of the affected population to cope independently. Humanitarian emergencies produce massive and complex needs requiring a coordinated international response, which will not be available forever. GMH professionals engage the affected community in re-establishing self-reliance and empowering them to take an active role in their recovery by accessing their healing resources. The GMH professionals emphasize partnering with the community in this and supporting their efforts to restore social connections and the fabric of social life.

Meeting MH and humanitarian needs can be complicated. Beside difficulties with meeting the overwhelming needs, the whole humanitarian aid experience has demonstrated that any helping intervention requires a delicate balance between providing assistance and mitigating the unintentional infliction of harm. This harm can also be recognized in interfering with pre-existing social and cultural coping, developing the relief dependence, and the weakening of the individuals' and the community's capacity for self-reliance and self-determination.

GMH interventions must always be collaborative, integrated, and coordinated. Humanitarian emergencies produce complex needs, that require interdisciplinary interventions. The global response demonstrated the limits of the narrowly siloed professional approaches. Establishing interdisciplinary collaborations and partnerships on the ground increases the efficiency of intervention, maximizes the use of resources, and avoids duplication of services and their fragmentation.

It started understanding MH needs as an interplay of life events, the circumstances of people's life, resilience, and other health and social factors.

Humanitarian competency is a necessary component of GMH's professional expertise. Understanding how the systems of humanitarian systems function allows GMH professionals to act as a part of collaborative humanitarian relief systems and maximize the benefits of the interventions. Being "system-savvy" helps to avoid redundancies and fragmentation and makes the environment and interactions with humanitarian agencies more predictable. It improves safety and prevents competition among actors and the overlap in service provision. When entering humanitarian space, the GMH providers become subject to humanitarian regulations that they must balance with the professional code of ethics, and always, prioritize their safety.

Humanitarian competencies are essential for all actors involved in humanitarian relief. Understanding how the humanitarian sector operates is necessary to conduct contextually appropriate interventions that utilize available resources and support. These inter-disciplinary and cross-sectoral competencies include knowledge of humanitarian values, regulations, and ethics, understanding the humanitarian systems and operations, and familiarity with the humanitarian professional culture. Having such competencies helps service providers define their role within the multidisciplinary team and form productive partnerships with other actors and people we serve.

Being a part of humanitarian action, GMH has responded to the call to strengthen professionalization, accountability, and ethics. Professionalization in GMH means developing standards of practice and training requirements. Accountability means using power responsibly. The inherent power disbalance between the humanitarian workers and the people served underscores the humanitarian responsibility and the role of ethics in everything the GMH professionals do on a disaster site.

Professional education for GMH specialists involves academic learning, practical skills, and humanitarian competencies. Humanitarian competencies imply the knowledge of humanitarian ethics and the code of conduct, understanding of the humanitarian systems and the humanitarian professional culture, and contextual, cultural, and geopolitical awareness. Other essential soft skills are open-mindedness, critical self-reflection, and cultural humility.

Professional competency in GMH work is a moving target. The humanitarian landscape is rapidly changing, exposing the limitations of preconceived knowledge and the reliance on rigid protocols. Specialized training is only as relevant as it allows us to adapt the competencies, knowledge, and skills to a new situation and context. Each emergency is unique and brings new challenges that are impossible to prepare for fully. The GMH professionals are responsible for continuing education, keeping their competencies current, and actively seeking professional consultations when needed.

Professional humility means being realistic about the limits of one's expertise and personal limitations. The most important takeaway from the book is being mindful of how little the MH field actually knows about the impact of humanitarian emergencies where human resilience is stretched to the limit, and about the most optimal ways to assist the impacted people. GMH work fosters professional curiosity and allows learning from every response.

GMH discipline continues developing its ground concepts, practices, and ethics. GMH has branched from the MH field and inherited some of its preconceived assumptions, which poorly translate into global realities. The international perspective opened the door for re-evaluating many MH concepts and tools and developing integrated multidisciplinary approaches. The paradigm shift from pathologizing human distress to focusing on resilience calls for developing GMH-friendly and contextually relevant concepts, assessments, and interventions.

The GMH providers must adhere to the highest standards of practice, conduct, and professional integrity. In GMH work, the guidance and regulations arrive from three sources: the professional codes of ethics, the humanitarian code of conduct, and GMH-specific ethics. Ethical regulations require that service providers are aware of the potential harm associated with helping interventions, such as forming relief dependency or interfering with the natural process of overcoming, and actively work on minimizing this harm.

In a humanitarian space, any ethical and moral indiscretion comes at a high price. Due to the extreme vulnerability of people served and the public and often political visibility of GMH work, the cost of problematic decision-making and ethically questionable practices can be extremely high. Any mistake can negatively impact the safety of the beneficiaries and the aid workers, as well as funding for programming and the delivery of aid.

GMH's work prioritizes population-focused responses. This approach aligns with public- and global health and humanitarian relief focus but conflicts with the traditional MH framework. MH interventions historically have emphasized the person-centered approaches. In the humanitarian context, balancing personal and collective needs requires MH providers to conceptual reconcile the outcomes measured on the individual and the populational level.

Overall, the GMH service prioritizes relief response over humanitarian development. Both groups of interventions are essential. The crisis relief and addressing immediate needs ease concerns that GMH interventions will be used to impose the neocolonial agenda and tell people how they must live their lives. Development remains important for meeting long-term goals and sustaining recovery. The solution can be found in developing integrated interventions that would allow providers to respond to pressing needs and concurrently focus on resilience, building the local capacity, including the referral system development, and training the local MH workers.

All MH interventions must be ethically justified and carefully planned. Any programming includes ensuring the confidentiality of sensitive health information, provisions for unplanned changes, termination, sustainability, and aftercare. Planning is necessary to reduce harm and avoid making people feel abandoned after the program ends.

In GMH work, self-awareness and self-care are ethical requirements. In humanitarian emergencies, GMH providers are often exposed to severe trauma, moral ambiguities, and increased security risks. This emotionally intense experience can cloud professional judgment, create cognitive biases, lead to burnout, and compromise decision-making and risk assessment. To provide ethically sound services, GMH providers must be aware of their own needs, know when to self-care, and when to seek professional assistance. Many humanitarian organizations have widely implemented ongoing MH support for field workers and peer support to assist aid workers with re-adjustment.

Recommendations for the Future

Much has already been accomplished in the GMH field. Still, many challenges remain for this specialty to truly establish itself as a discipline recognized by the public, MH, and humanitarian professional communities.

There is a need to prioritize the development of the GMH-specific assessment tools, and evidence-based interventions that are humanitarian context friendly.

While many agree that MH work is important, only a few understand what this work really encompasses. We cannot just assume that other professionals, humanitarians, and beneficiaries know about our work and realize its benefits. To strengthen the professional image, GMH must actively use publications, education, and mental health promotion to increase its visibility in the professional community.

We need to be prepared already now to respond to future disasters, conflicts, or outbreaks. We must make sure there are enough trained GMH responders to help increase their future engagement and that there are no gaps in access to the services should they be needed.

There is also a need for trainers with GMH expertise. There is a tremendous need for training, and there are not enough trainers skilled both in MH and humanitarian work. Specialized modules can include professional skills for psychiatrists, psychologists, or social workers. There is also a need for interdisciplinary and cross-sectional modules that facilitate multidisciplinary collaborations and coordination on the ground, and these tabletop exercises must be conducted for MH specialists and professional humanitarians. Regardless of primary specialty, all training must routinely include modules on managing burnout, recognizing countertransference, fantasies, cognitive distortions, self-awareness, and self-care when responding to emergencies.

The respective professional boards and associations must formally recognize the GMH specialization to solidify the accomplishments and move forward. This recognition is vital for ensuring professional standards and the quality of work and for developing minimum training requirements, oversight, regulations, and, possibly, certifications in the GMH field.

GMH often occurs in remote places with limited professional supervision and oversight access, which elevates the responsibility of the deploying organization to exercise oversight, maintain work standards, and ensure quality. All NGOs must have a whistleblowing mechanism to express confidential concerns about ethical indiscretions.

Humanitarian competency is only one part of the professional expertise in GMH. Much more must be done to increase the humanitarian professionalization of proxy specialists across disciplines and sectors who directly or indirectly address MH needs.

Glossary of Global Mental Health Terms

Accountability is a commitment by humanitarians to use power responsibly. Strengthening accountability involves increased engagement, empowerment, and inclusion of the affected population in decision-making processes on their behalf (Strengthening Accountability, n.d.; OCHA Business Brief, 2021).

Armed conflicts are "the confrontations occurring between governmental armed forces and the forces of one or more armed groups, or between such groups arising on the territory of a State party to the Geneva Conventions of 1949" (https://ihl-databases.icrc.org/en/ihl-treaties/gci-1949/article-3/commentary/2016#125).

Aspirational values are humanitarian values meant to ensure human rights in complex environments fraught with controversy and political battles. They set the directionality or moral compass for MH interventions.

Burnout is "a psychological syndrome emerging as a prolonged response to chronic interpersonal stressors on the job. The key dimensions of this response are an overwhelming exhaustion, cynicism, detachment from the job, and a sense of ineffectiveness and lack of accomplishment" (Maslach & Leiter, 2016).

"Cargo cult mentality" in MH references the presumption that the imitation of Western treatment practices will bring a cure. This phenomenon got its name after the incident during World War II observed by the indigenous people of Melanesia. They reportedly were impressed by the arrival of aircraft on their islands carrying various supplies. Lacking an understanding of what airplanes were, they resorted to magical thinking, crafting bamboo models of planes and control towers in a superstitious hope that it would lure aircraft and deliver more material goods" (Feynman, 1974; Hall, 2016).

Child soldier is "any person under 18 years of age who is part of any regular or irregular armed force in any capacity" (UNICEF, 1997). The recruitment and use of children by armed groups is a serious violation of child rights and international humanitarian law.

E. Cherepanov, *Humanitarian Work for Global Mental Health Providers*, Contemporary Humanitarian Action and Emergency Management, https://doi.org/10.1007/978-3-031-74268-2

Compassion fatigue refers to the phenomenon where some MH providers develop symptoms of post-traumatic stress disorder (PTSD) after empathizing with a client who experienced traumatic stress (Figley, 1995).

Complex emergencies (CEs) are emergencies characterized by "extensive violence and loss of life; displacements of populations; widespread damage to societies and economies; the need for large-scale, multi-faceted humanitarian assistance; the hindrance or prevention of humanitarian assistance by political and military constraints; and the significant security risks for humanitarian relief workers in some areas" (OCHA, 1999). Examples include armed conflicts, political violence, or epidemics.

Complex political contexts (**CPCs**) are the situations recognized in both low- and high-resource settings and any place where belonging to a particular political, religious, tribal, ethnic, or gender identity group or expressing political convictions make a person a target of violence, institutional discrimination, and systematic persecution (Cherepanov, 2018, 2023). CPCs refer to regions with recent or ongoing authoritarianism, dictatorship, oppression, or government-sponsored political violence resulting in gross violation of human rights.

Contextuality is an awareness of the complex and unique factors influencing MH needs, the priorities in meeting them, and the choice of interventions (Wessells, 2009). Among these factors are characteristics of the current situation, remote or recent history, cultural traditions, and geopolitical influence.

Convergence of interventions occurs when GMH providers from different schools of thought and training use similar interventions and share a similar understanding of their goals. These shared interventions involve active listening skills, offering emotional support, encouragement, empowerment, and assisting with accessing the resources and problem-solving.

Convergence or "flocking" (Barton, 1970; Cherepanov, 2018; Cone et al., 2003) is the unorganized, spontaneous movement of volunteers and supplies to a disaster area. This pro-social behavior can have a disruptive effect on disaster relief activities.

Countertransference is a cognitive aberration that is common when working with trauma. It can occur when a client's experience triggers providers' traumatic memories and elicits strong emotional reactions and personal overinvolvement that can compromise the provider's ability to respond to the client's needs and may lead to professional boundaries violation.

Crisis intervention is a modality of MH interventions that is a form of secondary prevention and is not considered a treatment. Psychological First Aid (PFA) and other types of crisis interventions assist people in crisis to access their sources of strength and resilience, link to resources, and regain their functionality and sense of self-efficacy.

Deploying agencies manage and oversee humanitarian relief operations. They are directly involved in hiring, administrative and program management, arranging transportation, and logistics. Many arrange systems for security risk monitoring and MH support for volunteers.

Development aid is humanitarian assistance that addresses chronic or long-term issues and facilitates systems changes in the community or society. An example can be developing community-based support for survivors of gender-based violence. It is different from the relief, which focuses on meeting immediate needs.

Disaster is a situation of severe disruptions in the community functioning that exceed its capacity to cope using its resources. Disasters can have natural, technological, or mixed causes, as well as various factors that influence the exposure and vulnerability of a community (https://www.ifrc.org/our-work/disasters-climate-and-crises/what-disaster).

"Disaster syndrome". This term was first used to label "stunned, shocked mental state," allegedly common in the impact phase of disaster" (Wallace, 1957). This assumption has long been disputed. In fact, panic and disaster syndrome are rarely reported (Glass, 2001). Instead, disasters tend to evoke community resilience and not social breakdown (Auf der Heide, 2004; Jacob et al., 2008).

Do No Harm is a ground principle that calls on humanitarian organizations and actors to consider the unintended consequences of their interventions and take action to minimize the negative impacts and maximize positive impacts on peace (OCHA Business Brief, 2021).

Dual loyalty dilemmas in GMH refer to situations where a GMH provider encounters conflicted commitments. There are instances when loyalty to the deploying organization and the commitment to the beneficiaries collide. There may be situations when the values at the provider's place of origin (e.g., human rights) contradict cultural or political values shared by beneficiaries. There may be instances when the providers' understanding of their humanitarian mission conflicts with local laws, i.e., assisting illegal immigrants arriving by boat (Cherepanov, 2018, 2021).

Ethically questionable practices are ethical in some situations but can appear unethical in others (Cherepanov, 2018). In the instance of trauma tourism, people travel to disaster sites to satisfy their professional and personal curiosity instead of helping victims, which can be a legitimate goal in many other circumstances.

Ethics for Global Mental Health is the system of professional, multidisciplinary, and humanitarian values, competencies, and standards that provide guidance and a frame of reference for reasoning the complex professional and moral dilemmas arising within the humanitarian context (Cherepanov, 2018).

Existential despair is a state of despondency and low morale that can develop as a result of witnessing mass suffering and dying. Humanitarian workers may start questioning the value of their contributions, the significance of their impact, and the meaning of their work. Existential despair can be a sign of burnout.

Failed states are countries where the government loses the ability to govern effectively, for instance, and fails to control violence (Tyagi, 2012).

Fragile states can emerge in post-conflict or political transition states or due to prolonged political or economic crisis or impasse. Such states' characteristics include weak governance, limited administrative capacity, chronic humanitarian crises, persistent social tensions, and often, violence as the legacy of armed conflict and civil war (Tyagi, 2012).

Genocide is a legal term that refers to "acts committed with intent to destroy, in whole or in part, a national, ethnic, racial or religious group." The five acts qualified as genocide are: killing members of the group, causing them serious bodily or mental harm, imposing living conditions intended to destroy the group, preventing births, and forcibly transferring children out of the group (1948, the United Nations Genocide Convention In: United Nations, 2019).

GINGOs stands for Grassroots International Volunteer-driven, Non-governmental Organizations with small annual budgets. The qualifying range varies based on multiple factors.

The Global Burden of Disease (GBD) is a measure used to assess the population's health status and its impact on economic development and the population's well-being. GBD is measured by a metric called DALY or *Disability Adjusted Life Years*. Conceptually, one DALY is the equivalent of losing 1 year in good health because of premature death, disease, or disability (Kabajulizi & Francis Awuku, 2022).

Global Mental Health (GMH) is a field of study and practice concerned with providing psychological aid and MH support to people affected by humanitarian crises. It makes GMH a discipline with a dual MH and humanitarian professional identity (Cherepanov, 2019). Typically, such activities take place in the international setting, but they can also include care for refugees in their resettlement areas. The word "global" in global health usually refers to the scope of the problems, not their location (Koplan et al., 2009).

"Helper's" fantasy is a cognitive bias when MH providers identify their role as a Helper whose mission is to respond to any cry for help and do everything themselves with little regard for the person's resources, strengths, and resilience.

Humanism is the belief in being kind to other people and treating them with respect, even if they do not share the same beliefs or values. A humanitarian is someone who shares these beliefs and does good work for the benefit of others.

Humanitarian action is the system of humanitarian relief and development activities tasked with "orchestrating a humanitarian response to protect lives, prevent and alleviate human suffering, reduce vulnerabilities, and enhance capacity to cope and recover" (ALNAP, 2022, p. 26).

Humanitarian actors are the stakeholders of humanitarian action. They can be affected people (beneficiaries), volunteer aid workers, and a wide range of large and small organizations, including businesses and donor agencies, who possess the knowledge, skills, and resources to support the humanitarian response and improve the overall effectiveness of aid delivery (OCHA Business Brief, 2021).

Humanitarian competencies include knowledge of the context of humanitarian work, understanding of humanitarian relief systems and regulations, cultural and geopolitical awareness, and the ability to conduct contextually appropriate research and interventions.

Humanitarian emergencies and crises affect an entire community or a group of people in a region. It involves high levels of mortality or malnutrition, the spread of disease, and health emergencies (Humanitarian Crises, n.d.). Examples are disasters, armed conflicts, famines, and epidemics that threaten a community's health, safety, or well-being. Such events produce massive humanitarian needs, exacerbate vulnerabilities, and exceed the community's capacity for coping. They expose people to profoundly disempowering experiences of trauma and victimization and compromise community and family support and access to care.

The humanitarian impunity bubble is the illusion of invincibility that creates a false sense of safety, reassuring and sometimes empowering perception of the apparently coherent and predictable spaces (Allan, 2015). According to Allan, humanitarians sometimes live in their bubbles, relying on abstract rules and norms and not noticing real-life danger.

Humanitarianism is the system of beliefs and practices of people who try to help people who suffer and improve their living conditions (Humanitarianism. Oxford English Dictionary).

"Humanitarian mode" is an overpowering state of mind that emerges when humanitarians hear of a new disaster. They immediately disengage from routine life and become entirely different people who start perceiving reality through humanitarian needs lenses (Otegui, 2022).

Humanitarian negotiations are the interaction between humanitarian organizations and their counterparts. They are conducted to establish and maintain the presence of humanitarian organizations in crisis environments, ensure humanitarian access to people in need, deliver humanitarian aid, and implement protection activities (What is Humanitarian Negotiation?, n.d.).

Humanitarian principles are the fundamental values that provide aspirational guidance to humanitarian action. They are principles of humanity, neutrality, independence, and impartiality (OCHA Humanitarian Principles, 2011).

Humanitarian relief provides immediate response to an emergency or disaster. It aims to meet the population's immediate, urgent, and pressing needs. That is different from humanitarian development, which addresses long-term issues.

Humanitarian research is the systematic collection and analysis of data that applies to qualitative or ethnographic data (that can be observed) or quantitative data (that can be measured). Humanitarian research includes needs assessments, psychiatric epidemiology (study of distribution and cause of mental illness), monitoring and evaluation, social sciences research, and data collected for advocacy (IASC, 2007).

Humanitarian settings or humanitarian contexts are a broad range of emergencies where humanitarian relief activities occur (Tol et al., 2011). These situations include disasters, armed conflicts, famines, or political dysfunction.

A humanitarian system is a network of interconnected institutional and operational entities through which humanitarian action is undertaken when local and national resources are, on their own, insufficient to meet the needs of a population in crisis (ALNAP, 2022, p. 28).

Humanity is a fundamental humanitarian principle which states that human suffering must be addressed whenever it is found. Humanitarian action aims to protect life and health and ensure respect for human beings.

Iatrogenic harm is damage induced as a byproduct of an intervention by a service provider or caretaker of any type or from a procedure or technique (Caplan &

Caplan, 2001). For example, a MH provider can tell a client who realistically struggles with life adversity that their reactions are pathological and must be treated.

Impartiality is the fundamental humanitarian principle that states that humanitarian action must be carried out based on need alone, giving priority to the most urgent cases of distress and making no distinctions based on nationality, race, gender, religious belief, class, or political opinions (OCHA Humanitarian principles, 2011).

Independence is a fundamental humanitarian principle that states that humanitarian action must be autonomous from the political, economic, military, or other objectives (OCHA Humanitarian Principles, 2011).

Inter-Agency Standing Committee (IASC) is the longest-standing and highest-level humanitarian coordination forum in the United Nations. It brings together the executive heads of organizations and consortia to formulate policy, set strategic priorities, and mobilize resources in response to humanitarian crises (UN/IASC, 1992).

Internally Displaced People (IDPs) are people who had to flee their homeland to another region within the same country. IDPs are technically refugees but not according to the legal definition of a refugee (https://www.unhcr.org/us/about-unhcr/who-we-protect/internally-displaced-people).

International Humanitarian Law (IHL) is a set of rules that seek to limit the effects of armed conflict. IHL is binding on state and non-state actors, regulating the methods and means of armed conflict and granting protection for non-combatants (OCHA Business Brief, 2021).

International Trauma Questionnaire (ITQ) is an assessment tool, which is "a brief, simply worded measure, focusing only on the core features of PTSD and CPTSD, and employs straightforward diagnostic rules. The ITQ was developed to be consistent with the organizing principles of the ICD-11." It is translated into multiple languages (Cloitre et al., 2021).

Medical humanitarianism involves medical and other health-related activities undertaken in conditions born of conflict, neglect, or disaster. It has a growing presence in international development and global health. Médecins Sans Frontières (MSF) is the largest medical humanitarian organization.

Mental health is "a state of mental well-being that enables people to cope with the stresses of life, realize their abilities, learn well, work well, and contribute to their community" (https://www.who.int/health-topics/mental-health).

Mental Health and Psychosocial Support (MHPSS) is the composite term for integrated mental health and social support interventions and any local or outside support to protect or promote psychosocial well-being and/or prevent or treat mental disorders in an emergency (IASC, 2007).

Mental health recovery is "the process of change through which individuals strive to improve their health and well-being, live a self-directed life, and strive to achieve their full potential" (SAMHSA, 2004).

Meta-analysis is a statistical analysis method that examines data from multiple independent studies of the same subject to determine overall trends (Oxford's English dictionary, s.v. "meta-analysis").

Military humanitarianism is the use of military force to further a humanitarian cause. Such interventions were born out of the international community's failure to respond to tragedies such as the Rwandan genocide in 1994 and the Srebrenica genocide in 1995 and remain a highly controversial approach (Gusterson, 2019).

Misanthropy is a disdain for humankind and disappointment in humanity (Mysanthropy. n.d.). In humanitarian work, this attitude is associated with trauma, depression, and burnout.

MONGO is the abbreviation that stands for "My Own NGO." It refers to the professionals who travel to disaster and conflict-impacted areas as individual citizens with no organizational affiliation (Paul, 2019; Polman, 2013).

The neocolonial mentality is the attitude of internalized racial, ethnic, or cultural superiority felt by people from Western countries who aid low-income countries (Nunning, 2015).

Neutrality is the core humanitarian principle which states that humanitarian actors must not take sides in hostilities or engage in political, racial, religious, or ideological controversies (OCHA Humanitarian Principles, 2011).

NGOs (Non-Governmental Organizations) are voluntary non-profit groups or institutions with a social mission that operate independently from the government (What is an NGO?, n.d.)).

Operational guidance offers strategic guidelines on providing multilayered and interconnected GMH and psychosocial interventions. In humanitarian work, operational guidance is provided mainly by IASC (2007), but there are other sources of direction for specific interventions.

"The original sin of Mental Health" is a naïve belief that we, as experts, know better what people need and how they are supposed to feel, along with the conviction that people cannot cope without the MH providers' assistance.

Participatory action research (PAR) involves researchers and participants working together to define problems and negotiate solutions (Reason & Bradbury, 2008).

Peacebuilding is "any work that seeks to effect change in the key driving factors or actors of existing or renewed armed conflict that would bring a sustained peace" (Church, 2007).

Political violence is perpetrated by the government administration to achieve political goals or force the opposition into obedience (Conteh-Morgan, 2003). Political violence is not random. It targets people based on their collective identity (ethnicity, race, religion, political beliefs, or sexual identity) and is endorsed or facilitated by the government. Genocide or political oppression are examples of political violence.

Professional fantasies are cognitive biases recognized in the response to an emergency. In a predictable way, they alter the perception of the professional role. Acting out these fantasies increases the risks of violating professional boundaries, contributing to burnout, impacting the quality of work, and leading to reckless behavior (Cherepanov, 2018, 2020). The common fantasies are the Helper, Rescuer, and Superman fantasies.

Psychological First Aid (PFA) is a form of crisis intervention that provides immediate MH relief, support, and practical assistance to people affected by a disaster. It is well suited for humanitarian emergencies. The intervention consists of several modules that can be adapted to different situations and cultures (Brymer et al., 2006). The World Health Organization, War Trauma Foundation, and World Vision International (2011) recommended PFA for conflict-affected areas.

Public Health interventions aim to detect, prevent, and respond to diseases (Oxford English Dictionary, s.v. "Public Health").

Refugee camps are temporary facilities built to provide immediate temporary protection and assistance to people who have been forced to flee their homes due to war, persecution, or violence (Refugee Camps, 2023).

Refugees are people who are unable or unwilling to return to their country of origin due to a well-founded fear of being persecuted for reasons of race, religion, nationality, membership of a particular social group, or political opinion (ICRC, 1949).

Rescuer fantasy is a belief that one must rescue or save another person from something bad. This belief is posited as a motive for specific actions or choices (Oxford Dictionary, s.v. "rescuer fantasy").

Resilience is the capacity to withstand or to recover quickly from difficulties (Oxford Languages Dictionary, s.v. "resilience"). In MH, it refers to a person's ability to cope with changes and challenges and to bounce back during difficult times.

Responsibility to Protect or R2P is a nonbinding norm holding that outside powers have a responsibility to intervene in response to a government's failure to protect its population from mass atrocities such as genocide, even when it violates the government's sovereignty. R2P doctrine is used to justify the justification for military humanitarianism, which remains controversial and unevenly applied (World101, 2023).

Safety imperative means the absolute priority of safety. In humanitarian work, safety imperative refers to the fundamental premise of prioritizing safety for both the beneficiaries and the providers.

Self-care involves paying attention to one's needs, practicing self-compassion, and setting aside time for activities that enhance overall well-being, contributing to physical and mental health improvements.

Sexual exploitation in humanitarian space is the situation in which the aid workers abuse their position of power and trust and take advantage of the vulnerability of refugees, asylum seekers, or forcibly displaced persons to obtain sexual favors from them (Preventing Sexual Exploitation, n.d.). People in need of humanitarian assistance must be protected from sexual exploitation and abuse and have access to channels to report it and have it addressed (OCHA Business Brief, 2021).

Social determinants of health (SDOH) are economic, political, social, and other non-medical factors that affect daily life and influence physical and mental health outcomes. They are the conditions in which people are born, grow, live, and age. Food insecurities, lack of adequate housing, and poor access to health and mental care negatively affect health and MH. They are linked to social inequity, the unequal distribution of income, wealth, influence, and power (Braveman & Gottlieb, 2014).

Superman fantasy is a cognitive bias that suggests that a flight-in-and-out MH provider (i.e., "Superman") can solve the problem. This attitude excludes collaborative work, working with the team, or delegating tasks.

Temoignage comes from the French verb "temoigner," which translates as "to witness." For humanitarians, this means a willingness to speak on behalf of the people we assist and to bring abuses and intolerable situations to the public eye (MSF, n.d.).

Torture is the intentional infliction of severe mental or physical pain or suffering by or with the approval of state agents (PHR, n.d.).

Trauma aggregation is a phenomenon associated with collective traumas. It emerges when individual trauma experiences aggregate or create a shared mental space where people share similar experiences (Cherepanov, 2020). Trauma aggregation allows people to relate to and support each other, which adds to resilience.

The treatment gap measures the accessibility of health and MH services. The treatment gap is measured as the percentage of individuals who require care but do not receive treatment (Kohn et al., 2004, p. 859).

Virtue ethics refers to navigating ethical dilemmas through the lens of prioritized values (Behnke, 2005). This approach to ethics has been finding growing support among humanitarian and GMH professionals.

Vulnerability in humanitarian emergencies refers to individuals and groups with less access to resources and limited ability to cope, problem-solve, and understand what is happening. Its meaning is the opposite of resilience.

A volunteer offers their services in any capacity (Oxford English Dictionary). In the humanitarian sector, some volunteers respond to humanitarian emergencies work for free, others receive a stipend or are paid by foundations or grants, and some choose to invest their funds in exchange for the opportunity to help others.

Voluntourism is a combination of volunteering and tourism, a form of tourism in which travelers participate in voluntary work, typically for charity (The Oxford English Language dictionary, s.v. "voluntourism"), often providing limited (if any) real benefits to the communities they believe they are helping.

War crimes are serious violations of international humanitarian law (ICRC, 1949). Examples are genocide, use of torture, or war rape.

"The war on terrorism" was a name for the international military campaign that was launched by the US and UK governments and their allies after the September 1, 2011, attacks in the US (Schmitt & Shanker, 2005). The campaign has made the environment even more dangerous for humanitarians.

War rape is the use of sexual violence as a tactic of war to humiliate, dominate, instill fear, or forcibly relocate civilian members of a community or ethnic group (OHCHR, 2008). The political agenda of the war rape differentiates it from other forms of gender-based violence (García-Moreno & van Ommeren, 2012; Hagen & Yohani, 2010).

References

Allan, T. (2015). Life beyond the bubbles: Cognitive dissonance and humanitarian impunity in northern Uganda. In S. Abramowitz, C. Panter-Brick, & P. Piot (Eds.), *Medical humanitarianism: Ethnographies of practice* (pp. 96–119). University of Pennsylvania Press.

ALNAP. (2022). *The state of the humanitarian system. ALNAP study*. ALNAP/ODI.

Auf der Heide, E. (2004). Common misconceptions about disasters: Panic, the "disaster syndrome" and looting. In M. R. O'Leary (Ed.), *The first 72 hours: A community approach to disaster preparedness* (pp. 340–380). iUniverse Publishing.

Barton, A. (1970). *Communities in disaster: A sociological analysis of collective stress situations*. Anchor.

Behnke, S. (2005). On being an ethical psychologist. Monitor on Psychology, 36(7), 114.

Braveman, P., & Gottlieb, L. (2014). The social determinants of health: It's time to consider the causes of the causes. *Public Health Reports, 129*(Suppl 2), 19–31. https://doi.org/10.1177/00333549141291S206

Brymer, M., Jacobs, A., Layne, C., Pynoos, R., Ruzek, J., Steinberg, A., Vernberg, E., & Watson, P. (2006). *Psychological first aid (PFA) field operations guide* (2nd ed.). National Child Traumatic Stress Network & National Center for PTSD. https://www.nctsn.org/

Caplan, G., & Caplan, R. (2001). *Helping the helpers not to harm: Iatrogenic damage and community mental health*. Routledge.

Cherepanov, E. (2018). *Ethics for global mental health: From good intentions to humanitarian accountability*. Routledge. https://doi.org/10.4324/9781351175746

Cherepanov, E. (2019). Ethical dilemmas in global mental health. *BJPsych International, 16*(4), 81–83. https://doi.org/10.1192/bji.2019.10

Cherepanov, E. (2020). Responding to the psychological needs of health workers during pandemic: Ten lessons from humanitarian work. *Disaster Medicine and Public Health Preparedness, 16*(2), 734–740. https://doi.org/10.1017/dmp.2020.356

Cherepanov, E. (2021). Mental health interventions in complex political contexts. *Intervention, 19*(2), 149–154. https://doi.org/10.4103/intv.intv_14_21

Cherepanov, E. (2023). Refugees from countries with complex political contexts: Politically informed approach to health and mental health services. *Frontiers in Public Health, 11*, 1323259. https://doi.org/10.3389/fpubh.2023.1323259

Church, C. (2007, 12–13 April). Corruption and peacebuilding: How they may collide? In *The Nexus: Corruption, conflict and peacebuilding*. The Fletcher School, Tufts University, The

E. Cherepanov, *Humanitarian Work for Global Mental Health Providers*, Contemporary Humanitarian Action and Emergency Management,
https://doi.org/10.1007/978-3-031-74268-2

Institute for Human Security. Retrieved from http://fletcher.tufts.edu/corruptionconf/pdf/Church.pdf

Cloitre, M., Hyland, P., Prins, A., & Shevlin, M. (2021). The international trauma questionnaire (ITQ) measures reliable and clinically significant treatment-related change in PTSD and complex PTSD. *European Journal of Psychotraumatology, 12*(1), 1930961. https://doi.org/10.1080/20008198.2021.1930961

Cone, D. C., Weir, S. D., & Bogucki, S. (2003). Convergent volunteerism. *Annals of Emergency Medicine, 41*, 457–462.

Conteh-Morgan, E. (2003). *Collective political violence: An introduction to the theories and cases of violent conflicts*. Routledge.

Feynman, R. P. (1974). Cargo cult science. *Engineering and Science, 37*(7), 10–13. https://calteches.library.caltech.edu/51/2/CargoCult.pdf

Figley, C. (1995). *Compassion fatigue: Coping with secondary stress disorder in those who treat the traumatised*. Brunner/Mazel.

García-Moreno, C., & van Ommeren, M. (2012). *Mental health and psychosocial support for conflict-related sexual violence: Principles and interventions*. World Health Organization. https://www.unicef.org/protection/files/Summary_EN_.pdf

Glass, T. A. (2001). Understanding public response to disasters. *Public Health Reports, 116*(Suppl. 2), 69–73. https://doi.org/10.1016/2FS0033-3549(04)50146-2

Gusterson, H. (2019). Drone warfare in Waziristan and the new military humanism. *Current Anthropology, 60*(S19), S77–S86. https://doi.org/10.1086/701022

Hagen, K. T., & Yohani, S. Y. (2010). The nature and psychosocial consequences of war rape for individuals and communities. *International Journal of Psychological Studies, 2*(2), 14–25. https://doi.org/10.5539/ijps.v2n2p14

Hall, H. (2016, March 15). Cargo cult psychology. *Science-Based Medicine*. https://sciencebasedmedicine.org/cargo-cult-psychology/

Humanitarian Crises. (n.d.). Maltester International. Available at https://www.malteser-international.org/en/current-issues/humanitarian-crises.html

IASC. (2007). *Guidelines on mental health and psychosocial support in emergency settings*. Interagency Standing Committee.

International Committee of the Red Cross (ICRC). (1949). *Geneva Convention of 12 August 1949*.

Jacob, B., Mawson, A. R., Payton, M., & Guignard, J. C. (2008). Disaster mythology and fact: Hurricane Katrina and social attachment. *Public Health Reports, 123*(5), 555–566. https://doi.org/10.1177/003335490812300505

Kabajulizi, J., & Francis Awuku, D. (2022). Do non-communicable diseases influence sustainable development in Sub-Saharan Africa? A panel autoregressive distributive lag model approach. *Health Policy and Planning, 37*(3), 337–348. https://doi.org/10.1093/heapol/czab131

Kohn, R., Saxena, S., Levav, I., & Saraceno, B. (2004). The treatment gap in mental health care. *Bulletin of the World Health Organization, 82*(11), 858–866.

Koplan, J. P., Bond, T. C., Merson, M. H., Reddy, K. S., Rodriguez, M. H., Sewankambo, N. K., Wasserheit, J. N., & Consortium of Universities for Global Health Executive Board. (2009, June 6). Towards a common definition of global health. *Lancet, 373*(9679), 1993–1995. https://doi.org/10.1016/S0140-6736(09)60332-9. Epub 2009 Jun 1. PMID: 19493564; PMCID: PMC9905260.

Maslach, C., & Leiter, M. P. (2016, June). Understanding the burnout experience: Recent research and its implications for psychiatry. *World Psychiatry, 15*(2), 103–111. https://doi.org/10.1002/wps.20311. PMID: 27265691; PMCID: PMC4911781.

Médecins Sans Frontières (MSF). (n.d.). *Advocacy and Temoignage*. https://msf.org.au/advocacy-and-t%C3%A9moignage

Mysanthropy. (n.d.). In Merriam-Webster's Dictionary http://www.merriam-webster.com/dictionary/misanthropy

Nunning, V. (2015). Fictions of empire and the un-making of imperialist mentalities: Colonial discourse and post-colonial criticism revisited. *Forum for World Literature Studies, 7*(2), 171–198.

OCHA. (1999). *OCHA orientation handbook on complex emergencies*. Office for the Coordination of Humanitarian Affairs OCHA. Available at: http://reliefweb.int/sites/reliefweb.int/files/resources/OCHA%C2%A0ORIENTATION%20HANDBOOK.pdf

OCHA. (2011). *Humanitarian principles*. UN Office for the Coordination of Humanitarian Affairs (OCHA). https://reliefweb.int/report/world/ocha-message-humanitarian-principles-enar

OCHA Business Brief. (2021, December 8). *Introduction to the humanitarian system. Connecting business initiative*. Available at https://www.connectingbusiness.org/sites/default/files/downloads/publication

OHCHR. (2008). *Rape: Weapon of war*. United Nations Human Rights, Office of the High Commissioner. http://www.ohchr.org/en/newsevents/pages/rapeweaponwar.aspx

Otegui, D. F. (2022). *Symbolic approach to humanitarian action: It takes one to know one*. Springer International Publishing.

Paul, B. K. (2019). Channeling disaster aid: Process and problems. In B. K. Paul (Ed.), *Disaster relief aid* (pp. 43–99). Palgrave Macmillan.

Physicians for Human Rights (PHR). (n.d.). *Torture*. https://phr.org/issues/torture

Preventing sexual exploitation and abuse (n.d.) UN.org. In: https://www.un.org/preventing-sexual-exploitation-and-abuse/content/agencies-funds-and-programmes

Polman, L. (2013). *The crisis caravan: What's wrong with humanitarian aid?* Henry Holt and Company. http://rbdigital.oneclickdigital.com.

Reason, P., & Bradbury, H. (Eds.). (2008). *The SAGE handbook of action research: Participative inquiry and practice*. SAGE.

Refugee Camps. (2023). *USA for UNHCR*. United Nations, Refugee Agency. https://www.unrefugees.org/refugee-facts/camps/?utm_medium=website_source=archdaily.com

SAMHSA. (2004). *National Consensus Statement on Mental health Recovery*. Center for Mental Health Services, SAMHSA.

Schmitt, E., & Shanker, T. (2005, July 26). U.S. officials retool slogan for terror war. *New York Times*. http://www.nytimes.com/2005/07/26/politics/us-officials-retoolslogan-for-terror-war.html

Strengthening Accountability to Affected People. (n.d.). IASC. Geneva: Switzerland. Retrieved from https://interagencystandingcommittee.org/strengthening-accountability-affected-people

Tol, W. A., Barbui, C., Galappatti, A., Silove, D., Betancourt, T. S., Souza, R., Golaz, A., & van Ommeren, M. (2011). Mental health and psychosocial support in humanitarian settings: Linking practice and research. *Lancet, 378*(9802), 1581–1591. https://doi.org/10.1016/s0140-6736(11)61094-5

Tyagi, J. (2012). Weak states. In G. Ritzer (Ed.), *Wiley-Blackwell encyclopedia of globalization*. https://doi.org/10.1002/9780470670590.wbeog809

UN. (2019). Genocide background. *Office on genocide prevention and the responsibility to protect*. http://www.un.org/en/genocideprevention/genocide.shtml

UNICEF. (1997). *Cape Town Principles and best practice on the prevention of recruitment of children into the armed forces and demobilization and social reintegration of child soldiers in Africa*. https://openasia.org/en/wp-content/uploads/2013/06/Cape-Town-Principles.pdf

United Nations General Assembly (UN/IASC). (1992). *The Inter-Agency Standing Committee (IASC) (resolution 46/182 and resolution 48/57)*. http://www.un.org/Docs/journal/asp/ws.asp?m=A/RES/46/182

Wallace, A. F. C. (1957). Mazeway disintegration: The individual's perception of socio-cultural disorganization. *Human Organization, 16*, 23–27.

Wessells, M. G. (2009). Do no harm: Toward contextually appropriate psychosocial support in international emergencies. *American Psychologist, 64*(8), 842. https://doi.org/10.1037/0003-066X.64.8.842

What is an NGO? (n.d.). *NGOSourse*. Retrieved from https://www.ngosource.org/what-is-an-ngo

What is Humanitarian Negotiation? (n.d.). *Frontline negotiations*. Centre of Competence on Humanitarian Negotiation. Retrieved from https://frontline-negotiations.org/what-is-humanitarian-negotiation/

World Health Organization, War Trauma Foundation, & World Vision International. (2011). *Psychological first aid: Guide for field workers*. WHO.
World101. (2023, April 10). The rise and fall of the responsibility to protect. *World101*. https://world101.cfr.org/understanding-international-system/building-blocks/rise-and-fall-responsibility-protect

Additional Resources and Further Readings

These essential readings are suggested for those interested in additional studies of theory and practice of GMH work.

Bemme, D., & Kirmayer, L. J. (2020). Global mental health: Interdisciplinary challenges for a field in motion. *Transcultural Psychiatry, 57*(1), 3–18. https://doi.org/10.1177/1363461519898035
Berkowitz, S., Bryant, R., Brymer, M., Hamblen, J., Jacobs, A., Layne, C., Macy, R., Osofsky, H., Pynoos, R., Ruzek, J., Steinberg, A., Vernberg, E., Watson, P., National Center for PTSD, & National Child Traumatic Stress Network. (2010). *Skills for psychological recovery: Field operations guide*. https://www.ptsd.va.gov/professional/treat/type/skills_psych_recovery_manual.asp
Betancourt, T. S., McBain, R., Newnham, E. A., & Brennan, R. T. (2014). Context matters: Community characteristics and mental health among war-affected youth in Sierra Leone. *Journal of Child Psychology and Psychiatry, and Allied Disciplines, 55*(3), 217–226. https://doi.org/10.1111/jcpp.12131
Bickley, S. (2010). *Safety first revised: A safety and security handbook for aid workers*. International Save the Children Alliance. http://www.eisf.eu/resources/library/
Bouchet-Saulnier, F. (n.d.). *The practical guide to humanitarian law*. Médecins Sans Frontières (MSF). Retrieved from https://guide-humanitarian-law.org.
Brymer, M., Jacobs, A., Layne, C., Pynoos, R., Ruzek, J., Steinberg, A., Vernberg, E., & Watson, P. (2006). *Psychological first aid (PFA) field operations guide* (2nd ed.). National Child Traumatic Stress Network & National Center for PTSD. https://www.nctsn.org/
Cherepanov, E. (2018). *Ethics for global mental health: From good intentions to humanitarian accountability*. Routledge. https://doi.org/10.4324/9781351175746
Cherepanov, E. (2019). Ethical dilemmas in global mental health. *BJPsych international, 16*(4), 81–83. https://doi.org/10.1192/bji.2019.10
Cherepanov, E. (2020a). *Understanding the transgenerational legacy of totalitarian regimes: Paradoxes of cultural learning*. Routledge. https://doi.org/10.4324/9780429030338
Cherepanov, E. (2020b). Sexual and gender-based violence as warfare. In R. Geffner, V. Vieth, V. Vaughan, A. Rosenbaum, L. Hamberger, & J. White (Eds.), *Handbook of interpersonal violence across the lifespan*. Springer. https://doi.org/10.1007/978-3-319-62122-7_106-1
Cherepanov, E. (2023). Refugees from countries with complex political contexts: Politically informed approach to health and mental health services. *Frontiers in Public Health, 11*, 1323259. https://doi.org/10.3389/fpubh.2023.1323259
Chiumento, A., Khan, M. N., Rahman, A., & Frith, L. (2016). Managing ethical challenges to mental health research in post-conflict settings. *Developing World Bioethics, 16*(10), 15–28.
Cosgrove, L., Mills, C., Karter, J. M., Mehta, A., & Kalathil, J. (2020). A critical review of the Lancet Commission on global mental health and sustainable development: Time for a paradigm change. *Critical Public Health, 30*(5), 624–631. https://doi.org/10.1080/09581596.2019.1667488

Dyregrov, A., Gupta, L., Gjestad, R., & Raundalen, M. (2002). Is the culture always right? *Traumatology, 8*(3), 135–145. https://doi.org/10.1177/153476560200800302

Frounfelker, R. L., Miconi, D., Farrar, J., Brooks, M. A., Rousseau, C., & Betancourt, T. S. (2020). Mental health of refugee children and youth: Epidemiology, interventions, and future directions. *Annual Review of Public Health, 2*(41), 159–176. https://doi.org/10.1146/annurev-publhealth-040119-094230

Hilhorst, D. (2005, December). Dead letter or living document? Ten years of the Code of Conduct for disaster relief. *Disasters, 29*(4), 351–369. https://doi.org/10.1111/j.0361-3666.2005.00297.x. PMID: 16277645.

IASC. (2007). *Guidelines on mental health and psychosocial support in emergency settings.* Interagency Standing Committee.

IASC. (2015). *Guidelines for integrating gender-based violence interventions in humanitarian action: Reducing risk, promoting resilience and aiding recovery.* Inter-Agency Standing Committee.

IASC. (2020). *Operational considerations for multisectoral mental health and psychosocial support programs during the COVID-19 pandemic.*

Illich, I. (1974). *Medical nemesis: The expropriation of health.* Calder & Boyars.

International Federation of Red Cross and Red Crescent Societies (IFRC and ICRC). (1994). *Code of conduct for the International Red Cross and Red Crescent Movement and NGOs in disaster relief.* https://www.ifrc.org/document/code-conduct-international-red-cross-and-red-crescent-movement-and-ngos-disaster-relief

Kivlehan, S., & Kayden, S. (2023). *Humanitarian aid workers. CDC yellow book 2024. Travel for work & other reasons.* Center for Disease Control and Prevention. Retrieved from https://wwwnc.cdc.gov/travel/yellowbook/2024/work-and-other-reasons/humanitarian-aid-workers

Kohrt, B., & Mendenhall, E. (2016). Anthropological perspectives on global mental health. In *Global mental health: Anthropological perspectives* (pp. 341–361). Left Coast Press.

Lambert, J. (2015, January 27). Ethical considerations for research with victims of political violence and human rights violations. *StressPoints.* https://www.istss.org/education-research/traumatic-stresspoints/2015-january/ethical-considerations-for-research-with-victims-o.aspx

Leach, A. (2015, February 5). Exporting trauma: Can the talking cure do more harm than good? *The Guardian.* Retrieved from https://www.theguardian.com/global-development-professionals-network/2015/feb/05/mental-health-aid-western-talking-cure-harm-good-humanitarian-anthropologist

Mackenzie, A. (n.d.). *How to avoid white savior complex and why that's important.* Retrieved from https://themuttonclub.com/how-to-avoid-white-savior-complex/

Pittaway, E., Bartolomei, L., & Hugman, R. (2010). "Stop stealing our stories": The ethics of research with vulnerable groups. *Journal of Human Rights Practice, 2*(2), 229–251. https://doi.org/10.1093/jhuman/huq004

Reason, P., & Bradbury, H. (Eds.). (2008). *The SAGE handbook of action research: Participative inquiry and practice.* SAGE.

Saul, J., & Simon, W. (2016). Building resilience in families, communities, and organizations: A training program in Global Mental Health and Psychosocial Support. *Family Process, 55*(4), 689–699. https://doi.org/10.1111/famp.12248

Slim, H. (2015). *Humanitarian ethics: A guide to the morality of aid in war and disaster.* Oxford University Press.

Sphere. (2018). *The Sphere handbook: Humanitarian charter and minimum standards in humanitarian response* (4th ed.). www.spherestandards.org/handbook

Summerfield, D. (2004). Cross-cultural perspectives on the medicalization of human suffering. In G. M. Rosen (Ed.), *Posttraumatic stress disorder: Issues and controversies.* Wiley. https://doi.org/10.1002/9780470713570.ch12

Summerfield, D. (2012). Afterword: Against "global mental health". *Transcultural Psychiatry, 49*(3–4), 519–530. https://doi.org/10.1177/1363461512454701

The Code of Conduct for the International Red Cross and Red Crescent Movement and NGOs in Disaster Relief. (1996, February 29). *Annex VI. The international review of the Red Cross,*

No. 310. Retrieved from https://www.icrc.org/en/doc/resources/documents/article/other/code-of-conduct-290296.htm

Tol, W. A., Kohrt, B. A., Jordans, M. J., Thapa, S. B., Pettigrew, J., Upadhaya, N., & de Jong, J. T. V. M. (2010). Political violence and mental health: A multi-disciplinary review of the literature on Nepal. *Social Science & Medicine, 70*(1), 35–44. https://doi.org/10.1016/j.socscimed.2009.09.037

Tol, W. A., Barbui, C., Galappatti, A., Silove, D., Betancourt, T. S., Souza, R., Golaz, A., & van Ommeren, M. (2011). Mental health and psychosocial support in humanitarian settings: Linking practice and research. *Lancet, 378*(9802), 1581–1591. https://doi.org/10.1016/s0140-6736(11)61094-5

Tol, W. A., Stavrou, V., Greene, M. C., Mergenthaler, C., van Ommeren, M., & García-Moreno, C. (2013). Sexual and gender-based violence in areas of armed conflict: A systematic review of mental health and psychosocial support interventions. *Conflict and Health, 7*, 16. https://doi.org/10.1186/1752-1505-7-16

Watters, E. (2011). *Crazy like us: The globalization of the Western mind.* Robinson.

Wessells, M. G. (2009a). Do no harm: Toward contextually appropriate psychosocial support in international emergencies. *American Psychologist, 64*(8), 842. https://doi.org/10.1037/0003-066X.64.8.842

Wessells, M. G. (2009b). Supporting the mental health and psychosocial wellbeing of former child soldiers. *Journal of the American Academy of Child and Adolescent Psychiatry, 48*, 587–590.

World Health Organization, War Trauma Foundation and World Vision International. (2011). *Psychological first aid: Guide for field workers*. WHO.

Index

E. Cherepanov, *Humanitarian Competencies for Global Mental Health Professionals*, Contemporary Humanitarian Action and Emergency Management, https://doi.org/10.1007/978-3-031-74268-2

MIX
Papier aus verantwortungsvollen Quellen
Paper from responsible sources
FSC® C105338

If you have any concerns about our products,
you can contact us on
ProductSafety@springernature.com

In case Publisher is established outside the EU,
the EU authorized representative is:
Springer Nature Customer Service Center GmbH
Europaplatz 3, 69115 Heidelberg, Germany

Printed by Libri Plureos GmbH
in Hamburg, Germany